The **Essential** Guide TO

# Grief and Grieving

by Debra Holland, M.S., Ph.D.

**ALPHA**

A member of Penguin Group (USA) Inc.

**ALPHA BOOKS**

Published by the Penguin Group

Penguin Group (USA) Inc., 375 Hudson Street, New York, New York 10014, USA

Penguin Group (Canada), 90 Eglinton Avenue East, Suite 700, Toronto, Ontario M4P 2Y3, Canada (a division of Pearson Penguin Canada Inc.)

Penguin Books Ltd., 80 Strand, London WC2R 0RL, England

Penguin Ireland, 25 St. Stephen's Green, Dublin 2, Ireland (a division of Penguin Books Ltd.)

Penguin Group (Australia), 250 Camberwell Road, Camberwell, Victoria 3124, Australia (a division of Pearson Australia Group Pty. Ltd.)

Penguin Books India Pvt. Ltd., 11 Community Centre, Panchsheel Park, New Delhi—110 017, India

Penguin Group (NZ), 67 Apollo Drive, Rosedale, North Shore, Auckland 1311, New Zealand (a division of Pearson New Zealand Ltd.)

Penguin Books (South Africa) (Pty.) Ltd., 24 Sturdee Avenue, Rosebank, Johannesburg 2196, South Africa

Penguin Books Ltd., Registered Offices: 80 Strand, London WC2R 0RL, England

International Standard Book Number: 978-1-61564-111-6
Library of Congress Catalog Card Number: 2011905827

13   12   11      8   7   6   5   4   3   2   1

Interpretation of the printing code: The rightmost number of the first series of numbers is the year of the book's printing; the rightmost number of the second series of numbers is the number of the book's printing. For example, a printing code of 11-1 shows that the first printing occurred in 2011.

*Printed in the United States of America*

**Note:** This publication contains the opinions and ideas of its author. It is intended to provide helpful and informative material on the subject matter covered. It is sold with the understanding that the author and publisher are not engaged in rendering professional services in the book. If the reader requires personal assistance or advice, a competent professional should be consulted.

The author and publisher specifically disclaim any responsibility for any liability, loss, or risk, personal or otherwise, which is incurred as a consequence, directly or indirectly, of the use and application of any of the contents of this book.

Most Alpha books are available at special quantity discounts for bulk purchases for sales promotions, premiums, fund-raising, or educational use. Special books, or book excerpts, can also be created to fit specific needs.

For details, write: Special Markets, Alpha Books, 375 Hudson Street, New York, NY 10014.

**Publisher:** *Marie Butler-Knight*
**Associate Publisher:** *Mike Sanders*
**Executive Managing Editor:** *Billy Fields*
**Senior Acquisitions Editors:** *Paul Dinas,*
*Brook Farling*
**Development Editor:** *Lynn Northrup*
**Senior Production Editor:** *Kayla Dugger*

**Copy Editor:** *Jan Zoya*
**Cover Designer:** *Rebecca Batchelor*
**Book Designers:** *Rebecca Batchelor,*
*William Thomas*
**Indexer:** *Angie Martin*
**Layout:** *Brian Massey*
**Senior Proofreader:** *Laura Caddell*

# Dedication

*This book is dedicated to all who've shared their stories and their grief with me. (I've changed most of your names and some of your circumstances for your privacy.) You've been the inspiration for this book (not to mention giving me a lot of the content). I'll never forget your loved ones.*

## Dedication

# Contents

## Appendixes

# Introduction

This is a book about grieving, and for the most part it's about the death of someone you care about. But it also covers losses in other areas that still have an emotional impact, such as the loss of a marriage or a job.

If you've picked up this book, it's because you have experienced (or are experiencing) grief, or a person you care about is struggling with the loss of someone or something he or she holds dear. First of all, I want to reassure anyone who is mourning: you're not alone, and you're not crazy. The kaleidoscope of feelings you're experiencing is normal.

Because grief is often an unknown reaction, it catches us off guard. It's similar to feelings that we've felt before, such as disappointment or sadness, yet it can be accompanied by even more emotions and reactions. Grief is also different in diverse circumstances. One of the benefits of educating yourself about grief is that sense of relief that comes from knowing what is normal. Being able to identify what you're feeling and why you feel the way you do helps put your feelings into perspective. They aren't any less intense, just more understandable.

You can begin your grief recovery right away. That doesn't mean it won't be a long and painful journey. For some, it will be. However, your journey starts with the belief that you'll recover, even though right now you may fear you never will. It might feel as if you'll be bogged down in grief forever.

The goal of this book is to help you understand grief, so you can find strength during your grief journey, cope, and eventually recover. You'll adjust to the changes within yourself and the changes in your life.

I have been a marriage and family therapist for 25 years, and a corporate grief counselor for 10. In that time, I'm heard thousands of people share their grief with me. I've heard stories that have brought me to tears, and ones that lifted my spirits. I've been privileged to help so many. They've taught me so much.

The grief journey isn't easy. For the majority of people, it's probably the most difficult time of their lives. But it's not one we can escape. Sooner or later we will lose people, circumstances, and things we love. Those losses will throw us out of balance as we struggle to find our way through the pain and other reactions we feel.

## How to Use This Book

*The Essential Guide to Grief and Grieving* is a basic overview of grief, intended to familiarize you with the mourning process so you can understand what you are going through and better cope with the rollercoaster of emotions you're experiencing. It's also helpful for the people around those grieving to better learn how to support them. In addition, this book will provide other resources to enable you to delve deeper into the educational and recovery process.

The book is divided into four parts:

**Part 1, Loss and Grief,** offers an overview of grief, grieving, and loss. You'll learn the reactions you may have when you're grieving, and the challenges you may expect on your journey. You'll learn what you're feeling is normal—perhaps painful and horrible, but normal.

**Part 2, Bereavement,** is about death—mostly of people you love—and bereavement. But you can also grieve the loss of co-workers, classmates, friends, neighbors, celebrities, and pets. You'll learn how to (and how not to) support the bereaved.

**Part 3, Loss in Other Life Circumstances,** is about relationships, but not just romantic ones, such as marriage. This part also covers the failed relationship with your work that leads to job loss, and the relationship with your body as it changes due to aging and illness. It also discusses the loss of your home, another powerful relationship loss.

**Part 4, Recovery,** is more than self-care, although that's included here. It's also about what you can do to support yourself in your grief. These chapters can set you on the path to recovery, help you open your heart again—to love and be loved—and give you the courage to take on new life challenges.

## Book Extras

Throughout the book, you'll see additional pieces of information in sidebars. Here's what to look for:

| | |
|---|---|
| survival strategies | These tips give you advice for coping with grief or helping other people cope with grief. |

| cautions and concerns | These sidebars contain cautions to help you avoid some common grief pitfalls. |

| Definition | Check these sidebars for definitions of words or phrases that may be unfamiliar to you. |

| Expressions of Grief | These quotes will help you understand and relate to others who are grieving. |

You'll also see a fifth, name-changing sidebar that presents interesting facts, case histories, or other extended background information you should know.

## A Last Word Before We Begin …

My wish is that this book gives you hope that you'll eventually recover from your grief. You'll be forever changed by the grief journey. The information here will help sustain you through your grieving experience and guide you to recovery. Your life will be different, but perhaps even better in some (or many) ways. You *can* feel joy again.

## Acknowledgments

It sometimes takes a community to write a book, and I'm blessed to have a lot of people to acknowledge:

My acquisitions editor, Paul Dinas, who with patience and humor guided me through this process. My development editor, Lynn Northrup; production editor, Kayla Dugger; and copy editor, Jan Zoya.

My agent, Jessica Faust.

My boyfriend, Don Napolitano, who's cheerfully allowed me to retreat to my office and work, instead of spending time with him. Thanks for all the support, the wonderful dinners, *and* cleaning up the kitchen afterward.

My wonderful family, immediate and extended, has always supported me. I'm more grateful than I can express to have them in my life. Special thanks to my uncles, Peter Junger and Larry Codner, who've rescued me from computer issues many times over the years. Thanks also to my beloved grandparents, and my father, Robert Holland, who taught me about bereavement.

I've had so many friends support me in writing this book. I can't mention you all, but you know who you are.

To Louella Nelson, writing teacher extraordinaire, who taught me how to write fiction, and thus (hopefully) made this nonfiction book a better read.

To the writing community of RWA, especially the women (and a few men) of the Fantasy, Futuristic and Paranormal chapter. Whenever I had a question, someone on the FF&P online loop had an answer or something to contribute. Thanks SO much.

To my critique partner, R. J. Sullivan. Bob, thanks for setting aside your own work to critique my chapters. I appreciate all the help you've given me over the years. You're definitely the Comma King!

Some other friends have read some chapters and given me feedback. Joe Maizlish; Bart Palamaro; Ottilia Scherscel; Heidi Telpner, R.N.; Charity Gallardo; Linda Leszczuk; Kelly Whitely; Delle Jacobs, LCSW; Charlotte Maclay; and Mary Ellen Bowman, I'm *so* grateful for your help.

To friends who contributed some ideas, Pastor Bob Mooney; Shannon Holland, LCSW; Raphael Gunner, Ph.D.; and Terry Jordan, LCSW, thanks so much.

My church, Messiah Lutheran of Yorba Linda, including Pastor Bob Mooney and Pastor Ron Baesler.

Adventure boot camp and my fitness instructor, Suzanne Stringfellow, and all my friends in class, especially Wendy Swarts, kept me sane and in shape throughout the intense process of writing this book. Thanks, ladies.

Thanks to Shihan Brad Wenneberg and my fellow blackbelts at American Martial Arts Academy for teaching me how to get through intense experiences. I thank Mike Oats and Steve Hoppel, for taking over my morning karate class so I could write. Now it's back to training for third-degree blackbelt!

To two special women, Jonna Lannert and Kathleen Givens. You left too soon, and I miss you.

## Trademarks

All terms mentioned in this book that are known to be or are suspected of being trademarks or service marks have been appropriately capitalized. Alpha Books and Penguin Group (USA) Inc. cannot attest to the accuracy of this information. Use of a term in this book should not be regarded as affecting the validity of any trademark or service mark.

# Part 1

# Loss and Grief

You're grieving. Or someone you care about is grieving, and you want to understand what that person is going through and learn how to support him or her. You're hit with powerful emotions and other reactions that you don't know what to do about. You may wish all the painful emotions would just go away and you could get back to your normal life.

In this part, we look at what grief is and the kinds of things, such as loss, that cause us to grieve. We touch on misconceptions about grieving and how they can hurt or inhibit your grieving process. We expand on various kinds of loss and the way they affect you. We also explore trauma, because a traumatic experience sometimes causes grief as well as traumatic reactions—or something that causes you grief may also feel traumatic. Knowing about the effects of trauma enables you to take better care of yourself if you're in this situation.

# chapter 1

# The State of Grief

Everyone grieves

Grief can be complicated

People grieve differently

Myths that can impede the grieving process

Grief is a complex emotion that's often not understood, especially if you haven't experienced it before. Sometimes a person doesn't know he or she is grieving. For example, we don't usually associate "grief" with a job loss. Because of this, we might not completely heal because we don't know we're hurting in this area. However, unresolved grief is often an unfinished issue in people's lives. It can underlie anger, acting out, and depression, and it can cause problems in other areas, such as physical health, emotional well-being, job performance, or a romantic relationship.

## What Is Grief?

Grief is a profound feeling of sadness and pain caused by an important loss, change, crisis, or failure, either actual or perceived. Although grief is usually associated with *bereavement,* many types of loss, such as a job, a move, a failed relationship, or health problems, can lead to grief. There is a whole range of grief, from mild sadness—missing someone or something that's over in a few days—to abject suffering that can last for many years.

**Bereavement** means to be deprived by death. Someone whose spouse has died, for example, is said to be bereaved.

Because grief is often an unknown reaction, one you usually don't experience until you have an important loss, it catches people off guard. It's similar to other feelings you've felt, yet grief is still a unique experience. Grief is also unpredictable. It also differs in various circumstances, so you might not recognize it. Even if you've been through times of grieving before, no event feels the same. You can't anticipate what your grief will be like, or how long it will take to recover.

When you're grieving you can feel like you're going crazy or something is wrong with you. One of the benefits of educating yourself about grief is the sense of relief you receive from knowing what are normal reactions. Learning that you're grieving helps you make a shift in your coping. You have an emotional label for your reactions; you aren't weak, crazy, or overreacting. As painful as it is to settle into your grief, you can also have a sense of relief, as in, "Now I understand what's happening to me. I'm grieving!"

The ability to identify what you're feeling and why you're feeling it helps put your emotions into perspective. They aren't any less intense, just more understandable. Without the fear of being "crazy" or the pressure to change, you have more emotional resources to manage your grief. You can allow yourself to feel instead of worrying about your reactions.

When Ben's wife died from a cancer that quickly progressed, he took bereavement leave for six weeks before returning to his job. While at work, he was able to compare his pre-loss performance and his post-loss functioning, and could see a distinct difference, which worried him. He began to question how he was handling his grief and wondered if he'd come back to work too soon. Yet he also loved his job, and his boss and co-workers supported and cared about him.

Ben brought his concerns to me. "I'm so up and down. Sometimes I'm fine, then I'm struggling," Ben told me. "Sometimes I feel sad, and I've teared up a few times at work. I can't concentrate much." He gave me an anxious look, which eased when I reassured him that his reactions were normal. "Sometimes I feel like my muscles are sore, especially my shoulders, for no reason that I can tell," he added.

"That's normal, too," I said. "You've been carrying the weight of your world—your wife's illness and death—on your shoulders. You've probably been very tense in the last few months." Ben straightened in his chair. He looked relieved. Now he could stop worrying and focus on work and his recovery.

**cautions and concerns**    Even though aches and pains are a normal reaction to a loss, make an appointment with your doctor to rule out any physical causes.

Grief is complex and multilayered. Many in the depths of grief find words inadequate to explain how they feel. Others, especially those grieving the death of someone close to them, use words like "raw," "unpredictable," "empty," "terrified," "isolated," "confused," "exhausted," and "wild" to describe their emotions.

To grieve means to acknowledge in your heart, and to others, that your loss meant something to you, and that now you must honor the importance and pain of that loss. The reality of the grief journey—the sadness, tears and fatigue, the alteration of normalcy, changes in family, distancing of some friends and family—can be confusing, lonely, and difficult. Times of grieving can be the darkest, most troubled of our lives. Some who become mired in their grief can grieve for the rest of their lives.

However, you need not grieve forever. Part of recovery involves the knowledge that you need to give yourself the space to grieve for as long as it takes. Your journey from pain to recovery begins with the belief that you will come to terms with your loss. When you become discouraged, remind yourself, "I will recover. It will just take time."

## A Universal Experience

Grief is a universal human experience, a theme that winds through the seasons of our lives. No one escapes the pain of suffering losses through death and other circumstances. As the years pass, we will experience times of our own *mourning*, and we'll support others through their sorrow. Sometimes, we'll go through a period of little or no loss. Other times, losses will pile on us in a weight that we think we cannot bear. Then there are those in-between phases, where we have space to recover before the next crisis hits us. Or the loss is small enough to heal quickly.

**Definition**

While grief is an emotion, **mourning** is a state of being, a time of grieving where the individual focuses on his or her sadness. This length of time is different for everyone. There is no "normal."

Because grief and grieving eventually happen to all of us, it's important to know how to cope in the best way possible. While what works for one person won't necessarily work for another, there are many similarities to the grieving process. Often your best resource is others who've been through the same experience. They can support you throughout the crisis and to recovery. But family and friends can still listen and be there for you even if they haven't had the same personal experience with grief.

## Not Just Sadness and Disappointment

Grief is different from sadness and disappointment, although those feelings are included in the bundle of emotions that are part of grief. Most people have experienced sadness and disappointment before. Often things that cause these emotions first happen during childhood and adolescence. Learning to deal with these feelings is part of growing up.

Grief is characterized by pain and sadness, but a lot of other feelings and reactions comprise grief. (Chapter 3 delves further into grief reactions.) While sadness is a response to loss, you might also experience it from the following:

- Loneliness

- Someone or something hurting you

- The pain of others (including animals)

- Feeling troubled

- An unhappy event or one or more painful circumstances in your life
- Feeling discouraged and/or hopeless
- Pain from your past
- Feeling "blue" or "down"

We all experience disappointments, both large and small, throughout our lives. You feel disappointed when someone or something doesn't meet your expectations. You can be disappointed in yourself, in others, in things, in an ideal, or in an experience. The more you risk, the more you can feel disappointed by failure. Most disappointments are easily set aside, but others remain life-long feelings. If the pain of the disappointment is sharp, and the person doesn't let it go, it can turn into bitterness.

However, you can utilize disappointment to grow and change. You can reevaluate what caused your disappointment and use it to increase your efforts. You can head in a different direction, or let go of someone or something. You can also channel your sadness and disappointment into creativity. Your feelings can inspire stories, art, poetry, and music.

## Grief Is Different for Everybody

Grief often has an abrupt beginning—an event happens, and you're plunged into mourning. Other times, the loss is gradual, and you might have a corresponding slow build-up of grief. Sometimes it might take you a while to realize you're grieving. According to grief experts Russell Friedman and John W. James, authors of *The Grief Recovery Handbook* (see the Resources appendix), more than 40 events can cause grief. However, there may be far more than 40 events. We assign personal meaning to times, places, feelings, objects, our bodies and health, people, and pets. A loss that to many people isn't a big deal (something that might not even register on their emotional scale, such as the loss of a pet) may be very meaningful to someone else. Because grief is emotional, it doesn't always make sense.

**Cautions and Concerns**

It's important not to judge the grieving of others, because we can't determine for someone else what's important or how he or she should feel and behave.

There are some similarities and patterns to the grieving process. However, grief is as individual as the person who feels it. No two people will grieve the same way. Everyone's emotions are unique to them. The effects of a loss, and the amount and way someone will grieve, can be based on many factors, such as …

- Spiritual beliefs.

- Life experiences, especially of other losses.

- Types of loss suffered, and the circumstances of the loss.

- Developmental and cognitive abilities.

- Meaning assigned to the loss.

- Physical health, age, gender, and culture.

- Personality, temperament, and attitude.

- Family pattern of grieving.

- Social support and other meaningful activities in one's life.

## Misconceptions About Grief

A lot of myths exist about grief and grieving, especially when it comes to bereavement. Friends, family, co-workers, and even some religious advisors and counselors can cause harm to those who grieve, even though they mean well. They can give the wrong advice, or they can, subtly or overtly, criticize the person's grief journey.

Because of these misconceptions, the grievers may fail to *process* their grief in the healthiest ways. They may think something's wrong with them. Or they might try to avoid or suppress their feelings, which can lead to prolonged grieving and physical health challenges. Or they can become hurt and angry with those offering the "advice" and argue with them or withdraw.

definition

To **process** your grief means to allow yourself to feel your emotions instead of suppressing or avoiding them. You explore what you feel and why you feel the way you do. You come to accept your emotional state.

## It Will Pass

"Time will heal your pain" is a common misconception, as if the passage of days, months, and years is enough to make people feel better. People often toss this cliché at grievers, as if bestowing a great piece of wisdom. Even if it were true (which it isn't), what good does some hope of future relief do for someone who is grieving *now?* Often, after a loss, especially bereavement, people can hardly put one foot in front of the other. They're not sure if they can bear their grief for another 10 minutes, much less until a hypothetical future.

The truth is that time alone will not heal you. Time does help in that, eventually, you adjust to the loss. Time doesn't erase your emotions. You can still miss what and whom you lost. What the grievers do with the time is what makes the difference. If you just sit in a chair and stare out the window, waiting for time to heal you, you might be there a long time. You'll collect a lot of dust, but you won't make much progress.

| | |
|---|---|
| cautions and concerns | A small number of people may experience delayed grief. Initially, they may think they're fine (although perhaps they may be numb) and that feeling may last for weeks or even months before they begin to grieve. |

## Everyone Sympathizes

Most people do sympathize, but not everyone. Some people are too self-centered, busy with their own lives, or uncaring to feel for you, much less support you. But just because people sympathize doesn't mean they express their sympathy to you. They may do the opposite and avoid you. Or, if they say something, it may not come across in a helpful manner. Because most people don't receive education in talking about uncomfortable subjects, much less grief, they may handle the situation poorly for several reasons:

- They're uncomfortable.

- They don't know what to say, and are afraid they'll say the wrong thing.

- They don't like to see someone else's pain.

- They don't like the reminder that loss can happen to them.

- They're already negative people, so critical comments are consistent with their personality.

It's especially difficult for people to know the best way to support the bereaved. Many people would rather say nothing at all than say the wrong thing, and that can come across as uncaring. Most don't know that a simple sentence such as "I was sorry to hear about your loss" can make all the difference. Chapter 13 will go into greater detail about what to say (and what not to say) to someone who has had a loved one die.

People who are grieving often learn not to show how they feel. They try to share their feelings and perhaps aren't met with understanding, or maybe they're shamed by critical comments. To avoid the shame of others' implied or outright judgment or criticism, grievers often isolate themselves further to protect themselves. Yet that very isolation adds to the deep loneliness they may feel, and it lengthens (or even stalls) the recovery process. Chapter 18 goes more into how to take care of yourself when someone is unsupportive.

When Diana's house caught fire and burned down, she was traumatized and grief-stricken. But she found, when she tried to talk about losing her house in the fire, people kept telling her, "You should be grateful everyone got out safely." Diana was so very grateful that her family and their pets were all okay. But she was still upset about losing her house and wanted to share her feelings. Because she wasn't able to do so, she found herself becoming depressed.

While lack of understanding while you're grieving is often painful, the positive part of a loss may come from the unexpected support of some individuals or groups. For example, people you work with but don't really know give you a hug after the death of a family member, neighbors organize a clothing drive for your family after your house burns down, or strangers send money after reading about your loss in the newspaper. If you allow it, those who surprise you by reaching out can often balance (although not erase) the hurt of those you expected to be there for you but weren't.

## Distraction Helps

People are often told to "keep busy," as if distraction will make them feel better. Often grievers will try to exhaust their bodies so their thoughts will stay away from their grief and/or so they can sleep at night. Sometimes this is possible. Other times you'll feel tired *and* sleepless.

Dan and his 32-year-old son, Gary, worked for the same company. Gary was a fun-loving guy who enjoyed riding motorcycles. On one weekend trip, he was killed in an accident. Dan was devastated by the death of his son. He couldn't escape reminders of the pain because memories of Gary were around him at home and at work. While he and his wife deeply grieved together, when he was at work, Gary appeared to shut out his grief. He threw himself into his job and didn't talk much about his son. He became irritable and critical. Distraction was the only way he knew to avoid feeling his pain. His co-workers had no idea how much he was grieving.

Distraction does help, but only to a point. While meaningful occupation can be comforting, frantic busyness only serves to help the individual avoid feelings. Compulsive housecleaning, extensive yard work, and long hours spent on the job are all ways to avoid your feelings. However, some tasks such as cleaning and organizing your home are a way to feel in control of something (your environment) when you have no control over the death of a loved one or other losses.

In a recent workshop, I discussed ways of reducing stress and asked for examples from the audience. One participant mentioned that she cleans. I joked that cleaning would make me feel more stressed, and everyone laughed. But this is a good example of meaningful occupation. For this woman, cleaning has always helped her. Therefore, if she experienced a loss, using it as a way to cope would make sense for her. Even better would be if she'd allow herself to stop and reflect and perhaps cry when she dusted an object that reminded her of her loss. It's important to pick activities that help ease your stress rather than just exhausting you.

If you spent your time distracting yourself, your grief may remain underground, but not healed, and may spring up when you pause. It's important to balance periods of busyness with times of quiet. That might mean you'll start to feel and grieve when you pause. But that's what you need to do. Giving yourself this space is taking care of yourself.

Mandy discovered this for herself. She spent the first year after her beloved mother's death trying to distract herself through compulsive shopping, even though she'd never really liked to shop. She spent money she didn't have, which made her feel guilty. Finally, Mandy stopped shopping. As the reality of her mom's death set in, Mandy spent much of the second year in tears. It took a time of "real" mourning for her to move on from her deep grief.

**survival strategies**    One way distraction helps is to be of service in some way. Volunteer to assist those less fortunate. (There are always people who have it worse.) However, don't do this in the early phase of your grief. If you get too caught up in a cause, you may not have room to process your feelings.

## Don't Think About Sad Things

Grief isn't something that's controllable, yet some people believe it's better to try to restrain it. They'll tell you to put sad things out of your mind. Many grievers would love to follow this directive if they only could, but there's nothing they can do to control their emotions. They feel the way they feel, and they can't stop it. Whether they like it or not, their thoughts are preoccupied with their loss.

The lack of knowledge about grieving, accompanied by a suppression of feelings, can cause emotional blockage (or even damage), which can prolong recovery. It can also lead to physical stress or illness. People tell themselves, or are told by others, things like this:

- "Shrug it off."
- "Don't think about it."
- "Stuff happens."
- "Don't dwell on it."
- "What's done is done."
- "Think about the good things in your life."

Part of processing your loss is thinking about what makes you sad. You will return to your memories many times. Even though they may make you sad, they can also bring you comfort. Processing your grief, including the sadness, is a necessary part of recovery.

## It Could Always Be Worse

People tell themselves this phrase as a way to comfort themselves. There's nothing wrong with feeling some gratitude for the blessings you do have, even though you're grieving a loss. Holding on to gratitude is a helpful way to balance out your sorrow. Yet you can also use this platitude to cut yourself off from experiencing the full range of your grief.

When Nancy's 5-week-old son died suddenly, the only way she could get through the shock and pain was to tell herself, "At least it wasn't Donna." If she felt that much sorrow over the baby, how much more devastated would she have felt if she'd lost her 4-year-old daughter? Only years later did she realize she'd learned the "it could have been worse" philosophy from her mother, and had used it at the time because she didn't know how else to cope. With hindsight, she saw that if she'd been able to talk to supportive people, especially other mothers who'd been through the experience, she would have dealt with her son's death differently.

That doesn't mean you won't hear or read about someone else's grief story that is far worse than yours, and you can find yourself moved by their plight. These moments might give you some perspective and make you feel grateful for what you do have. However, these experiences must come from your own encounters in life, not those imposed on you by others.

People can use this cliché as a "band-aid" to try to put over the wound of someone's grief. They don't know how to *be* with your feelings, so they attempt to stop your pain. They think they can point you in another direction, which will make you feel better. While you might agree that things could be worse, it probably doesn't make you feel better.

Like anything else in life, it matters how you take care of yourself during your time of grieving. There are things you can do that aid in comforting and healing yourself. There are also things you can do that aren't beneficial. Chapter 20 will help you explore ways to cope with your grief.

## Essential Takeaways

- Everyone experiences times of grief.
- Grief is a complex and multilayered emotion.
- Everyone's grieving process is different and is based on several factors.
- Misconceptions about grief can interfere with the healing process.

# chapter 2

# Loss

Grieving and loss

Different types of loss

Living with regret

Coping with secondary loss

Recovering from loss

Part of being human is our capacity to love and to bond with people, things, and places. In addition, these connections provide us with identity, ideals, meaning, purpose, goals, dreams, roles, and a sense of security. Some connections can be deep and powerful. When we lose them, we experience grief.

## The Relationship Between Grieving and Loss

There are losses that disappoint us; make us sad, angry, ashamed, or resentful; and those where we simply shrug our shoulders and move on. Some losses motivate us to increase our efforts to overcome our problems. Then there are those losses, the most painful of all, which we grieve over. What differentiates grief from other reactions is the love and meaning we've given to the person, place, or thing we've lost. The more we love or need someone or something, and the more he, she, or it means to us, the more likely we are to grieve, and the longer and more intense our grieving experience.

# Types of Loss

A loss can be a cataclysmic event such as the sudden death of your child or a tornado that wipes out your community, or as seemingly insignificant as breaking a sentimental heirloom. Many people can make a list of the losses, large and small, they've accumulated over their lifetime. Some people have lives laden with loss. Others lead apparently charmed lives, with little impacting them. Most people fall somewhere in between. The longer you live, the more losses you'll experience.

Some people are more impacted by the losses in their lives. For them, it's not just the losses they experience, but also the way they experience those losses. In other words, it's not just what you're handed, it's what you make of it. Some people focus in a determined way on loss and negativity. Others are more balanced or optimistic.

Most people have busy, full lives. There's no space for a crisis or a loss to drop on you with all the attendant tasks that fall on your shoulders, as well as the complex grief reactions you experience. People may be surprised and dismayed to find an important loss can cause emotions that are more intense than any they have felt before. Your new must-do list and the depths of your emotions often leave you overwhelmed as well as grieving. Some losses might involve more busyness than others. While you're dealing with them, you may want or need to put some (if not all) of the rest of your life on hold. You'll have to take care of the urgent tasks before you can process your loss.

## People and Relationships

The loss of people we care about accumulates over our life span. For most of us, the greatest losses in our lives are the loss of close family members, the people we love deeply—children, spouses, parents, grandparents, and siblings. However, we can grieve the death of close friends, aunts, uncles, cousins, friends, co-workers, and pets. We can also become emotionally involved with public figures, even though we don't personally know them, such as professional athletes, movie stars, politicians, or singers and musicians, and grieve their deaths.

Beginning with the teen years, we can (sometimes often) experience the loss of love interests. Most people can still remember the pain they felt after the breakup of their first love or the pain of an unrequited crush. Although some people are married to their high school sweethearts, most people experience serial relationships, have their heart broken one or more times, and have to grieve the loss of multiple relationships. Aside from the death of loved ones, divorce is one of the most painful life experiences. Those who go through a divorce may grieve the loss of hopes and dreams and the good parts of their marriage for a long time.

## Loss as Positive Change

Not all losses are bad. Some involve life transitions that put closure to something we've accomplished, or end a certain period in our lives. They may also move us to a different place. While we might be happy about the change, we can still grieve how our life was before. For example, you find a new job. Obviously, that means better pay, benefits, or opportunities than the job you currently have. Yet you might miss valued co-workers, work you'd taken satisfaction in, tasks and goals you've accomplished, a familiar routine, and other things you value about your current job. You know at the new job you'll have a learning curve and new challenges, but it won't be the same. Even though you're excited, you may grieve for what and whom you leave behind.

Here are some other examples:

- Sending a child off to college and missing him—grieving that your "baby" has grown up and left you

- A young adult in her first semester of college who is homesick and grieving friends and former life

- Buying a new home and leaving behind friends in the old neighborhood, favorite haunts and activities, an organization you belong to, or the familiarity of your surroundings

- Grieving the single life and independence you're giving up when you get married

- Having your first baby, and grieving the loss of freedom and peaceful nights

- Landing a job after being unemployed for a while, and missing the time you spent with your family and the projects around the house you worked on that you must now put aside

J. K. Rowling, author of the *Harry Potter* series, struggled with grief after she'd finished writing the last book in the series. At first she felt ecstatic about the accomplishment, but then the grief hit her. She described the feeling as "a bereavement," and said it was "huge." Even though she had known the series was going to end, she'd lived with the characters for 17 years. And they were more than characters to her—they provided an escape from some of the difficult challenges she'd had in her life. When the grief hit her, she wept uncontrollably. The only time she'd ever cried like that had been when her mother had died.

It's important to take the time to acknowledge and process your grief. Often, people think they shouldn't feel sad or mourn because the next stage in their life is supposed to be (and actually is) a good thing. You can feel positive about your future and still grieve your past. By allowing yourself to process your emotions, you're able to work through them more quickly. Then you'll feel ready to take on the challenge of your new opportunity and appreciate and enjoy your changed circumstances.

**Cautions and concerns**

Disenfranchised grief occurs when the person incurs a loss that he or she thinks is shameful (or thinks his or her emotions are shameful), and therefore feels it can't be talked about, openly mourned, or acknowledged by others. Some examples are AIDS death, rape, testicular or prostate cancer, suicide, and losses due to gambling debts or drug addictions. The inability to openly grieve increases the impact of the loss.

## Anticipatory Loss

Sometimes, when we know a certain loss is in our future, we can grieve before that event actually happens. For example, a loved one is dying of cancer, our company has announced terminations that will take place in 90 days, or our house is in foreclosure. Anticipatory loss involves foreknowledge that you, your circumstances, or someone you care about will change in a way that you'll find painful.

Sometimes the stress before the event is so intense that when the actual loss occurs, we can feel relief. For example, when a loved one is slowly dying, we endure the heart-wrenching experience with him. By the time the individual passes away, we are relieved he is released from suffering. It's not that we aren't sad, or wish our loved one could be back with us, hale and hearty; we're just relieved he is finally free from pain and suffering.

With bereavement, family members can become more connected with the dying loved one. They have the opportunity to make amends for past wrongs; share memories, stories, and love; and make the physical, mental, and spiritual preparations for the death. Even though they know the death is coming, their grief is still as strong (or stronger) when the loved one passes. However, they may have few regrets because they handled everything beforehand.

Often the anticipation of the loss, and what you and others are going through, can take a toll on family members. When someone is dying, for example, sometimes loved ones withdraw from him or her as a way to avoid seeing someone suffering. Or they become angry or irritable so as to keep their fear and sadness at bay. They may bicker with each other, or even become estranged.

John's family had a hard time watching the big man wither away from cancer. The constant pain, frequent nausea, and exhaustion wore away at him and them. Most of his family rallied around him, spending a lot of time at his house. But one of his daughters couldn't take the stress. She'd burst into tears as soon as she saw her father, and started avoiding family gatherings. This caused some upset feelings on the part of the rest of the family, which lingered after John's death.

The relief you feel after the death may last for months. It's not until we've gotten over the trauma of watching our loved one die that grief might appear. This might take several months, or even a year. (Chapter 4 goes into more detail about trauma.) Sometimes the anniversary of the death will jump-start the stalled grieving process.

## Impact of Multiple Losses

Emotions from loss can accumulate, and with each one, the grief can build because the pain from the past contributes to your current feelings. It's as though each major loss layers on top of the last one. This can cause people to feel like the recent loss reopens the old wounds. This is especially true with bereavement. People coping with multiple losses may say things like:

- "I'd just gotten over (previous death) and now it's all come up again."

- "I'm dealing with the death of my (relationship) and now I have to feel this (new loss), too. It's too much."

- "My mom died 13 years ago, and the loss of my friend has brought it all up again."

Multiple losses can also make people feel as if life has given them too many blows, and they're not sure if they can pick themselves up and go on. They're tempted to give up, and perhaps actually do so (at least for a while). Other people may be more determined and keep forging on in the face of difficulties.

Expressions of Grief

"I lost many of my friends after my daughter died. They thought I should be getting over her death."

—Catherine, whose 14-year-old daughter died suddenly

# Loss and Regrets

The grieving process often involves regrets. If you've lost someone or something, you think back, seeing your mistakes (or what you now judge to be mistakes). You wish you could turn back time, make changes. I usually see three types of regrets.

## Type One

The first kind of regret focuses on prevention of the loss and usually begins with the words, "If only ..." and regards actions you wish you'd taken (or not taken):

- "If only I'd dragged my husband to the doctor, he might still be alive."

- "If only I hadn't fallen asleep at the wheel, I wouldn't have gotten into an accident and wrecked my car."

- "If only I'd locked all the windows, my house wouldn't have been broken into."

- "If only I'd kept my teenager at home that night instead of allowing her to drive to that party."

- "If only I'd worked harder at my job. My company might not have laid me off."

## Type Two

The second type also starts with "If only …" and involves actions you wish the victim had taken (or not taken):

- "If only my husband hadn't stepped on the ice, he wouldn't have slipped and frozen to death."

- "If only my wife had worn a seatbelt, she wouldn't have had the car accident that crippled her."

- "If only my friend had eaten healthy, instead of subsisting on junk food, he might not have had that heart attack."

- "If only my son hadn't left the door unlocked, we wouldn't have been robbed."

- "If only the sitter hadn't taken her eyes off my little girl, she wouldn't have drowned in the pool."

## Type Three

The third type of regret involves wanting to change something about yourself or what you did or didn't do in the past. You may wish you'd been a better person in some way. Or you can feel bad about something you left unsaid or undone. Conversely, you may regret some thing(s) you did say or do. People with this type of regret say things like:

- "I wish I had spent more time with my children when they were little instead of working so much. I didn't realize how fast they'd grow up, and that I'd be left with an empty house."

- "I should have told my wife more often that I loved her. I thought we'd have forever."

- "I used to complain about my son—how messy he was, how inconsiderate, how I had to force him to do his homework. If I had him back, I'd never complain again."

- "I never thought I'd get divorced. I took my husband for granted. I loved him too little, scolded, nagged, and complained too much."

As life goes on without a loved one's presence due to death, dementia, divorce, or abandonment, you can regret that a loved one is not present to witness your accomplishments or those of your family members. While most of the time you might feel fine, you can especially miss them when a special event or achievement happens.

> **cautions and concerns**
>
> While it's normal to have regrets, especially in the beginning of the grieving process, it's important not to dwell on them. The more you feel regretful, the more you can sink into self-loathing, depression, or bitterness. If you cling to your regrets, you can also become stuck in your grieving. Talk to friends, family, a grief counselor, or a psychotherapist about how you feel. Often others are able to put things into perspective for you.

## Secondary Losses

When grieving a death or another type of loss, we must cope with the primary loss as well as secondary losses that accompany it. A secondary loss occurs because of the primary one. Any secondary losses probably wouldn't have happened if the primary event hadn't transpired. For example, you're laid off from your job (primary loss), run out of savings (secondary loss), and the bank forecloses on your house (secondary loss).

Here are other examples of secondary loss:

- Relationships with friends, family, neighbors, and co-workers
- Our role in our family, community, job, or organization
- Our financial, social, or job status
- Income and/or financial security
- How we define ourselves
- A feeling of safety
- Our sense of control over our lives

Sometimes you might be aware of the secondary losses at the same time as the primary one. You may have to grieve all of them at once. Other times, you only gradually become aware of the secondary losses. Therefore, the time of grieving may be further impacted and extended.

You might also grieve the secondary loss. For example, your parents die, and you have to sell your childhood home. Or your secondary loss might not be about grief, but other things that may have an effect on your grieving. For example, if you wreck your car, you might have to deal with the physical effects, such as soft tissue damage and the resulting neck and headaches. You grieve the loss of the car, and also your sense of security. It's also possible you might not be aware of any grief for the secondary loss. Either it's too nebulous, or it's swallowed up or overshadowed by the primary problem.

## Financial Loss

For many people, an important crisis or loss also brings a financial burden, like medical or other bills, or a decreased income. Sometimes you have time to plan for the financial problem. For example, you have a 90-day notice of a layoff. Other times, events unexpectedly drop on you—you were laid off and escorted out the door of the company. Having to worry about money when you're struggling with difficult emotions adds stress to your grieving process. Or financial stress might interfere with it altogether as you fight for a way to survive. Lack of money can also limit the choices you have for coping.

Six months after Angela's mother died, all she was doing was struggling—with grief over the loss of her mother, to pay bills she'd never had before, and to keep her father from giving up on life. In the midst of all this, she realized she'd have to sell the only home she'd ever known. It was the only way the family could pay off her mother's hospital bills.

Also, the loss may not be just about the money. Often it's about a feeling of security and peace of mind. Now people have to deal with reduced income, and feelings of fear, anger, and betrayal in addition to their grief. In turn, financial problems can cause or exacerbate other situations or problems. For example, a couple can start arguing over money, thus stressing their relationship at the very time they need to team together.

## Loss of Ideals and Values

Losses aren't always about people or possessions. It's not uncommon to grieve for intangibles. Sometimes these can be primary losses, like when you have to give up a dream you've worked hard for. However, it's more likely that they are secondary losses. When someone you love dies, or you lose a job or a home, or your good health deteriorates, you can also lose the meaning those people, experiences, or things brought to your life, as well as your sense of purpose.

**Expressions of Grief**

"How can I be a father if my child is dead?"

—Dan, about the death of his only daughter

Some other examples of intangible grief are the loss of hopes, dreams, and expectations; a role or identity; innocence; a time and place; concepts and beliefs; and trust.

While writing this chapter, I took a break for lunch, preparing leftover soup and biscuits. I sprinkled the biscuits with water—a trick of my grandfather's (who died when I was 9) to bring back their freshness. Suddenly I was stabbed by sadness, remembering the Sunday breakfasts my grandfather would cook. He'd make a special trip to the bakery to buy our favorite rolls. I could visualize their shape, the crisp outside, and soft middle.

Tears came to my eyes, and I mourned, not just the loss of my beloved Opa, but of that time—surrounded by the love of my grandparents and other family members—as we ate a meal together.

Because these losses are more abstract rather than tangible, it's easy to suppress or ignore them. Or perhaps you might not even realize you're grieving one or more. This lack of awareness can cause a vague feeling of unrest or dissatisfaction. You may make impulsive or unwise decisions in order to escape the feelings. Stopping to pin down and process your grief will enable you to access your life with "clear eyes" and make healthier choices.

## Ongoing Loss

Some losses are ongoing. Instead of an event, like a death or loss of your job, this type of loss lingers. Your grief can feel unending because you are living with the continuous loss. You cannot forget because the reminders are all around you.

Here are some examples:

- Living with a debilitating illness, loss of limb, or brain injury
- Living in a house partially destroyed by a fire, earthquake, flood, or tornado and having no money to fix it or move to another one
- Losing a community due to war or natural disaster and living as a refugee
- Losing a job and being unable to find a new one
- Losing a home and becoming homeless

These kinds of losses also cause ongoing stress that can cause mental, emotional, and physical problems. In these instances, you usually have multiple losses because, in addition to the ongoing loss, you have several (or many) secondary losses. You might be so busy struggling to survive (and taking care of your family) that your grief is suppressed.

# Bouncing Back

A loss doesn't always have to remain negative. A serious loss can force a person to grow. It can also cause people to acquire knowledge and skills they didn't have before. Sometimes a loss propels people into a different situation that they wouldn't have chosen on their own. For example, a job loss may cause someone to start his or her own business.

Steve Jobs, co-founder and Chief Executive of Apple, Inc., is an excellent example of this. Right after his 30th birthday, in 1985, Steve had a falling out with the Apple board and ended up being fired from the company he co-founded. He was devastated and felt like a public failure. After a few months of not knowing what to do, he created a new company, NeXT, Inc. He also developed Pixar Animation Studios. NeXT was later bought out by Apple, bringing him back into the Apple fold. What Steve learned at Pixar, he was able to apply at Apple, leading to the successful creation of the iPod, iPhone, and iPad. Without the detour forced on him by the termination, Apple would not be the successful company it is today.

In real life, people overcome many things. The human spirit is remarkably resilient and has a tremendous capacity for healing. People can recover from the most debilitating situations. We have the ability to develop and draw on inner strengths such as personal commitment, persistence, courage, a positive attitude, love, and understanding. As painful and difficult as life changes are, they can also lead to increased personal strength, lessons learned, and a recovery that's different, and perhaps even better in some ways, than our existence before the loss.

## Essential Takeaways

- We need to honor our feelings of loss, no matter how insignificant the loss seems to others.
- We can grieve for various types of losses.
- Many losses are accompanied by secondary losses.
- After a loss we often struggle with regrets.
- Losses force us to grow in ways we may not have chosen on our own.

# chapter 3

# How People React to Grief

Grief reactions encompass all areas

Physical and emotional functioning

Mental, behavioral, and spiritual functioning

Tracking your grief journey

When we first undergo a loss, crisis, or major life event, we can feel confused and disoriented. We've just experienced a profound event that has changed our lives in some way. We may feel unable to think clearly or absorb what's happening. The loss might not make sense. It may take hours, days, weeks, or even months before the change feels "real."

## Grief Reactions

Grief may be experienced and expressed in physical, emotional, mental, behavioral, and spiritual ways. These feelings and reactions often intertwine. They might seem uncomfortable at times, especially if you're dealing with multiple effects. Yet they are a normal part of the mourning process.

Before you even experienced your loss, you might have struggled with certain physical, mental, and emotional symptoms. Or you might have never experienced the reactions before, and they manifest for the first time after your loss. If you've overcome them, they may return as you're grieving. Or if they still exist, they may become stronger. For example, if you had problems with anxiety, you might now become more anxious and occasionally have panic attacks. Some symptoms tie together; for example, a panic attack will cause shortness of breath and heart palpitations. It may also make you want to avoid situations that might upset you. In addition, you might have to cope with the symptoms you currently have, plus new grief reactions.

Expressions of Grief

"I keep asking why, but there's no answer."

—Len

You can have different reactions at different times in your grieving process, and they may change as time goes on. For example, in the beginning, you may feel shaky and agitated. Your thoughts are chaotic. You have no appetite and can't sleep. You cry often. Six months later, you may eat and sleep too much. Your thought processes are normal, but you're still sad and deeply miss what or whom you lost. You may still cry, but not as much as the beginning. A year later, you feel more like yourself. You have more good days than bad, although sometimes you're still sad. On a bad day, you might cry, but for not as long as before.

## Physical Effects

The physical effects that can accompany grief sometimes take healthy people by surprise. While stress headaches or fatigue may not seem unusual to them, they might not have anticipated the aches and pains or some of the other affects that can accompany grief. Sometimes the physical pain hurts enough to temporarily drown out your emotional pain. Or you can feel like a physical and emotional wreck.

When you feel physical effects, it's important to take care of yourself. Your symptoms may be worsened by poor lifestyle choices. If you start to feel worse—in more pain or exhaustion—you may cause other physical and emotional problems. In addition, the pain or fatigue can impact other areas of your life.

Nineteen-year-old Nathan lived with his single mother while attending college. When she died in a car accident, he experienced low energy and headaches, and lay on the couch watching television, sleeping, and sometimes crying. He subsisted on easy-to-obtain junk food and gained 30 pounds in six months. The extra weight and lack of ambition made him feel ashamed. It wasn't until he started participating in an online bereavement forum that he became "unstuck," moved off the couch, and began to join in life.

**MISC.**

**Men and Emotions**

Men may have a more difficult time than women getting in touch with their feelings. The male brain is more geared toward action rather than emotion. This is because in ancient times, the warrior/hunter needed to compartmentalize his emotions and focus on survival tasks. Men (both then and now) are also socialized from childhood not to feel or display "weak" feelings such as grief, fear, or sadness.

Some of the following physical effects are common and some are not. But all are within the range of normal (as long as they don't last too long or interfere with most of your day-to-day functioning). They include the following:

- Sobbing, sighing
- Trembling, chills, sweating
- Digestive disorders (nausea, indigestion, diarrhea, constipation)
- Change in sleep patterns—excess sleeping, difficulty falling and/or staying asleep, nightmares
- Feeling faint, weak, dizzy, or lightheaded
- Change in weight—gain or loss because of tightness/emptiness in stomach—and not feeling hungry, or overeating to fill the emptiness
- Change in sex drive—increase or decrease, more or less connection with a partner
- Shortness of breath, tightness in chest
- Tightness or soreness in the throat
- Easily startled or jittery

- Restlessness, agitation, clumsiness
- Weakened immune system

**cautions and concerns**

If your symptoms persist, check with your doctor to rule out any health problems.

It's important not to neglect your health, especially if you have others depending on you. It's easy, due to fatigue and feeling overwhelmed, to let personal self-care slide to the bottom of your to-do list. Your immune system may be weakened due to the loss and the grief and stress you're experiencing. You don't need to make it worse and add illness or disability to your time of grieving. Taking care of your body helps support the emotional and mental parts of yourself. Chapter 20 will give you tips for self-care.

## Emotional Effects

During a loss or other unsettling event, it's normal to have emotional reactions, which are different for each individual. Some people may feel more affected than others, even when they suffer the same loss. Some people are unsettled by the feelings they may never have felt before (or never felt with such intensity). They may not know how to cope with grief, especially when they're dealing with a major loss.

**survival strategies**

Don't let others dictate what is emotionally right for you. Other people, especially if they haven't experienced a similar loss, can give you the wrong advice.

When Matt was terminated from his high-powered job, he felt like he'd been "hit with a two-by-four." His neck and shoulders hurt. He alternated between anger and numbness. He felt betrayed by his company and resented that they kept someone who wasn't even as good, but had a lower salary. Sometimes, he'd feel afraid for the future. "What will happen if I can't get a job?" he thought. Although he tried not to, he missed his work and his co-workers, especially his golfing buddies, who hadn't called since he was laid off. Although Matt was ashamed to admit it, he'd also broken down in tears a time or two, but only when no one was around.

Some other emotional grief reactions include the following:

- Sensitivity
- Regret, guilt
- Sadness, hopelessness, apathy
- Anxiety, panic or panic attacks, fear or phobias
- Agony, anguish
- Longing, loneliness
- Shame
- Depression, not wanting to live anymore, mood swings
- Minimizing (trying to not feel or make your feelings unimportant)
- Relief
- Abandonment, bitterness, blame
- Emptiness, lower self-esteem
- Powerlessness, helplessness, sense of being out of control

**Cautions and concerns** Many studies have concluded that women tend to cry about five times more than men. Tears can be a normal way for women to express their feelings. However, women are also more at risk for depression and some types of anxiety disorders than men.

Tears are a common reaction to grief. Physically, the act of shedding tears during a highly emotional or stressful event removes toxic substances from the body. Tears also contain leucine enkephalin, which is a natural pain reliever.

Emotionally, tears are a type of language. They communicate that something is wrong—you're in pain, you're sad, or you're hurt. They (usually) cause other people to soften toward you, to empathize, or to try to console you. Although men don't usually cry tears of anger, it's not uncommon for women to feel mad and cry (and hate the fact that they are doing so).

We don't just cry from negative emotions; we can also tear up when moved by beauty, love, pride, sentimentality, and human or spiritual connection. Tears of grief can vary from a few seconds of moist eyes to deep, wrenching sobs, lasting for hours. When we see someone crying, we, too, can start to cry, both from our own sadness and from our empathy for the mourner.

## Mental Effects

While mental reactions can persist for weeks and even months after a loss, they are usually strongest in the hours and days right afterward. The confusion and disorientation start to disappear as you adjust to what's happened.

When Paul's wife abruptly left him, his business also suffered because he was distracted and had a hard time concentrating and making decisions. The utilities were shut off because he forgot to pay the bill. When no one was around, he'd break into tears. Most nights, he had a hard time sleeping. He constantly replayed scenes from his marriage, wondering what went wrong. His buddies tried to get him to go out with them, but he didn't want to talk or socialize.

Some mental reactions include the following:

- Short attention span—difficulty focusing, concentrating, and comprehending
- Forgetfulness
- Surreal sense
- Vivid dreams/nightmares
- Difficulty making decisions
- Feeling overly critical

While most mental symptoms wear off within a few days or weeks, a few may persist. Don't make important decisions while in this state. If possible, make sure you take safety precautions. For example, if you're having a hard time concentrating, let someone else drive. Most of all, be kind to yourself. Don't berate yourself for forgetfulness or making mistakes.

When men are under extreme stress or are depressed, they're often irritable. But they're not very in touch with why they're irritable. They tend to blame outside circumstances and other people rather than recognize what they're really feeling inside.

## Behavioral Effects

Sometimes your behavior during grief is in line with your personality. For example, if you already enjoyed solitude and solitary activities, you might retreat into isolation. Or you might find yourself going against your normal personality—you usually enjoy solitude, but now crave the company of others. You can't bear to be alone with your thoughts and feelings. Sometimes these are behaviors you deliberately choose, such as socializing. Other times, you may find yourself doing them without much conscious thought, such as wandering aimlessly around the house, neighborhood, or office.

There's nothing wrong with solitude if you need to be alone to think, feel, and come to terms with your loss. Just make sure you don't completely isolate yourself from friends and family. Those connections are important. Talking to others about your memories and feelings helps you heal.

Some other behavioral effects of grief include the following:

- Avoidance, shutting down
- Needing to be with others, excessive partying
- Erratic, irrational behavior
- Being frantically busy or overactive in certain areas, like work
- Needing to talk about the deceased
- Dependency on other people
- Difficulty with communicating
- Identification, where you wear something from the deceased or that reminds you of them
- Apathy or disinterest in things you used to find pleasurable

You might also experience phantom behaviors, where you glimpse the deceased in a crowd. For a second you may think the person is really there. Your heart can leap, only to crash into reality when you remember that he or she can't possibly be there. Or you might think you see the deceased and at the same time, know you're just seeing someone like him or her. But you feel a poignant wish that it were true. Or, if you're in a familiar area, you might search for the beloved face in the crowd, even though you know it won't be there. Sometimes these phantom encounters can happen years after the death.

Two months after Katie's boyfriend, Matt, died in a motorcycle accident, she was at a shopping mall, and saw a tall, brown-haired man in the distance. There was something about his walk and the set of his shoulders that made her think, "Matt!" Her heart leapt, and she hurried after him, all the while knowing it couldn't be true. But she couldn't stop the hope that propelled her to catch up with him. Then he turned and she saw his profile. Not Matt. She burst into tears.

**Cautions and concerns** Many people don't like to discuss major personal problems with others, especially subjects like divorce, illness or death of a family member, or a serious illness of their own. Yet studies show that people who try to suppress or deny their feelings may have increased health problems.

## Spiritual Effects

Losses can cause some painful spiritual effects in our lives, as we struggle to find meaning from the experience and process our grief. It's not uncommon, especially right after a loss, to question, blame, or become angry with God. We can wonder if God has deserted us or if we've done something for which we're being punished. The following are some reasons we may become angry with God:

- The death of a child or other special person

- A sudden, tragic accident

- If you prayed for healing and believed it would happen but it didn't

- A loss that's overwhelming

- A loss that doesn't feel fair

- If you've worked hard for something and it's taken away

- You feel betrayed by God

Some people previously might not have given much thought to an afterlife, but the passing of loved ones (and other losses) can make them think of spiritual concepts they might never have considered before. They may discard their traditional beliefs after a loss, or they may form a new conception of God or of what they believe.

**survival strategies** | Sometimes people feel guilty about their anger with God, as if their emotions are sacrilegious. Yet, if you're a believer, it helps to express your feelings to God, anger and all.

People can also draw a great deal of comfort from their religious beliefs. They can feel spiritually sustained by their faith and supported by those from their fellowship who gather around them. They can feel grateful to be spared in some way from further losses. They might cling to the belief that they will be reunited with loved ones in an afterlife. They may have others stepping forward with unexpected support and feel a profound connection with the human spirit and a new appreciation of the goodness of people.

After a loss, people can become less materialistic or driven to succeed at work because they've experienced a shock that taught them what was really important. They can make different lifestyle choices. They may find a new balance between work and personal life. They may feel much freer without as many personal possessions.

Dr. Laura Schlessinger, a radio talk-show host and author, shared her family's reaction to their house burning down. After they rebuilt, her family didn't replace 75 percent of their possessions. She said they discovered they didn't need all that "stuff." They'd learned family was what really mattered.

These are some other ways you might have been spiritually affected:

- You're angry at a religious institution or the clergy.

- You lose faith in God.

- You feel a closer connection with God or a departed loved one.

- You desire to change and become a better person, create meaning in your life, or impact/change the world in some way.

# Moving Forward

Think about tracking your grief journey. It may help to note what you're feeling and doing. Write down your feelings and reactions in all areas—physical, emotional, mental, behavioral, and spiritual. By keeping a record in a journal, you'll be able to see small improvements. The more you focus on the improvements, the more you can feel hopeful instead of discouraged.

## Essential Takeaways

- Grief can change your familiar patterns of thinking, feeling, and acting.
- A loss can affect you in all areas of your life—your mood, health, interaction with others, work, and how you see yourself.
- Men and women often express their emotions differently.
- Shedding tears may help you cope better with what you're going through.

# chapter 4

# Grief and Trauma

Defining trauma

Experiencing a traumatic event

The different ways we react to trauma

Recovering from trauma

Often trauma and grief are intertwined because death or other loss can occur in a shocking way and a traumatic event also involves one or more losses. Both a traumatic event and the death of someone we love are severe stressors. When they happen together, we have to deal with both the affects of trauma *and* of grief.

## What Is Trauma?

Trauma involves an event outside our normal experience that frightens us and makes us feel helpless. The traumatic incident overwhelms our normal ways of coping, pushing us into an emergency state. Whether we are involved in the event or witness it, the more shocked, terrified, and powerless we feel, the greater we will be impacted. The acute stress we undergo may adversely affect our physical, mental, and emotional well-being. Most of the time, our reactions last only a few days. But the effects may also last a lifetime.

Tracy had just bought a snazzy new sports car, which she loved. Then one night, a drunk driver hit her, totaling her beloved car. Although she cried, her tears were as much about anger as grief. She found herself making stupid mistakes that were unlike her, such as locking herself out of the house. Even her boyfriend complained that she "had lost her brain." She had trouble sleeping for a few nights because, once she closed her eyes, she kept seeing the truck speeding toward her. She often replayed the incident in her mind. She broke out in tears the first time she had to get into the rental car because it made her miss her sports car. In addition, the first few days of driving, she felt vulnerable, imagining another accident. She knew she needed to buy a new car, but the research and decision-making seemed too overwhelming. It took several weeks before she felt normal again.

> **cautions and concerns**
> An ongoing painful and/or frightening situation such as physical, sexual, or emotional abuse; early childhood neglect; or the terminal illness of a loved one can also traumatize us.

## Traumatic Events

When we experience a traumatic event such as a car accident, fire, assault, robbery, natural disaster, or seeing someone die, we have a hard time processing what's happening. A traumatic incident can occur so rapidly that you don't really understand what's happened. One moment everything is normal, the next chaos has broken out. Often the complexity and (usually) unexpected occurrence makes it difficult to understand and absorb. Your thoughts have a hard time catching up with reality.

Some events, such as a robbery or an earthquake, may last only a few minutes. But while you're in the middle of one, it can feel like it takes forever to get over. Other traumatic experiences can last for hours, days, or even months. In describing their initial reaction, people use words such as "stunned," "disbelieving," "dazed," "overwhelmed," "incredulous," and "surreal."

The way in which an individual deals with a crisis, both when it's happening and afterward, is unique, and is based on that person's training, coping ability, personality, values, life experiences, fears, expectations, beliefs, and support system. For example, if you work in a hospital or are a police officer or firefighter, you might not be affected in the same way a kindergarten teacher is. Also, the more traumatic events you experience in your life, the more impact it has on you. You might have a harder time recovering from subsequent ones.

## War and Disaster

War or disaster is an extreme form of traumatic situation. Those who are caught in a war zone or experience a natural or human-made catastrophe must survive the event with all the fear and danger accompanying it. But they also have to live with the aftermath, which may be just as horrible (or even more so).

The terrorist attacks on 9-11, Hurricane Katrina, or the 2011 earthquake and tsunami in Japan are examples of disasters. The people involved lived through the catastrophe in fear for their lives, witnessed the horrors, and then had to keep experiencing the aftermath—destroyed buildings, bodies, and people searching for loved ones.

In war or disaster situations, you often witness destruction to most (or even all) of your surroundings or environment. In addition to the deaths of family, friends, and neighbors, there's the loss of possessions, homes, and perhaps the entire neighborhood or community. Often people struggle with immediate survival because of the lack of food, drinkable water, or shelter. Lawlessness can make you fear for your life and/or your home and possessions. Many times, you're so busy trying to survive or cope with the damage, you have no time to grieve. The grief might hit you later, when things have settled down, or it may come in the form of other reactions that you don't recognize as grief.

For some, the external triggers from war or disaster—such as destroyed buildings—can last for years. The constant reminders make it harder for survivors to recover. For example, without the Twin Towers, many people glancing at the changed New York City skyline are jolted into remembering what happened on that day, perhaps bringing up traumatic reactions.

**survival strategies**

Even if you weren't present during 9-11, Hurricane Katrina, or the earthquake and tsunami in Japan, you can still feel traumatized from viewing the images on television and experiencing intense emotions as you watch. Children are especially vulnerable. Limit your television watching during disasters and keep your children from watching. Read the newspaper (either the paper version or online) instead.

When in a war, both soldiers and civilians frequently fear for their lives. They are constantly on the edge, knowing danger could happen at any moment. They may not be able to trust anyone because it's difficult to know who are the enemies and who are genuine, friendly people. Soldiers must be ready to kill others, which can be emotionally difficult to do, in spite of training, or knowing others are the "enemy." The need to constantly be prepared to defend oneself or to actually kill someone takes a toll.

Because they don't feel safe while at war, and usually experience trauma, soldiers carry those feelings and reactions home with them. It's not uncommon for them to have a difficult adjustment back to civilian life. They may have multiple reactions, including *flashbacks* and nightmares. Not all flashbacks begin visually. Their mind and body can replay sounds and smells. They can also experience physical flashbacks, for example, from being grabbed or poked by a gun. They keep feeling the negative touch and then re-experience the trauma.

Research shows that soldiers who've returned home often speak less and become easily irritated. Even those with laid-back personalities can become angry. They may have difficulty feeling emotions, even with loved ones. Some are more debilitated by their traumatic reactions, causing a diagnosis of *Post-Traumatic Stress Disorder* (*PTSD*). Symptoms of PTSD last more than a month and interfere significantly with life. If untreated, they may continue for months, years, or even decades. Those with PTSD respond well to a combination of medication and psychotherapy.

definition

**Flashbacks** are thoughts that jump back to a traumatic event. It may feel as though you're re-living the experience. **Post-Traumatic Stress Disorder (PTSD)** is a medical diagnosis. The classic symptoms are flashbacks and nightmares. Sufferers can also experience irritability, angry outbursts, persistent fears, emotional numbness, and social withdrawal.

You don't have to be a soldier to have PTSD. Ordinary citizens can receive the diagnosis, too. Trauma, or several traumas, can pile too much stress and pain on you, and you just can't cope. It's not uncommon for sufferers to go a while before going to a doctor or counselor. Usually this happens because they don't understand what's wrong, don't know what to do, or are too ashamed to seek help.

## Primitive Responses to Fear

During the traumatic incident, you're under acute stress, and intense fear is a primary emotion. When that intense fear is accompanied by thoughts of, "I'm going to die!" or "I'm going to be hurt!" the body will respond by initiating what's called the "fight-or-flight response." This response is controlled by the more primitive part of our brain that harkens back to our caveman days. When ancient humans were afraid, it often meant something with sharp teeth and claws was headed their way. Their only choices were to fight—using rocks, sticks, or spears—or run away and hope they weren't caught. Fast forward thousands of years, and our bodies still respond to acute stress in the same way.

The evolutionary fight-or-flight response is a prewired automatic survival reaction for dealing with dangerous situations. It prepares the body to fight or flee from real or perceived danger. The fear and perception of danger causes a chain reaction in our brain, and alters the brain chemistry, bypassing the part of the brain that controls rational thought. The chemicals adrenaline, noradrenaline, and cortisol are released into the bloodstream. These cause a rise in blood pressure and blood sugar, rapid heartbeat, fast breathing, and energized muscles. Our senses sharpen. Our pupils dilate. Endorphins, which are the body's natural painkillers, are released. Unessential systems, such as digestion, shut down.

Most of the time in our modern society, we can't fight. Nor can we run. Another primitive response to danger is freezing. Ancient humans would hide behind a rock or a tree and hope who or whatever was stalking them would pass by. Nowadays, freezing is a likely response to fear. That doesn't mean you literally can't move (although some people are affected to this extreme), but you tighten all your muscles and take shallow breaths. You may react and handle the situation well—your body just doesn't have a chance to fight or flee, so you freeze the fear into your muscles.

**survival strategies**

Cardiovascular exercise that gets your legs moving helps to lessen the effect of traumatic reactions. Strenuous exercise activates your central nervous system and retrains your brain. It doesn't have to be long; 20 minutes will do. Go for a brisk walk; jog; bike; swim; play soccer, tennis, or basketball; or put music on at home and dance around the room with your kids.

## Thoughts, Emotions, and Trauma

It's not necessarily what happens during the traumatic incident that makes the most impact on you, especially if you aren't physically injured. When you experience a trauma, what you think and feel is as important (if not more so) as what actually happens to you.

In some frightening situations, such as robberies, we are preprogrammed through viewing movies, television shows, and the news that a robbery ends in injury or death. It doesn't matter that statistics about shootings during robberies are actually very low; it's what we *imagine* that makes the difference in our brain. Therefore, when you're a victim of a robbery, your mind easily jumps to thoughts of, "I'm going to die." Your brain plays a movie that involves shooting and lots of blood, detailing what's going to happen to you.

When two gun-carrying men robbed the store where Nicole worked, her first thought was, "They're going to kill me." The robbers demanded the money from the cash register, and, with shaky hands, she tried to scoop it up. "Hurry!" one robber ordered, pointing the gun at her. Images of her baby son flashed through Nicole's mind. "He's going to grow up without me," she thought. The robbers took the cash from the till and left. They'd been in the store for a total of 1 minute and 59 seconds. But the impact on Nicole lasted for months.

In circumstances like Nicole's, where a scary and traumatic situation is coupled with intense emotion, the brain experiences what you think as real. It doesn't matter that the robbers had no intention of killing Nicole, or that they actually did not harm her. In her mind, she was dead! In those seconds, she grieved the life she'd never have with her son, and she grieved for her son who'd have to grow up without a mother. Even though the horrible vision was only in her mind for a very short time, it registered on her subconscious as fact, and the effect on her body was as if it had really happened. As you can see by Nicole's experience, the thought about the trauma can be as debilitating as the reality.

## Personality and Trauma

People who are sensitive and imaginative are more apt to experience acute stress during what they interpret as dangerous situations. Because of their sensitivity, they tend to feel more frightened by encounters or experiences that would leave a less susceptible person unaffected. For example, sensitive children can feel scared when a parent raises his or her voice. A volatile parental argument might send the child scurrying under the bed for safety. A different child might continue playing with his or her toys and barely notice the fight.

Although Sherry didn't witness the death of her co-worker, David, when he was hit by a company van, she heard detailed descriptions from the witnesses. Although she didn't know David very well, she vividly kept picturing the van hitting him, sending his body flying. She found herself crying throughout the day, but tried to hide her reactions because her less sensitive colleagues (who also didn't know David well) didn't seem as affected.

Because of their vivid imaginations, sensitive people not only replay the incident as it happened, but imagine what might have occurred. Instead of focusing on the positive—"I'm safe"—they imagine the myriad things that could have gone wrong. For example, after a robbery, they keep thinking, "I could have died." If they dwell on the fear fantasy they've created, they keep their anxiety level high and their body revved up in the fight-or-flight response. It's like living in a horror movie that they replay over and over. They become stuck in what could have happened.

These "what could have happened" anxieties can be strengthened by others. It's not uncommon for parents, spouses, and friends to make statements like, "You could have been killed!" If friends and family react in fearful, protective ways, they can reinforce the victim's stress and fear. Luckily, this type of thinking is one of the easiest traumatic reactions to dissipate. Once people learn that they continue to stress their body by the negative fantasy they've "made up," they can usually work on stopping their thoughts and calming their physical reactions when they begin to replay the "what could have happened."

## Reactions to Trauma

If we experience a traumatic event, it's very common for us to have a wide range of emotional or physical reactions. These are normal reactions to an abnormal situation. Our mind and body can remain alert for danger, even after the danger no longer exists. Sometimes things remotely associated with the event (even if it's just our thoughts) can set off the reactions (or over-reactions).

The amount you're exposed to the event and the loss you suffer will make a difference on how adverse your reactions are. The timeline of your reactions to the traumatic stressor begins with your response to the event and continues as long as you have symptoms. When you know the common reactions, you can identify those that stem from your traumatic experience.

## Physical Reactions

It doesn't matter how strong you are or what shape you're in, you can still have physical reactions to a traumatic event. Some of the most common physical reactions are these:

- Shakiness, weakness, or dizziness
- Heart palpitations, difficulty breathing, or panic attacks
- Being easily startled/jittery
- Nausea, headaches, sore muscles
- Difficulty sleeping, usually because of replaying the incident; waking up drenched in sweat
- On the verge of tears when thinking about the event, or wanting to cry, but can't
- Appetite changes, not wanting to eat, or eating too much

## Mental Reactions

When our bodies release a surge of adrenaline because of the traumatic event, it impresses the memory into our brain, which makes it difficult to forget what happened. Remembering the traumatic incident can make us anxious. The negative memory can easily be triggered, which is why people avoid places, objects, smells, and wearing certain clothes that remind them of the event. In addition to flashbacks and nightmares, here are some mental reactions:

- Intrusive thoughts

- Hyper-alertness

- Avoidance behavior that includes trying not to think of or feel about the incident, and avoiding the place where it occurred

- Feeling vulnerable, including unsafe at home

- Numbness, confusion, difficulty understanding the details of what has happened

- Wanting to isolate, or not wanting to be alone

- Difficulty with focus and concentration

- Replaying the event over and over

After Nicole was robbed, she was shaky and tearful. As soon as she arrived home, she hugged her young son and wouldn't let go of him for a long time. She even took him to bed with her. That night, she couldn't sleep, imagining that the robbers had followed her home. She'd doze off, then startle awake at every sound. It took a week before she was able to sleep without her baby.

**cautions and concerns** The risk of traumatic reactions may increase from the severity of the trauma, childhood abuse, or a history of mental illness.

## Emotional Reactions

After a traumatic event, people can struggle with various emotions. Sometimes, these are intense. The feelings may seem as if they come out of nowhere. You may be aware that the emotion is linked to the incident, but you don't know why you're feeling it now. You may have missed the subconscious cue that triggered your reaction. Some common emotional reactions are guilt, anger, helplessness, anxiety, irritability (a "short fuse"), depression, shock or numbness, and fear (which may feel irrational).

Those who were exposed to the traumatic incident may re-experience the trauma when they return to the place where the original event occurred. It may take the form of fear and anxiety, accompanied by thoughts of "I need to get out of here."

Emotional stress can change brain function. Preliminary brain research is showing that a single exposure to acute stress affects information processing in the cerebellum, which is the area of the brain responsible for motor control, movement coordination, and learning and memory formation.

Although a few people may suffer acute reactions, such as depression, anxiety disorders, and PTSD, most people get better on their own. Their symptoms will usually subside after a few days, and disappear completely after a week or two. Knowing about these reactions will help you not feel crazy, especially when you have reactions that don't feel like your usual ways of responding.

## Delayed Reactions

Traumatic reactions may unexpectedly surface weeks or even months after the event. They may seem like they appear for no reason, and you can wonder what's happening to you. By that time you may not think to relate your symptoms back to the trauma.

If you've experienced a traumatic incident, it's important to remember you may have delayed reactions, so if you start to feel different in some way, you can link them back to the event. It also helps to educate close friends and family members about trauma. Sometimes they're the ones to see the differences in you. They also might be better at remembering that what's happening to you now may be related to your previous trauma.

# The Double Whammy of Trauma and Grief

When you're dealing with both trauma and grief, you're hit with a double whammy. Your traumatic reactions might get in the way of your grief. Or you can feel impacted by both. For example, if you were present when your loved one died, then you might have flashbacks of the body. For some, it might be difficult to get that picture out of their minds. You can cry and grieve every time you think of the person as he or she looked in death. The more severe and sudden the cause of the death you witnessed, the more you may experience trauma symptoms. The combination of trauma and grief might feel incapacitating.

Jeff belonged to a bicycle group that met every Saturday. On one of their outings, the group rode around a corner, Jeff in the lead. He swerved out a yard too far, moving from the bike lane into the street, where he was struck by a car. All his friends witnessed the event and tried to help him, but he died at the scene, leaving everyone traumatized and grief stricken. They banded together for a group counseling session, which helped them understand their reactions and process their feelings. It still took time before all the friends were willing to ride their bikes again.

It doesn't just have to be the loss of a person that can bring on grief and trauma. Traumatic events also involve the destruction of property and pets, and you may grieve their loss. You might also feel empathy and concern for others who are affected by the experience.

Let me relate a story that in a small way illustrates how trauma can color your grief. My cat Angel was 4 years old—middle aged in cat years. She was a delicate white Persian, with beautiful translucent blue eyes. One night I came home from work, and, as she walked toward me, her hindquarters collapsed. She dragged herself the rest of the way, terror in her eyes. I scooped her up and rushed her to the vet. Hours and several tests later, the vet showed me her X-rays, and pointed out a tumor on her spine. Gently, he advised me to euthanize her.

He led me to a room where Angel was brought to me. I cuddled her and cried, kissed her head, told her how much I loved her, and said goodbye. Then the vet came in, and I laid Angel on the table. The vet was very kind, and he told me that it would be over in less than a minute. I stroked her, and watched the life fade from her eyes.

For the next few days, I cried and grieved. But I also realized I had trauma symptoms. I kept having flashbacks to Angel's empty blue eyes. I often felt shaky, and had some nightmares. I'd never been present when a beloved pet died, so I hadn't known what to expect. Plus, I'm a sensitive person, which made me more vulnerable to the experience, although other, less sensitive people, might not have been as affected. I made sure to write about my feelings, which helped me feel better. I also talked to other pet lovers who understood.

If I hadn't witnessed the death, I still would have had grief from Angel's passing—sadness, missing her, tearfulness, and having a hard time sleeping without her customary presence next to my legs. But I wouldn't have had the traumatic symptoms of flashbacks, nightmares, and shakiness. I'm not sorry I made the choice to be with her. I just had to pay a price for that decision. My traumatic reaction lasted two days, although I missed Angel for a long time.

## Coping with Grief-Related Trauma

Traumatic stress and grief can affect your academic or work performance. It can make you distance yourself from friends and family. The reactions can cause problems in your relationships, especially if you have family members, friends, and co-workers who are also affected by the event.

The effects of trauma can have a severe impact on your grieving. It's important to diminish (with help, if necessary) the traumatic reactions so you can achieve enough physiological stability to have energy available for grieving and adjustment processes. When you begin to confront your traumatic reactions, you might feel uncomfortable or frightened. You don't like reliving the experience. But research shows that those who have experienced a trauma and avoided talking about it are more susceptible to a variety of illnesses. Talking about what you went through with others who are supportive is one of the best ways to cope. It helps you assimilate what happened. The more you process your emotions, especially during the first week after the trauma, the more improvement you'll have in your long-term health and emotional well-being.

While intrusive thoughts of the trauma are normal and often outside your control, let them play out but don't dwell on them. Try to switch your thoughts to a positive image, for example, your child laughing or you petting your dog or cat. Remind yourself that you're safe. The intrusive thoughts might jump back in your mind, but, as much as possible, keep calmly switching them. For example, change, "I could have been killed!" to "I'm grateful that I'm safe."

### Breathe In, Breathe Out

misc.

One of the best tools we have to reduce stress and trauma is our breathing. When we're afraid or stressed, our muscles tighten, causing our breathing to become shallow, and depriving ourselves of some oxygen at the very time we need it the most. Taking some deep breaths can calm and center us. Deep breathing during a stressful event (or during later recollections of the event) will help us cope with it better. For natural breathing, when you take a deep breath, your belly should expand. When you exhale, your belly should pull in.

Track your traumatic reactions in a notebook or journal. For each one, note the severity and how quickly it fades. They should lessen within a few days and disappear completely within a few weeks (although you might have one or more re-emerge for a short while). If the reaction(s) interferes with your normal life, or lasts more than a few weeks, you should seek help from a counselor who specializes in trauma.

A few years after the trauma of her parents' death, Anne went to a psychologist and was diagnosed with PTSD. "It explained all the black holes in my memory and all my bad behaviors," she said. Anne felt better, in part, because she could put a name on the cacophony of emotions and issues inside her.

Feeling alone or abandoned makes trauma harder. Having a social network and coping strategies appear to offer some protection from the acute stress reactions. Social support can give you resilience. Other things you can do to help yourself are these:

- Set limits with others during those times you don't feel like talking.

- Rest, eat healthy, exercise regularly.

- You may find practicing yoga and meditation to be helpful.

- Take a good multivitamin and omega-3 (salmon or krill oil) supplement to support your body and brain.

- Avoid caffeine. You're often jittery enough, and caffeine will only make it worse. (Remember, caffeine isn't just in coffee and tea. It's also in many soft drinks.)

- Avoid using drugs, alcohol, or sleeping pills.

- Engage in a mix of activities you've previously found satisfying and enjoyable.

- Choose your support system carefully. A buddy who thinks a night of drinking will fix you isn't the best person for you to be around right now.

Those who survive a traumatic experience often feel a renewed appreciation for their lives. They may reassess what's really important to them and make changes. Their self-confidence can increase because they've survived a horrible experience. They may feel stronger and more capable.

## Essential Takeaways

- A traumatic event is a frightening and extremely stressful situation that can overwhelm our normal coping methods.
- Experiencing a trauma can be a shock to your whole system, and you can have unfamiliar emotional and physical reactions to the event.
- When you have a harrowing loss, you can experience both trauma and grief reactions.
- After a period of trauma and grief, you can feel stronger than before.

# Part 2

# Bereavement

In this part, we look at the grief journey. We start with some historical perspectives of death and some theories about grief, and then cover the various emotions you might feel. We talk about the people you've loved and lost—those nearest and dearest—such as parents, spouses, and children. But we also cover other relatives, co-workers, classmates, teachers, and pets. Sometimes you're taken by surprise by the strength of your feelings about someone's death. We may expect to grieve the most for close family members, and we do. Yet a favorite teacher's death or the loss of a beloved pet can hurt more than the passing away of some relatives.

We also go over how to support the bereaved. There are things you can do and say that are helpful and comforting, and there are things you can say and do (with the best of intentions) that can cause pain to those who are grieving.

# chapter 5

# Perspectives About Death

Historical overview of death

Modern attitudes about death

Applying the five stages of dying to grief

Different circumstances, different emotions

People in wealthy industrial countries have come to believe death is more "normal" for the elderly than for those who are younger. Children are not supposed to die, and parents expect to outlive their offspring. For the most part, in the United States and other industrialized countries, older people do die more frequently than younger ones. However, what's come to be seen as the "natural order" of life is really a modern concept.

Before the twentieth century, people mostly died at home, surrounded by familiar faces and in their own bed. Friends and family might come to pay their last respects. Death was taken for granted as a (painful) part of life. Nowadays, even though we know death is a part of life, we have managed to isolate ourselves from that awareness. Thus, death can become a shocking and intrusive reality.

## The Historical Perspective

For much of human existence, most people lived on the edge of life and death. Survival, except for the wealthy, was difficult. People obtained fresh meat by hunting game or slaughtering farm animals for food. Without food or the means to obtain food, people starved to death. Without a fire, they could freeze to death.

Up until the early to mid-twentieth century, people were very aware of the circle of life. Illness and death were not isolated occurrences. People resided in close-knit communities, often with several generations living nearby, or even in the same house. Without hospitals, people were born at home, nursed through illness and injury by family members, and usually died in their own beds. After death, loved ones washed and dressed the body. The deceased was often laid out so neighbors and friends could come pay their respects.

**Expressions of Grief**

"I'm not supposed to bury my child. He was supposed to grow up and someday bury me."

—A father who'd lost his young son

## Before the Mid-Twentieth Century

For most of human existence, death, and thus grieving, was a pervasive part of life. The average lifespan for much of human existence was about 20 years. By the time of the Romans, life expectancy was around 22 to 25 years. By 1900, the worldwide life expectancy was about 30 years.

Babies and children were far more vulnerable than adults. Parents knew they'd lose one or more of their children before they reached adulthood and also knew that some would die as adults. In Colonial New England, for example, 40 percent of babies failed to reach adulthood. In fact, in some cultures of the past, parents didn't name their babies until their first or second birthdays because of the likelihood of their babies dying. Perhaps a name signified attachment, something they didn't dare risk until they knew the child had survived babyhood.

Pregnancy and childbirth were often dangerous experiences for women. Lacking modern birth control, most women could expect to endure multiple childbirths. With each birth, a woman risked her life. Mortality rates for women in childbearing age groups were higher than for men of the same age.

To personalize these statistics, I'll use a well-known historical figure, Thomas Jefferson, author of the Declaration of Independence, and the second President of the United States. His wife, Martha, bore six children, five girls and one boy. Their son lived only a few days. One daughter died at 4 months, one at 17 months, and another between ages 2 and 3. Only two of his children—Martha, the eldest, and Mary, the fourth child—reached adulthood. Mary lived to age 25, only to die from childbirth. Jefferson's wife also died a lingering death from the complications of childbirth. Only Jefferson's daughter, Martha, outlived him.

Jefferson was an upper-class, educated man. The Jefferson family had access to the best food and (what passed for) medical care of his time. If he endured so many losses, imagine the death rate and suffering of poorer families.

In 1930, the average life expectancy at birth in the United States was 58 for men and 62 for women. In 1930, the death of a 58-year-old male may have generated comments such as, "He lived a full life." By 2006, life expectancy had risen to 75 for white men and 80 for white women. Today if a 58-year-old man dies suddenly, his family and friends feel he passed away "before his time." In addition to their grief, his family and friends could feel cheated of what "should" have been the rest of his life.

## Modern Medicine Changes the Statistics

It was only in the 1950s, after the development of penicillin and other sulfa drugs, that mortality rates for the general population shifted from children and child-bearing women to elderly adults. Public Health Measures, improved nutrition, and control of infectious diseases are also credited with adding to the increase in life expectancy. The health of the elderly greatly improved in the 1980s and 1990s. During the twentieth century, humans added more than 30 years to the average lifespan.

# American Cultural View of Death

Without the constant reminders of our mortality faced by previous generations, it's been easy for modern humans (in industrial countries) to relegate death to the "back burner" of life—something to be dealt with "someday." Many people think they won't have to deal with dying until they're old.

We have come to take the modern way of life and death for granted. More people experience the death of a loved one, or multiple deaths of family, later in their life. In the United States, we have generational family relationships that relatively few people possessed in the past.

Think of the average 50-year-old in the United States today. She may have both parents living. It's also possible that one or more grandparents are still alive. Her own offspring are healthy—children, grandchildren, and perhaps great-grandchildren. Before she lives out the allotted lifespan, more grandchildren and great-grandchildren are expected.

## Attitudes Toward Death

Today, people usually die in hospitals (although more and more dying people are cared for at home, under the auspices of hospice), which cut them off from the general public. As dying and death became isolated from everyday life, people grew uncomfortable with the thought of death, much less the reality. Humans have a tremendous capacity for denial, especially when it comes to things that they'd prefer not to think about. Because the idea of death is avoided or denied, people can often believe, "That's something that happens to other people." Therefore, it's a shock when the reality of death intrudes on their lives.

## Extending Life to Cheat Death

Modern medicine has saved and prolonged the lives of countless people. However, it's not infallible. Medicine cannot cure everything, and, although it can keep death at bay, it cannot stop the inevitable. Yet most people believe that doctors can save them or their loved ones. There's often a sense of relief when someone goes into the hospital because now they will be healed. It can be quite a shock, when, contrary to expectations, the individual dies.

The other contemporary preconception is that if you eat right, take your vitamins, exercise, and don't smoke or drink too much or do drugs, then you'll live longer than someone who has poorer habits. And while taking care of ourselves does enhance our health, the quality of our lives, and often does extend life, people are still going to die. This is especially shocking when someone leads a vigorously healthy life, yet still passes away while relatively young.

Thirty-six-year-old Michael was an avid cyclist, who was careful with his diet and stayed fit and trim. One day after work, he and some colleagues took a 15-mile ride, stopped for dinner, then rode home. Michael pulled ahead of the other guys, and then collapsed. His friends administered CPR, but it was too late. The paramedics told them that Michael had died instantly, probably of a heart attack. In the grief group the next day, one of his colleagues said in a bitter tone, "He did everything right, and he's dead. It doesn't do any good to take care of yourself. I might as well eat cake every day."

In spite of Michael's early death, we can't know that Michael didn't prolong his life through his healthy lifestyle. Perhaps Michael would have died several years earlier if he hadn't taken care of himself. His family might not have had him as long if he hadn't eaten well and exercised regularly.

## Concept of Fairness in Death

As adults, we logically know that life isn't fair. Yet we still have this little-kid feeling that life *should* be fair. Children have a strong sense of equality and are offended when they're not treated fairly. Do you remember as a child when your brother or sister would receive something good and you didn't? Remember your "that's not fair" feeling? If you have children, you probably hear that complaint as well. Even though we've grown up, we still carry that little-kid concept of fairness.

"It's not fair/right" is often said when someone dies who is either young, a caring person, or talented (or any combination). We may feel if *we* were in charge of life, good people would live long, productive lives and not leave us. Some people even think it's the "bad" people who should die young, not the good ones.

It's not uncommon for the bereaved to think or say, "It's not fair. Why did *my* loved one have to die?" It's not that you want someone else to die; you just want your loved one back. You think it's wrong that he or she was taken.

Shauna had waited a long time to marry and have children. She was pregnant with her daughter when they discovered her husband had cancer. He passed away when their baby was six weeks old. "I'm angry because he left me," she said. "I have to do this all by myself. I didn't plan to raise a child alone. It's not fair! Why couldn't I have had more time with him?"

# The Elisabeth Kübler-Ross Model

In the 1960s, Swiss-born psychiatrist Elisabeth Kübler-Ross (1926–2004) studied people who were dying. She found that most people, when given a terminal diagnosis, experienced specific, progressive reactions. In 1969, she published *On Death and Dying*. The book brought the public's attention to the callous treatment of terminally ill people at the time. Because of her work, the care and treatment of the dying considerably improved. Today, the dying are treated in a much more sensitive and humane manner.

## The Five Stages

In her book, Elisabeth Kübler-Ross reported five distinct stages of dying:

1. Denial
2. Anger
3. Bargaining
4. Depression
5. Acceptance

The five-stages model caught the attention of doctors, psychologists, and the public. It wasn't long before the stages of dying became the stages of grief, and the five fluid stages became crystallized in the public's consciousness.

Denial usually happens in the minutes, hours, or days after the death or the news of the death. It's really the initial shock and disbelief about the death, rather than a complete inability to accept that the person has died. It takes a while for the reality to seep in. Denial serves as a kind of buffer. It gives you time to make sense of the bad news. Even though you hear the news of the death, see the loss, and feel the absence of the deceased, it's hard to believe they're gone. You can believe on one level, but not on another. You can know the loss is true, but you don't feel it's real. Frequent comments at the beginning of this stage may include the following:

- "No, not (name)!"
- "It's not true!"
- "This must be a joke!"
- "This must be a mistake!"
- "You're kidding!"

Very soon these thoughts are followed by the realization, "He wouldn't joke about this!" Even though you might hear the truth and perhaps respond by feeling sad or crying, it still doesn't feel real. You can't accept the death.

Later, people tend to say, "I can't believe she is gone." They may also make statements about expecting to see or hear the person again. They'll say, "I keep expecting her to call me," or "Around 5:30, I start listening for the sound of his car in the driveway."

Disbelief is more prevalent and strong when the dying process is quick or sudden. It's difficult to reconcile your mind to the truth. In your mind, the memory of the deceased is so strong, it's hard to believe he or she is really gone. With a long, drawn-out death, it's harder to feel disbelief, especially if you've been present to see the person's deterioration and had time to prepare for the death. However, if you closed your eyes to the reality of the dying and managed to stay in denial out of desperate hope, despite the reality, then you may feel disbelief.

We become angry when we've lost someone because we care. If we didn't care about him or her, we probably wouldn't feel angry. Anger is a powerful feeling, and we can use it to mask feelings we might have underneath such as sadness, fear, pain, or helplessness. You may have anger …

- At the person for dying.
- That your loved one was taken, and you're left behind.
- That you don't have more time with him or her.
- With doctors, nurses, and hospital staff.
- With family members.
- At anyone who contributed to (or caused) the death.

- With the deceased for not taking better care of him or herself, or for carelessness that lead to the death.

- Because this isn't how it's supposed to be.

Most people move through the anger stage and are able to process the other emotions they have. Others can get "stuck" in this stage, becoming angry people. They seem like they're not themselves. They have a short fuse, and become irritable with those around them. Some may have a personality change unless they find a way to work through their pain and anger.

After Maria's mother died when she was 19, her primary feeling was anger. Although she didn't realize it, she radiated the feeling toward those around her, alienating many of them. Months later when she started acting more friendly, Maria's co-workers told her, "We thought you didn't like us. You were angry all the time." Maria was astonished to hear the feedback, and hastened to explain that she wasn't mad at them, just at her mother for leaving her.

Bargaining means you try to negotiate with God, or with "life," that your loved one returns to you. Even though you know your loved one is dead and can't come back, emotionally you want the pain to stop. You fantasize about having him or her with you again. When you bargain, sometimes you add what you'll do if the loved one returns. "Just bring him back, God, and I'll never ask for anything else again." You could also negotiate how you'll treat the deceased if they are restored to you. "I'll tell her I love her 10 times a day."

Bargaining is especially prevalent when you're still feeling disbelief. "Please, God, let this not be true." But the further you move into your mourning, the less you'll feel able to bargain. That doesn't mean you stop fantasizing about your loved one, but the illusion that you can bargain to have them return becomes less and less real.

You can reach a stage in your grieving where you're so focused on your sadness, so absorbed by your loss, it's difficult to get out of bed, do your usual activities, or care much about yourself or others. You lack energy, and may not even care that you're so fatigued. You might have thoughts of giving up or dying. You feel depressed.

When Tammy lost her husband after three years of marriage, she struggled with low spirits. "I wasn't supposed to be by myself," she said. "I was sad, angry, and depressed. I just wanted to crawl in bed and pull the covers over my head. For the first few months, I spent days in bed."

**Cautions and concerns** Be cautious if a doctor tries to put you on antidepressants or tranquilizers early after your loss. By suppressing your feelings, medication can interfere with your grieving process.

When you lose someone you care about, you have a good reason to feel depressed. It's a normal reaction that you need to ride out until it's over. Grief-related depression and clinical depression have similar symptoms and may be misdiagnosed. Chapter 6 discusses grief and depression in depth.

Acceptance means that eventually you make peace with the fact that your loved one is gone. You adjust to the reality of his death, and the fact that this is how your life is without him. That doesn't mean you like it or that you are finished with your mourning. You start to live a new life without your loved one.

## Limitations of the Stages Model

The problem with using Elisabeth Kübler-Ross's original stages model is that it takes the myriad reactions that comprise grief and forces them into five boxes. The stages work well for people who are dying, but they don't always fit those grieving a death or other losses. While some people may find themselves grieving in the five stages, most people don't.

Grief, especially the grief of bereavement, doesn't unfold in orderly stages. Some people might not pass through any of the stages. The reality is that grief is individual and fluid. Painful emotions may come in waves, they may "pop up" unexpectedly during times of feeling "normal," or a certain emotion may be continuously present before gradually subsiding.

If people try to squeeze themselves into the five-stages model, they may find they don't fit. They may feel something is wrong with them if they don't. Or others can try to force the bereaved into a certain stage and criticize them if they show a different reaction. The stages don't take into account that someone's passing, while sad, can also be a loving and spiritual experience.

In my latest personal bereavements—my father and my grandmother—I didn't experience any of the stages of grief. Much of this was because their deaths were expected, and I'd prepared for them. I had nothing left unsaid with them at the time of their passing. I did have deep sadness and a spiritual sense of letting go. I missed them, and sometimes still do, but I also know that their loving memory is always with me.

Elisabeth Kübler-Ross's 2005 book (with David Kessler) is much more fluid than the adaptations by other clinicians that have evolved from her earlier work. In *On Grief and Grieving: Finding the Meaning of Grief Through the Five Stages of Loss* (see the Resources appendix), the authors discuss how people may skip stages or go back and forth between them. However, the idea of stages is deeply embedded in our cultural psyche, and the interpretation others put on your grief journey can still be stringent.

# Reactions to Circumstances of Death

While you're going to grieve a loved one's death no matter how it happened, the cause of the death makes a difference to the mourning process. Different types of deaths elicit different emotions. If a death was sudden or unexpected, accidental or natural, a suicide, or caused by violence, family and close friends may have a hard time coping.

When someone dies from natural causes, even if you think she died too young, there is a good reason—her body gave out. Therefore, there is the sense that it was her "time" (regardless of whether you feel it was the "right" time). But when someone dies in an accident or is murdered, there's a feeling of outrage and unfairness because the person's life was cut short. It doesn't feel right.

## Sudden Versus Lingering Death

There are pros and cons to passing away suddenly or dying a lingering death. In a sudden death, the person doesn't suffer (at least not for long). But there's no time for the individual or her loved ones to prepare themselves for the passing. Thus the death is shocking, and people don't feel a sense of acceptance.

Living in a pain-wracked, deteriorating body is a horrible experience to endure. As the dying individual suffers, so does his family. Yet with a lingering death, the dying person (and his loved ones) has a chance to come to terms with the death. This gives them an opportunity to do the following:

- Say goodbye

- Get their affairs in order

- Mend broken fences

- Share stories and pass on family history

- Make amends for past harms or neglect

- Make peace with dying

- Take care of spiritual matters

Sometimes what's supposed to be an extended dying process takes a sudden turn. Everyone knows or has heard stories of people who've beaten the odds or at least have extended their lives a few weeks, months, or years past the timeline the doctors gave them. Thus, families and friends of the person with cancer or other terminal illness hope and believe this will happen with their loved one.

However, the ravages of cancer or other illnesses can cause the person to go downhill far faster than anticipated. Therefore, people are caught off guard because they expected to have more time with the person—to prepare themselves, to interact, or to say goodbye.

## Accidental Versus Natural

With an accident, people can feel angry because someone or something has ripped their family member or friend from them. They can have a belief the accident could have been prevented "if only" the victim had done (or not done) something differently. And not just the victim, if only others involved in the accident had done things differently, then the deceased would still be alive. They may feel as if their loved one's life was cut short.

Sometimes friends, family, or co-workers think if they had been present, the deceased wouldn't have died.

On Super Bowl Sunday, Marty had a party for his buddies. His wife, Anne, who disliked football, went shopping. One of the guys, lacking childcare, brought his 3-year-old son. The men quickly became involved in the game, and the boy wandered outside. He fell in the pool and drowned. Each man at the party was racked with guilt. So was Anne. A former lifeguard, she *knew* if she'd been home, the boy wouldn't have been unattended near the pool. Even though she'd never met the child, his death deeply affected her, and haunts her to this day.

Accidental death can bring up feelings about the randomness of life and death. Whether or not the accident was someone's fault, people are shocked by the death. They can think things like, "This person left the house this morning, expecting to return home." They can wonder if an accidental death will ever happen to them or their loved ones. They can feel more vulnerable about life for a while.

With a natural death, people aren't usually upset with the deceased unless they feel the person contributed to her own death in some way. If she ate poorly, allowed herself to become overweight, didn't exercise, avoided the doctor, or smoked, then others can feel angry or frustrated because she could have lived longer. The same can happen if she took risks or put herself in harm's way.

Loved ones are most likely going to feel angrier with the deceased if he died from doing something stupid. For example, a man who died from a fall off the roof because he was too stubborn to have a roofer take care of a broken tile, or a teenager who crashed her car because she was texting. They can blame the deceased for his or her death.

### Car Crash Stats

MISC.

According to American Automobile Association (AAA), approximately 100 people in America die each day from car crashes. During the past 25 years, more than a million people have died and about 75 million people have been injured in car accidents. Most crashes are due to driver error and are preventable.

The carelessness, distraction, stubbornness, and stupidity that cause accidents are deplorable, but understandable. We've all had such moments, which could have led to serious consequences, but didn't. As angry and sad as we might feel when our loved one is killed in an accident, there's still an element of understanding. That doesn't happen with a murder or suicide.

## Suicide

For the family and friends left behind, suicide is perhaps the most painful of all types of death to comprehend because they feel as though it was a choice. In addition to their grief, they may suffer shock, pain, guilt, anger, and regrets, and believe it all could have been prevented. They may feel burdened with a tremendous (although often irrational) sense of responsibility for the death. When a suicide happens, it leaves people with questions, some of which will never be answered:

- Why did he kill himself?

- Why didn't I see something was wrong?

- Why didn't she tell me something was wrong?

- What could I have done differently?

- Why didn't he get help?

- How could she do this to the people who love her?

MISC.

**Suicide Stats**

Several sources place suicide as the eleventh leading cause of death in the United States. In 2007, 34,598 people in the United States committed suicide. That's 94 people a day, 1 every 15 minutes.

While it's difficult to believe for those who haven't experienced it, suicidal individuals are in deep (perhaps secret) pain and depression. They can have twisted, unrealistic thinking. They think their suffering will never end. They don't understand the damage they will do to loved ones because they believe family and friends are better off without them. They can't see any other solution to their problems. To them, it's the only answer.

Although suicides can happen for no apparent reason, they usually occur for a specific reason, such as:

- Mental illness, including depression (which may be coupled with substance abuse)

- An event happens, and the individual can't live with the consequences (for example, financiers who jumped to their death after the stock market crashed in 1920)

- A secret problem the individual can't deal with any more or doesn't want to face

- An angry, "I'll get back at them/him/her!" reaction

- A loss that's too painful to bear

survival strategies

A simple mnemonic can help you remember suicide warning signs—IS PATH WARM:

**I**dealism

**S**ubstance abuse

**P**urposelessness

**A**nxiety

**T**rapped

**H**opelessness

**W**ithdrawal

**A**nger

**R**ecklessness

**M**ood changes

## Violence

Some acts of violence are deliberate. In a homicide, the murderer sets out to cold-bloodedly kill someone. Other times, it's a robbery gone bad or the victim(s) were in the wrong place at the wrong time. The killer might not have originally planned to hurt anyone. Even though the murder(s) might have been carefully planned out, to most victims and loved ones, the act of violence was unexpected and random.

The bewildering violence of a murder shocks and outrages family, friends, and the community. It feels so wrong that a killer(s) took the life of someone you care about. There's a feeling of anger, unfairness, and, perhaps, injustice. The anger you experience can feel deeper and more bitter than your reaction to other losses, and the grief journey can feel turbulent and last a long time. The following are part of what makes the grieving process so tumultuous:

- The family member(s) may feel pain and shame from being a suspect in the investigation.

- The police may not catch the killer.

- The family may have to wait months or even years before the case goes to court, and when it does, loved ones may experience many weeks in court.

- You can feel traumatized by seeing photos and hearing about the murder.

- The jury/judge may not give the verdict/sentence that's wanted.

- You may feel more vulnerable (for yourself and your family) because your sense of safety has been violated.

Often the family and friends feel the verdict, and having the killer behind bars, will bring them emotional closure. For some, it may, but most still feel pain and emptiness from the loss. They may have focused on the court case to the exclusion of everything else, including processing their grief. And now, months or even years after the death, they must finally work through their grief.

## Death from Active Duty

Usually families have a great deal of pride about their loved one's service. They know their son or daughter has undergone intensive, difficult training. They are performing jobs few people can do. They are often in constant danger. While on active duty, they can live with deprivation and hardship.

Families brace themselves for the tragic news—a son or daughter has died. Even though young men and women (and their loved ones) know they are placing their lives on the line when they enlist, they may still have the belief, "It won't happen to me." The death means the family's greatest fear has come true.

Family members and friends may take comfort in the idea that their loved one died for a cause. The soldier died for his country. He died promoting the cause of freedom. However, like most deaths of loved ones, that comfort won't be enough to cover the pain of their loss. Regardless of how their loved one died, he is gone, and will be missed.

> **survival strategies**
>
> Don't just say to family members, "She died for our country." The words by themselves can come across as another platitude. You can use the statement as part of a longer message: "She died serving her country, and I'll never forget her sacrifice."

For the homecoming of the body or the funeral, community members can turn out in droves to honor the fallen, regardless of whether they previously knew the soldier or the family. Support from the community can feel uplifting to the family. They can feel their soldier touched others through his or her service and death, and didn't die in vain. The community support means that their soldier lives on in the memory of others.

## Essential Takeaways

- Up until the last 50 years, death was a more prevalent part of human life.
- People tend to isolate themselves from the idea of death.
- Adapting Elisabeth Kübler-Ross's five stages of dying model to grief isn't accurate for many people.
- How the person died makes a difference in the grief of loved ones left behind.

# chapter 6

# The Grief Journey

Everyone's journey is different

A variety of emotions

Grief and depression

One step forward ... two steps back

Getting through the holidays

Coping with unexpected surges of grief

The grief journey is a winding road that starts with the foreknowledge of a death, or the actual death itself. The journey may meander through a dark forest of despair. You may pause in isolated spots for a while. Sometimes you'll walk alone; other times you may have company. Whether you trudge, walk, or run won't make any difference to how long it takes you to make the journey. You may feel as if you'll never emerge from the dark forest. But eventually, you'll step out of the trees and feel the sun upon your face.

## Each Journey Is Different

Everyone is unique. We all have our own circumstances, passions, personalities, talents, and relationships. Therefore one person's grief will be different from everyone else's, even someone who has shared the same loss. Our reaction to the loss and journey from mourning to recovery is our very own. But we are also all human. Therefore, in some ways, our grief will be similar to all other human beings.

# Feelings Associated with Bereavement

When you lose someone you care about, there's a gap in your life and a hole in your heart. If the death is recent, the deceased is often (if not constantly) in your thoughts. You are preoccupied with your loss. You may not feel like yourself. You can feel off balance and disoriented. You may dwell on whatever "unfinished business" you had with the deceased. And you usually can come up with some—from as little as, "Why didn't I kiss him goodbye that day?" to a major act that you now wish to atone for, but can't.

The sharp pangs of grief can go on for long periods of time. Although the pangs may become dull, they don't go away. You still have emotional triggers. You can experience various emotions throughout your grief journey. Some may continually be present. Others may come and go. A few will only exist for a short time, and then vanish.

In addition to the feelings mentioned in Elisabeth Kübler-Ross's five stages of dying, which many have adapted to grief—denial, anger, bargaining, depression, and acceptance (see Chapter 5)—there are many more emotions associated with the grief journey due to bereavement. These emotions include guilt, loneliness, despair, sadness, resentment, envy, frustration, and shame. Often, you can feel many of these emotions at the same time, which may lead to *conflicted grief.*

Definition

**Conflicted grief** is when you have several strong (and what feel like contradictory) feelings about your loss. Or your thoughts and emotions about the loss seem in conflict with each other.

## Guilt

Guilt is a feeling brought on by negative thoughts, either your own or because of things people say to you. Usually guilt involves thinking the following:

- I'm not good enough.
- I'm not doing enough.
- I should have done something different.

- I shouldn't have had negative thoughts about (the person who died).
- I'm still alive; I laugh and feel happy; my life is good.

**Expressions of Grief**

"When my mom died, I expected the pain and sense of loss, but I don't think I was prepared for the guilt."

—Kendra

After a death, you are emotionally vulnerable and susceptible to guilt and regret. In the absence of a reason to feel guilty about the loss, the human mind seems to need to create one, no matter how convoluted or irrational the reason. Some people are able to think through their guilt and conclude that they have nothing to feel guilty for, and let go of the feeling. Others might know their thoughts aren't logical, but they can't shake their guilt. Some are unable to see how their irrational thoughts are causing them pain. The reassurances of others may be enough to help you let go of the remorse. Other times, no matter what anyone says, you continue to hang on to your guilt.

The hardest kind of guilt to process is when you've done something that caused pain to the deceased while he or she was alive or contributed in some way to the death. This kind of profound guilt and self-reproach can haunt you, perhaps for many years. It can contribute to *complicated grief*, which may need professional intervention.

**Definition**

**Complicated grief** is a chronic debilitating condition. Instead of slowly moving through the grieving process, you're mired in your mourning. Many studies show that every year in the United States, the grief of more than 1 million people becomes complicated, sometimes to the point of pathological.

If you did something to cause harm to the deceased, then guilt is an appropriate reaction. This is a painful opportunity for you to examine your motives and behaviors toward the deceased. From your soul-searching, you can decide to make some changes in your life or become a better person in some way. You can start treating people differently in the future.

Write a letter to the deceased or have an imaginary talk with him or her, expressing your remorse, and asking for forgiveness. Then imagine the deceased forgiving you.

## Sadness

Sadness is the most common emotion with grieving. Sometimes it's pervasive throughout your journey. Regardless of what other reactions you experience, you can still feel sad. When you lose someone, you may feel anything from mild unhappiness to deep heartbreak.

## Loneliness

For most people, grieving is a lonely experience. No one else—no matter how empathetic—can feel your emotions. You miss your deceased family member or friend. People withdraw, friends pull away, and others who are grieving struggle with their own loss. You're not much fun to be around. You can feel lonely in the midst of people.

## Despair

Some losses, such as the sudden death of a child or spouse, can send you into despair. You can feel as though you're in a deep, dark pit. You're despondent, heartbroken, and inconsolable. The agony can feel unbearable.

## Envy

It's not uncommon to envy others who have that special loved one when you don't. For example, after your spouse dies, you may envy others because their partners are still alive. You can also believe it's unfair if others don't appreciate their loved one. You can feel guilt about your envy, as if you're bad for feeling it. However, it's not that you don't want others to have their loved ones; you just want yours back.

## Frustration

Throughout your grief journey, you can feel frustrated. You can feel as though you have a short fuse or are often impatient. You're frustrated …

- With feeling so emotional.

- That grief is taking so long.

- That you have to learn to do new things.

- That your life has changed in a way you don't like and can't do anything about.

- That you're having this painful and difficult experience.

## Resentment/Bitterness/Hatred

People can feel these negative emotions …

- About the death.

- At the deceased.

- At their life now.

- At those responsible.

- Against others with intact families.

These emotions are often destructive, not only to you, but because they also push others away. No one wants to be around a bitter person (unless it's another negative person). It's important you work through your feelings. Chapters 20 and 21 go more into how to do so.

## Shame/False Pride

Mourners often feel (or are told) they have to be strong. When they have their normal grief reactions, they think they're weak. They may feel ashamed to ask for help because they think others might see them as weak or needy. They may also not want to burden family and friends.

## Fear

When you're bereaved, you may have a lot to feel afraid about. You can fear …

- Being alone.
- The future.
- Financial insecurity.
- Doing certain tasks.
- That you'll never stop grieving.

## Hopelessness

With a painful bereavement, you can lose hope. You may feel you'll never recover from the pain. Life looks bleak and hopeless. You may not want to go on. While these feelings can be a normal part of bereavement, when you experience them, it's a good idea to join a bereavement group or see a grief counselor or psychotherapist.

## Detachment/Numbness

In the beginning of your loss, you may feel numb. You're detached, and just going through the motions of life, for example, planning the funeral. Here are some other terms people use to describe these feelings:

- Robotic
- On automatic pilot (autopilot)
- Like zombies
- Moving in slow motion
- Like existing in a waking coma
- Moving in a fog

This numbness is often what accounts for others saying, "She's so strong." Or "He's holding up so well." The bereaved may be neither strong nor holding up well. They are numb. The detachment may last for days, weeks, or even months. When it wears off, they start to feel their grief.

Leslie was the doting mother of a beautiful 10-month-old daughter, Christa. Leslie had already started making party favors for the elaborate, 1-year birthday celebration she planned for Christa. Leslie often took pictures of her daughter and e-mailed them to her family, friends, and co-workers. The baby went everywhere with her. She even brought Christa to work several times so everyone could see her.

Christa became ill and developed pneumonia. After two weeks in the hospital, to everyone's shock, the baby died. When friends would try to talk to Leslie, they'd break down in tears. Leslie would hug them, patting their backs and saying, "It's okay. It's okay."

"Leslie's so strong," everyone marveled. "How can she be so strong? She loved that baby *so* much." It wasn't until after the funeral, when almost everyone had left the service, that Leslie turned to the family and friends sitting with her. "Okay, the joke's over." She started to cry. "I want my baby back."

# Feeling Depressed

For most people, the death of a loved one can be a very depressing situation. That doesn't mean something is wrong with them. Depression is a normal and understandable response to the loss. Sometimes people think depression is a feeling, but it's really an emotional state.

Sadness is not depression, although sadness is part of depression. You may also have a persistent down mood and lose interest in activities you used to enjoy. You can feel hopeless and worthless. Your energy is low, making it difficult to do anything. You may feel empty and anxious. You may stop eating much, or eat too much. You can have early morning awakening or oversleeping. You may feel there's no point in going on.

**cautions and concerns**

According to the American Cancer Society, one out of five bereaved people will develop major depression. Those who do so are often more vulnerable because of a history of depression or the lack of a good support system. It's also not uncommon for a period of depression to occur late in your grief journey. You may isolate yourself and feel lonely, but you need the space to process and come to terms with your grief.

You can think your depression is normal grief when it's really turned into complicated grief or clinical depression. Therefore, you avoid going for treatment, and your depression can worsen. Conversely, you can go to your doctor and receive antidepressants for your normal grief response. The medication may interfere with your grief journey by suppressing the emotions you need to process.

If your depression continues, seek help from a mental-health professional who specializes in grief. The treatment of depressive symptoms due to grief can be quite different than treating clinical depression. A doctor or clinician who specializes in grieving will support you in processing your emotions, as well as help you decide if you need medication.

## A Day-by-Day Journey

When you're grieving, each day doesn't get progressively better. You'll feel up and down, like you've taken two steps forward and three steps back. Some days you might feel fine, and then grief unexpectedly hits you. Other times, you might feel miserable for days. You can wallow in one place for a while, then speed through certain reactions. You can feel fearful and pessimistic about the future, but sometimes you might feel hopeful or have glimmers of optimism. Although you may still grieve for your loved one and often feel sad, you should find your life returning to normalcy after a few weeks or months.

As with any wound, grief takes time to heal. If you had surgery, you wouldn't expect to heal in a few weeks, would you? Even if your incision has closed, the internal healing takes much longer. While it might feel frustrating to have a long convalescence, it's understandable. Grief is the same way. When you grieve a loss, you need to emotionally convalesce.

| survival strategies | You'll need different kinds of support at various parts of your grief journey. Those who are there for you in the beginning aren't always the best help later on. |
| --- | --- |

It would be nice to know that your grief journey will end at a specific date. That would give you something to hang onto—"I only have to endure this for two more weeks." However, there's no time frame or cut-off date for grieving. It lasts as long as it lasts. While research has shown that mourning generally lasts from three months to a year, many people continue to experience intense grief for two years or more. Bereavement can last for many years. It's important that you don't compare your responses with others, or judge how long your (or someone else's) journey to recovery is taking. Feeling that you "should" be grieving like someone else will only hinder your recovery. Allow yourself to fully feel your grief. Your time of mourning will follow its own natural course to completion.

## Holidays and Other Speed Bumps

Often, when we think we have a handle on our grief journey, we hit a grief bump, which can come in the form of a holiday or other special event. Holidays are supposed to be times when family and close friends gather to celebrate a festive occasion, sharing love, joy, laughter, gifts, and thankfulness. It's a time to bond as a family and make wonderful memories for the future. Yet if a loved one has died, family holidays can become sad, painful, and empty.

The time of year your loved one died can make a difference. If a relative passed away in January, then by November and December the family has processed a lot of their emotions. Perhaps they've reached a state of balance. However, those first holidays can bring the pain up all over again, as if it were fresh. Those who've lost a loved one closer to the holidays, right before Thanksgiving, Hanukkah, Christmas, or Kwanzaa, can feel like the holidays are a mockery. How can they possibly feel joyous when their hearts are broken? Whether they attempt to celebrate or avoid their traditions altogether, the pain stays with them.

**survival strategies** Birthdays and anniversaries of the deceased are often sad days. Make some time to commemorate your loved one. Have a conversation with him or her. Place flowers near a picture, or post a message in remembrance on your Facebook page.

Holidays can also bring up sadness and grief for loved ones who died years ago. Celebrating traditions passed on from family members connects you with them. This is a time you can yearn for their presence and miss them. Your memories of prior joyful celebrations might feel bittersweet.

This happened with my grandmother. Every Christmas Eve, my family would attend church. When the congregation sang "Silent Night," my grandmother always cried. That hymn transported her back to her childhood, to her family gathered around the candle-lit Christmas tree as they sang carols. She missed her parents and siblings. She grieved their loss, as well as a time and place that no longer existed.

Conversely, the actual holiday might not be as bad as you think. The sadness and dread building up to the day can be far worse than the reality. Although you can feel the loss and miss the deceased, you can also have times of deep thankfulness for your blessings and gratitude for all the loved ones you have present. You can get caught up in the excitement of children celebrating, playing, and opening up presents. You can exchange stories and memories, causing laughter and tears. You feel a closer connection with your family.

The first Christmas after Stephanie's husband died, leaving her with a toddler and a newborn, she could barely cope with day-to-day life, much less a holiday. Her neighbors chipped in to buy her a tree. They came over and decorated her home and put up the lights outside. After Christmas was over, they took everything down. Because of their kindness, the family had a nice Christmas after all. In addition, they felt loved by those around them and appreciated the goodness of the human spirit. Through helping Stephanie, the whole neighborhood became closer. Not only did Stephanie develop a new "extended family," the neighbors formed a tight-knit community.

Here are some tips to help you weather the holidays:

- Share how you're feeling with trusted loved ones, especially the way your grief has changed or deepened due to the holiday.

- Reduce your stress. This isn't the year to worry about a perfect celebration. Only do what you feel is necessary.

- Simplify and change your traditions. Pick those you feel will be meaningful this year, or create new ones.

- Ask for help. Others will be happy to step forward to lend a hand. Let others know specifically what you need. Don't say, "Can you bring something for dinner?" Do say, "Can you bring dessert for 10 people?"

- Find a way to memorialize your loved one. Set out a special candle. Hang their stocking with the others and have everyone write a letter to the deceased. You can read them together on Christmas morning. Make an ornament with their picture on it or buy one that represents them in some way. Include the deceased in a family prayer.

- Don't let others direct how you should spend the holidays. Just because someone thinks it would be best for you to go away for the week, doesn't mean it's right for you.

- Be of service to others. Helping others is a way to give new meaning to the holiday and help you feel better. Prepare and serve food at a homeless shelter or organize a gift drive for some needy families and deliver the presents yourself.

- Realize that you might feel overwhelmed and exhausted, both from your reactions to the loss and from the stress and hectic pace of the holiday. As much as possible, get to bed early and take naps.

- You don't have to pretend to be happy. If you think your sadness might be a problem for others, have a little talk with them beforehand about how you and they will handle your feelings.

- Spend time with people who are supportive and caring. By now, you know who among your friends and family is supportive and who's not. Gravitate to the understanding ones and avoid the others.

During the holidays, you can't help but think about and miss your loved one. However, try as much as possible not to dwell on your pain. Imagine your loved one being present in spirit. Instead of his or her absence, focus on the presence of the other family members. Your loss helps remind you of how precious time is with your family. Appreciate and love each one of them.

## Unexpected Surges of Grief

When holidays and other special events loom on your horizon, you can brace yourself for the grief you feel is coming. Other times you have no warning of what's about to happen. Grief unexpectedly rises up and seizes you. Sometimes, the unanticipated grief can be harder to bear because it takes you by surprise and knocks you off balance.

Three months after my father's death, my two oldest nieces had a dance recital. I sat in the audience, watching them perform, smiling and happy. Then I realized my father wasn't there to see his granddaughters. It hit me that he wouldn't be part of their accomplishments as they grew up. They were young enough that they wouldn't really know or remember him. Tears came to my eyes, and I secretly brushed them away. Afterward, I learned my mom had the exact same grief reaction.

As you can see by my example, you don't close the door on every bit of your grief. Instead, you complete the journey into wholeness. Eventually, you will see progress in terms of weeks, months, or years. Although everyone's time-line of grieving is different, most people can tell when they're feeling better. More time passes between "down" days. Their reactions have lightened or gone away completely. They don't have the mood swings they used to. People might say, "I can tell I'm doing better than I was last year at this time." Or, "I'm more myself." While the up and down, back and forth of grieving is frustrating, patience is the key. Allow your journey to be what it is.

## Essential Takeaways

- Everyone's reaction to loss and their journey from mourning to recovery is different.
- A mass of emotions makes up grief, and may include guilt, loneliness, despair, sadness, resentment, envy, frustration, and shame.
- Depression is a normal and understandable reaction to a loss, but if it continues for too long, seek help from a mental-health professional.
- Holidays can be times of missing your loved one, but they can also be opportunities for families to come together and appreciate each other.
- Grief can unexpectedly hit you on days you think you're fine.

# chapter 7

# Death of Parents

Parental deaths at different life stages

When a dysfunctional or difficult parent dies

When one parent remains

Losing in-laws

Losing your second parent

Dealing with your parents' deaths

We only have two biological parents—a mother and a father (although others can step into those roles). Our parents were the first people who fell in love with us, and we with them. They were our primary teachers. We learned basic life skills and so much more from them. All our lives, they've been our biggest cheerleaders. We've basked in the pride they take in us. No one else knows our life story like they do. Our parents shape who we become. For better or worse, and often in between, our parents were the most formative influence of our childhood.

We know (even if we don't want to think about it) that there will come a time when our parents die, and we will be left without them. We want our parents to remain mentally and physically healthy and for their deaths to take place in the distant future. Yet at some point, we must face the painful reality of our parents dying and death.

# Death of Parent(s) When You're a Child

The age you are when your parents pass away makes a difference in how their death impacts you. If it happens early in your life, their loss can be quite damaging. The death of a parent when you're a child alters your whole world. Nothing is ever the same again. The structure of the family changes. You miss out on their loving care and guidance for the rest of your life. You'll have emotional hardships and challenges that you wouldn't have experienced if your parent had lived.

Expressions of Grief

"My mother died in an accident when I was six. All I knew was that my life was happy and filled with love on one day, and the next it changed to sadness and confusion."

—Lynne

Younger children may not remember much (or anything) about their deceased parent. They grow up with this gap in their memory where their mom or dad should be. Other people have to fill in the blanks, telling stories and sharing memories of who he or she was. But even that is an incomplete picture.

When one parent dies, the remaining parent is often grief stricken. He or she has to deal with funeral details and cope with unexpected and unwelcome life changes. Often grandparents, aunts, and uncles are similarly affected. There may be no one to focus on the child's emotional needs.

Jessica's dad was an Air Force fighter pilot and died in a plane crash when she was three. Her mom was only 27. Her mom's grief shaped Jessica's life. She grew up acting very responsible and careful because it was important to her mother that she stayed alive. Her mother sometimes told her that the only reason she survived was because she had a child to take care of. Jessica's entire life was formed by the understanding that sometimes people just disappear and never come home. It made her want to hold on to people and possessions and keep life from ever changing.

Children can feel vulnerable without one of their parents. They may worry that the remaining parent will die. Younger children may become fearful and clingy. Older children might try to grow up fast so they can take care of themselves if something should happen to the remaining parent.

The oldest child (or children) can be pushed (or choose to step) into the role of caretaker for younger siblings, or even the remaining parent. There might not be a lot of space for him or her to grieve because of the overwhelming responsibilities of the caretaking role. An older child might also receive praise from others for being "the man or woman" of the family—a horrible burden to place on a kid. Few individuals (if anyone) make time for the premature little adult, taking her away for an outing to allow opportunities to be a child for a while and to talk about what's going on with her.

The financial situation of the family often changes. It's not uncommon for the family to move after the death. Either they cannot afford to remain where they are, or they wish to live closer to relatives or a job so there's not a long commute.

Children can also lose extracurricular activities, due to the move, lack of finances, or lack of time or energy on the part of the remaining parent. The children might have to give up a beloved pet because no animals are allowed in the new apartment or the family can't afford it. These losses compound the children's grief from the death of their parent. (Chapter 19 discusses how to help children cope with the death of a loved one.)

Children who have lost one or both parents may grow up with abandonment issues. They may (consciously or subconsciously) fear losing someone else they love, and/or believe they aren't lovable or don't deserve love. When they grow up, this fear can play out in relationships. They can choose someone who fits their fear profile—the person is emotionally unavailable, or not the type to stay in a relationship. Or he or she chooses someone who would stay, but may end up driving the person away because of jealousies and insecurities. These failed relationships can reinforce their abandonment beliefs.

**survival strategies** People with abandonment issues and a rocky relationship history should consider counseling, so they can work out their issues, feel worthy of love, and choose healthier partners.

# Death of a Parent When You're a Young Adult

When you're 18 through your 20s, you may not be as equipped to lose one or both of your parents as when you're more mature. When you're a child, a lot of relatives and friends may step in to help you and your family. When you're older, you may find yourself on your own. You may not know healthy ways to cope with your loss. You may feel all alone with friends who don't understand and a family absorbed in their own grief. Your pain may push you into behavior and choices that are unhealthy. Now that you're a "grownup," there's no one to curb your acting out. Therefore, you can get yourself into a lot of trouble, which can have lasting consequences.

Both of Cathy's parents died when she was in her early 20s, and she tried to deny her pain, grief, and trauma. She partied and drank. She had sex with many guys. She spent a lot of money she didn't have. But the acting out didn't help. The destructive behavior just rendered her mindless enough not to think or feel. "The worst moments of stress and pain in my life," said Cathy, "bring back that yearning to return to the days when my parents were there with a way to fix every problem and every heartache."

# Death of a Parent When You're Older

As adults, we no longer depend on our parents for our emotional and physical survival. They've done their job. They've raised us. We no longer need them. Or do we? No matter how old we are, we have a child inside us that's attached to our mommy and daddy. Our parents are friends, sources of wisdom and life experiences, grandparents to our children, and custodians of family history and traditions. We may have years with them when we are more like peers. When they die, so do their roles in our lives and in our family.

You can grieve bits and pieces of your parents as they begin to age, change, and stop participating in many family activities. You see them grow frailer, and your heart can ache. Eventually they decline to the point that you're grieving your once-healthy mother or father—the one who's no longer there. At the same time, you can have a tremendous appreciation for them just knowing they won't be with you forever.

Our parents are deeply embedded in our emotional psyche. After all, we've known them all our lives. We've always been a son or daughter. When they pass, it's often hard for our subconscious to believe they're gone. For a long time after their death, we can have thoughts of them as if they're alive. We forget they're gone; then we remember and the reality crashes down on us.

This happened to Linda, whose mother died five years previously. She and her husband had finished a remodeling job on their bathroom. While Linda was admiring the room, she thought, "I should take a picture and send it to Mom. She'd really like to see how it turned out." Linda went to get the camera. Then the realization hit—her mother was dead. For a few minutes, Linda felt stabbed with pain, like she'd lost her mom all over again.

After your parents pass away, you can miss doing things with them. They're no longer a phone call or e-mail away. You miss getting their advice, approval, or love. As time goes by, you find you still have questions for them. You might want your mom's recipe to a traditional dish that's now lost. You might want your dad's advice in an area of his expertise. You wish you had their knowledge of family history—not just about their lives and that of past generations—but also of your life. They're the ones who can answer questions about your infancy and childhood, things you don't remember.

Even if you're ready to let go because of your parents' physical or mental condition, after their death, grief continues to hit you. Just because you're at peace with your parents passing away doesn't mean you're at peace with their physical absence in your life. You miss your parents at major life turning points—graduations, marriages, and births. You wish your children or grandchildren could have relationships with them. No matter how old you are, you can have times of missing your parents.

## Guilt

Guilt is often a prevalent feeling with parents. After all, they originated guilt-tripping you. They know how to push your buttons. Secondly, at the end of their lives, parents are often hard to take care of. They can be demanding, critical, and complaining. Their needs can seem never-ending. You may feel like a bad son or daughter while they are alive (even if they never say so) because you can't be there enough for them. Or, after the death of one or both of your parents, you can feel guilty, thinking you should have done more.

> **Expressions of Grief**
>
> "After my parents died, I felt relief. They weren't responsive (due to Alzheimer's) for a while before they died. Then I felt guilty, as if I was a bad daughter for feeling that way. It took me a while to work through that."
>
> —Sharon

When your parents become elderly and in need of caretaking, sometimes you're the one who guilts yourself. It's common to tell yourself (and others) that your parents did everything for you as a baby and child. Now it's your turn to take care of them. Sometimes, adult children can feel genuinely grateful to be close to and care for a parent. Others struggle. It's not their choice to be in a caretaking situation—of course, they'd rather their parents were healthy and able to take care of themselves.

Your parents' physical and/or mental condition can worsen to the point where you welcome the idea of their death, even though you might feel guilty about that. Or you can feel guilty for the relief you feel when they die because they're not suffering and you're released from caregiving responsibilities. It's important to remind yourself that guilt is normal and not something you need to beat yourself up about.

## Issues with Siblings

It's not uncommon for sibling issues to flare up at the final stage of a parent's life. There may have always been problems between brothers and sisters, which worsen now. Other times, new ones arise. Siblings have an acute awareness of fairness and that includes who does the most caretaking of mom or dad. The sibling who bears the brunt of the responsibility often feels resentful of other siblings.

Conversely, siblings can draw together at this time. Perhaps they reunite, traveling to be there before the death or to attend the funeral. Grieving together, sharing memories with their dying parent or with each other, can be a bubble of time when their focus is on their childhood family. They can feel a renewal of their love for each other.

# Grieving Difficult Parents

Dysfunctional parents can be a primary source of irritation and pain. You may have always had troubled relationships with them. Or problems may have developed later in your life as you've changed and grown and/or your parents have changed for the worse. No matter how awful your parents are (even if you've cut yourself off from them), you may have the secret hope that they will change and finally become the parents you've always wanted.

Sometimes, when a dysfunctional parent is dying, he or she does soften, make amends, and open up. For a little while, you do have the parent you've always wished for. When he or she dies, you grieve the "good" parent you had for only a short time. You can wish for more months with that parent.

Your parents may die without giving you a chance to work through your issues with one or both of them. When they do pass away, you may feel empty, hurt, and resentful. For example, you always craved their approval, but now will never have it. With the death, the hope that your parent(s) will change dies with them.

Veronica was a critical, even verbally abusive, woman who seemed to have no soft side. She never showed her two children, Tom and Maria, love and affection, and she made their lives miserable. When she passed away, both Tom and Maria spoke at her funeral, talking about what a difficult, unhappy woman she was. They even said they weren't sorry she'd died. Veronica had left behind a legacy of damage and hurt that her children had to live with and try to heal.

The death of a difficult parent can set you free from their drama, criticism, selfishness, abuse, or apathy. You no longer have to deal with their hurtful or destructive behavior. You can explore and heal from the damage they caused you. You can become a better mother or father to your own children, so you don't pass on the dysfunction to another generation.

# One Parent Remains

How your surviving parent handles the death of his or her spouse makes a difference to you. Your parent can be a "rock," he or she can fall to pieces, or anything in between. Adult children have their own grief, and may also have to support the other parent who has lost a spouse of many years. They may help manage the logistics of the death and afterward. They may struggle to keep the remaining parent from giving up on life. There may be no one to support the adult child and help with grief he or she is feeling.

**MISC.**

**Interesting Fact**

Forty-three million Americans look after someone age 50 or older.

Sometimes in a long-term marriage, when a spouse dies, the partner never seems to get over it. Something within him or her fades away. It can feel like a burden if you have to prop up your remaining parent for a length of time. You're grieving, trying to live your regular life, and now you might have caretaking duties, in addition to trying to emotionally sustain your parent. You want him to move on and find new meaning and even joy in life. You don't want your parent to grieve himself to death.

Grief can make an elderly parent become more frail, vulnerable, and helpless. He might not know some basic survival skills such as cooking, and/or there is some mental deterioration, which makes accounting and bill-paying difficult. Sometimes your parent finds his feet and eventually is able to go on. Other times he continues to go downhill, placing a greater burden on your shoulders.

Natalie took care of her elderly father, who was not doing well since her mother passed away two years earlier. Her father couldn't get over his wife's death. He seemed lost. He wanted Natalie to cook for him and do his laundry like her mom had. The burden had become too much for her. She couldn't keep doing everything for him, and she felt guilty. She had a long talk with her father, and together, they decided to hire someone to help with housekeeping and fixing meals.

cautions and concerns

Don't become so focused on comforting and supporting your surviving parent that you don't allow yourself your own grief.

Many adult children have problems when their parent begins to date again. They may feel threatened by the new person in mom or dad's life. They may worry that he or she will take the parent away from them, physically and financially. They can dislike the idea of someone else in mom or dad's place. The parent may make it harder on the children. He (it's more common with men) or she jumps into dating quickly, before the adult children have finished their grieving. They think their parent is acting foolish just because he or she doesn't want to be alone or feel grief. It's also difficult for the adult children if the new spouse is insecure, alienates the children, and/ or forces the parent to give up old traditions and normal extended-family time. Adult children can feel hurt and bitter about the parent's choices, which only compound their grief for the deceased parent.

However, not all bereaved parents rush into dating. Many take the time to process their grief and come to terms with their loss. When the time comes to date, they have a talk with their children, including them in on the decision and the reasons for it. Discussions can take place that involve each side expressing their feelings and fears. Because the children know beforehand, they can prepare themselves. They can understand more about their dad and mom's loneliness and need for a companion. Maybe they can even participate in choosing people for the parent to date. They can have a more open mind about the new man or woman because they don't feel as threatened.

Three years after my father died, my mother knew it was time to date, and she kept me in the loop every step of the way. When her friend introduced her to a man, Del, my mom accepted a date, even though she had initial reservations. One date turned into another. Soon my mother fell in love, and I got a kick out of her looking as smitten as a high school girl. She'd chosen wisely, a man whom the whole family could respect and soon came to love. Del has been a great companion for her, a loving father figure to me, and a wonderful "grandfather" for my nieces. I know my dad would approve of and be grateful for the care Del has taken of his family.

## Losing Beloved In-Laws

In-laws can be a thorn in your marriage, people you have a polite relationship with, or people who are very dear to you, maybe even closer than your own parents. Your in-laws have ties of blood and love to your children. You've all become woven into a family. You may even become the primary caretaker as they age. When they die, you can feel profound grief.

In addition to your own sadness, you are impacted by the emotions of your spouse and children. You may worry about supporting your loved ones in their time of grieving. You may have to cope with some distancing, acting out, or depressed behavior on the part of your spouse and children. It may take a while before the family feels like they return to normal.

### Spousal Support

MISC.

The way you support your spouse before and after the death of her parent will make a difference in your marriage later on. Beyond the necessary help you give your spouse in her time of grief, afterward she will always look back and appreciate your care. Or your spouse can resent what you did or failed to do.

Madeline's father developed a cough that he couldn't seem to shake. Finally, he had extensive tests, and the doctor discovered he had stage-four cancer. From that point on, he deteriorated rapidly. During his shocking decline, Madeline felt like she was living in a nightmarish trance. She could barely function, but tried to spend every minute she could with her father. Her husband, Sam, was also devastated by the news. After 25 years of marriage, he'd come to love his father-in-law like a father. Yet he recognized that his distraught wife needed his support. Sam did his best to pick up the pieces of life dropped by his wife. He held her when she broke down in sobs several times a week, and stayed by her side as much as possible. Madeline's dad died a month after his cancer diagnosis. Weeks later when Madeline had gotten over her shock, she was able to recognize and appreciate Sam's contribution during that dark time. Even in the midst of her grieving, she felt more in love with her husband. Now several years later, she still feels appreciative of his efforts.

Due to the stereotype of difficult in-laws, you may not receive much support for your grief. Other people might not understand what you're going through. They may even discount your feelings. Instead of holding your feelings in, try to find others who've lost a beloved mother- or father-in-law. It will help to talk to someone who understands.

## Losing the Second Parent

For many people, the death of their second parent doesn't double their grief: it can multiply it. They can have intense feelings from becoming orphaned. Although these emotions may be more intense if they're younger when they lose their parents, it's still a double loss that can rock their world in painful ways. There's this vast empty space where before you had your parents.

**Expressions of Grief**

"For me, losing my mother was shocking. It was unexpected. It opened a can of worms I had no idea how to deal with emotionally. When my father died, it was less unexpected, but the fact that it happened so soon after my mother hadn't given me any time to truly process and no time to grieve because I was still dealing with the business end of her death."

—Kristin

If there's physical time (years) between deaths, it may give adult children a better opportunity to grieve and work through the issues. They can cope better with the second death because they've already dealt with the first one. If there are only months or a few years between the deaths or they happen simultaneously, your sense of being orphaned can intensify. You may feel like you want to "go home," but you can't because the two people who represented "home" are gone.

When we have grandparents and parents living, we can pretend they are barriers between death and us. In the usual scheme of things, we begin losing grandparents first. Then one parent dies, followed by the other. We become adult orphans. That barrier of protection is gone. No one stands between death and us. Our awareness of our mortality increases.

## Wrapping Things Up

When you've just lost your remaining parent, you (along with your siblings) may have the responsibility of settling the estate. While you're grieving, you have to deal with property and possessions. You may have to go through the house and garage—every single drawer, cupboard, and closet—and clean out, give away, and sell a lifetime of possessions. It's a time-consuming and painful process. If you don't have siblings (or they live out of state) the

burden falls on you. You can be so busy organizing the funeral and everything else, you may not have time to grieve. It may hit you later.

If you didn't have problems with your siblings before, they can manifest
now as you struggle to divvy up valuable or meaningful property and possessions. This is also a time when unresolved issues with siblings can rear
their ugly heads. Feelings (sometimes old) of unfairness rise up. Sometimes
division of the estate just can't be done in a way that feels equitable to all.
What do you do when there's only one heirloom vase and all three sisters
want it? These problems can permanently divide family members.

If one or more siblings were the primary caretakers, they may feel entitled
to more of the estate and become upset if their siblings don't agree. Or the
parent may have willed them a larger share. If siblings weren't privy to this
agreement beforehand, they can disagree or feel resentful now. Or they may
think the caretaker does deserve more, but not that much more. The whole
process can exacerbate the grief journey.

## Coping with Your Parent's Death

Like any death, coping can vary due to how your parents died. Your parent's
unexpected death can knock your world off-kilter. You struggle to find your
emotional feet enough to organize the funeral and help other family members who are grieving, too. A sudden death might drop unexpected responsibilities in your lap when you're shocked and grieving. Your grief journey
might be longer and harder because you didn't have time to prepare.

Sometimes parents live a long and full life. When the time comes for them
to die, they're ready. They may have also struggled with health concerns
that make them (and you) resigned to the inevitable. After the death, you
can feel sad, and/or you can have some guilt. But you may not have the
intense grief others feel for different types of death.

A friend of Shawn's sent him booklets about dealing with grief. Reading
those, the main thing he felt about his father's death was guilt over *not*
feeling all those emotions discussed in the booklets. He was sad, but not
devastated. His father had lived a good, long life. With all his health problems, his passing wasn't a big shock. But in comparing himself to the people
in the booklet, Shawn felt like some kind of coldhearted, unnatural son.

Aging and illness can take a toll on your parent, until he or she is no longer the person you want to remember. Sometimes the last stage of life and the dying process can be traumatic. You might keep flashing back to memories of those final days and moments—ones you'd rather forget. You can switch your thoughts to happier memories, but it might take some effort.

Sara's mother, Vivian, was in a long-term-care hospital for four months before she passed away. Sara didn't want to remember her mother looking so old, tired, and worn. She went through family pictures and selected ones showing Vivian's beauty, liveliness, and happiness. She kept them in a basket for people to look at when they came by the house. Now whenever Sara thinks of her mother, she remembers her based on those pictures.

Losing a parent is a major life adjustment, and it's important that you take care of yourself emotionally and physically. Seek support from others who have lost parents and understand what you're going through. Be patient with your grieving process. It takes time to come to terms with the loss of a beloved parent. Recognize that for the rest of your life, you may have surges of missing your parents.

## Essential Takeaways

- Your age when you lose your parent factors into your grief.
- Losing a difficult parent can lead to conflicted feelings, including sadness and relief.
- When you lose one parent, you may feel you need to support your surviving parent.
- Losing both parents makes both losses all the harder.
- Losing a beloved in-law causes grief for the whole family.
- No matter how old you are, you have times when you miss your parents. Allow yourself to grieve during these times, no matter how long it's been since they died.

# chapter 8

# Death of a Spouse

Losing your other half

Caring for a dying spouse

Living alone

Making difficult decisions

Helping children cope with the loss

Moving on without your spouse

When you and your mate step into the rowboat of marriage, you prepare to set off down the river on the journey of your lives together. You each take an oar and begin paddling. Along the way, you learn how to row as a team. You may add children to your boat, make stops, go backward for a while or detour down a side stream, navigate around rocks and through rapids, weather storms, and enjoy lazy, sunny days on the slow-moving water. You look forward to your future destinations, and plan what you'll do when you get there. You're always together.

Then your partner dies, and you are left alone, attempting to row by yourself. You may be paralyzed with physical and emotional grief, and lack the necessary strength and energy to paddle on. Without your partner, your boat may go in circles, regardless of whether you're rowing hard or drifting aimlessly, and you make what feels like no progress. At times, you doubt you can continue your journey without your mate. It may be a long time before you figure out how to straighten the boat and make your way down the river alone. But eventually, you will learn to navigate your way alone.

## 'Til Death Do Us Part

Whether your mate dies suddenly or after a long illness, your whole life turns upside down. One day you are part of a couple (and all that it meant to you) and the next day you are single. Not only has your mate passed away, but your identity as a couple has also died. And you're forced to deal with your grief without support from the one you've traditionally turned to.

The loss can plunge you into a maelstrom of sadness, helplessness, longing, and other emotions. It's not uncommon to feel angry or resentful at your spouse for leaving you, as well as guilty because you're the one who's still alive. This dark time of grief may feel as though it will never end. At times, you might even want to die so you can be with your beloved. Because you've never experienced these turbulent emotions before, there might be days when you feel like you're going crazy.

Partners not only grieve the loss of their mate, but of familiar aspects of life. With the death of your spouse, you lose a role that you've had for (perhaps) many years—that of husband or wife. You also grieve alterations in your lifestyle. If the surviving spouse must deal with decreased income and other financial concerns, and perhaps must go back to work, or give up a home, he or she experiences more loss.

**Misc.**

**Depression and Marriage**

Studies show that people who have a good marriage and positive view of their spouse have less depression four years after the death than those who have a difficult marriage or negative view of their spouse. Highly dependent spouses have more depression four years after the death than independent ones.

The Social Security Administration estimates that each year one million Americans lose their spouses. Many of these people have lived long married lives. Other couples lose their partners early, sometimes when they have children whom they must then raise as single parents. Parenting is challenging enough when there are two parents sharing the decisions, burdens, and joys of childrearing. These suddenly single people struggle with their own grief as well as their concern with the feelings and well-being of their children. They try to be both father and mother, as well as the sole provider for the family.

The surviving parent may be overcome with grief and not be there for the children. This happened to Maryanne, who was 24 and had a 4-year-old daughter, Kelsey, when her husband passed away. With his death, she thought her whole world had crumbled. She was dazed and couldn't think straight for weeks. Her mother had to come live with her in order to cook and take care of Kelsey because Maryanne wasn't capable of attending to her own needs, or those of her daughter. It took Maryanne six months before she was able to care for Kelsey, and her mother could return to her own home.

A partner's death is devastating. For some spouses, the pain of the loss never truly goes away. Older couples may die within a year of each other, their will to live snuffed out with the life of their partner. For others, work and family, especially children and grandchildren, ease their grief by putting their own life into perspective. Finding the coping mechanisms that work for each individual is the key to mastering grief.

## Yearning

After your husband or wife has died, it's natural to be preoccupied with thoughts of your loved one, and wish for them to be back with you. During this period, spouses tend to focus more on the good qualities of the mate and gloss over the things that annoyed them. They often think back to their courtship and early marriage, remembering their loved one when he or she was younger. They dwell on the happy times of their marriage. This can be comforting, as well as make the bereaved spouse yearn for their partner and feel lonely without them.

**Expressions of Grief**

"If only I could hold her again. I'd settle for five minutes. To feel her in my arms, lay my cheek against the top of her head, smell her hair, and feel her squeeze me back. What I wouldn't give for that."

—Mike, a recent widower, about his wife, Carol

## In Mourning

The grieving spouse should recognize his need to mourn the loss of his spouse for as long as necessary. It's a mistake to try to push the loss aside after too short a period of time. Many who are grieving benefit from a formalized period of "mourning" because they (and others) recognize that this time is set aside to feel their sadness and come to terms with (although not get over) their loss. As long as you are "in mourning," others know they need to respect your feelings and support you. No one, including yourself, expects you to be "over it" in six months.

Of course, the mourning period is different for each person. There are many factors that affect it, such as …

- The length and quality of your marriage.

- The support from family and friends.

- Your ability to process your grief.

- The age of your children.

- How your spouse died.

- Your financial circumstances.

For most spouses, the mourning period usually extends beyond the first year, and for some, it lasts many years. You might spend much of the first year in shock and struggling to emotionally and financially survive. For some widows and widowers, the second year is even harder. The magical hope that their spouse might return has disappeared. The shock and numbness has worn off. Most people's support at the difficult times, such as holidays or anniversaries, has also waned. The second year can be just as painful and lonely, or even more so, as the first.

cautions and concerns

It's important to let go of any ideas of how long your intense grieving period will last. Your preconceived expectations can make things worse because you begin to think something is "wrong" with you. Or you can be too hard on yourself for continuing to grieve. Being kind to yourself is vital to easing the difficulties during your time of mourning.

# Loneliness

One of the greatest struggles for those who are newly widowed is loneliness. Learning to function on their own can be a difficult process for widows or widowers. For all their married lives, and perhaps several years before, they were used to having a companion, someone to talk to, do things with, share memories with, and sleep with.

For a short time after the death, friends or family members often offer daily support. The bereaved spouse is inundated with calls, food, visits, and cards, so he or she doesn't have much opportunity to feel alone. But as time passes, friends and family return to their regular lives, the calls, cards, and visits taper off. Loneliness sets in.

After the death, there's an absence of familiar rituals like having dinner and talking about the day, doing tasks together, or watching TV together. Now for the bereaved spouse, these activities become reminders of the past. Many widows and widowers say it's difficult to get used to coming home to an empty house, or sleeping alone. They find it hard to fill their lonely hours.

Most couples have a well-established social life—a niche they've made that includes friends and family, clubs, organizations, church or temple, hobbies, sporting events, and the activities of their children and grandchildren. After the death of a spouse, they can feel as if they no longer fit in. This is particularly true with other couples. You were used to going out with them as a couple. But the relationship has changed, and you might not be getting together as a threesome instead of a foursome. It's always best to discuss your feelings with them if their friendship is important to you.

The attitude of some longtime friends can contribute to a feeling of isolation. Some of them might not be as sympathetic as you'd expected them to be. Often, grief at the loss of a spouse is very unsettling for some people. As a result, they withdraw from your company, or worse, they don't understand what you're going through. You may want to build your friendships with other widowed or single people instead of trying to focus your efforts on relationships with couples.

One woman reported that her longtime friend called several months after the death of her husband to see how she was doing. Used to sharing her emotions with her friend, the widow mentioned how hard it was for her to cope. Her friend became impatient with her, saying, "Well, isn't it time you got over it?" The woman was stunned and hurt by her friend's reaction. She knew her friend had been married for 50 years and couldn't understand what she was feeling. Their friendship was never the same after that.

**survival strategies** No matter how lonely you are, don't rush into another relationship because you need companionship and/or want to stop the pain. Allow yourself as much time as you need to grieve and to heal. Take the time to get to know the new mate, or you might end up with someone who's not the best partner for you.

## Caregiving for a Dying Spouse

When a mate becomes seriously ill, most spouses become the primary caregiver. Watching their partner suffer from physical and/or mental deterioration is painful, stressful, and draining. Often their world narrows to their caregiving duties. It may be difficult for them to leave the ill spouse alone or find someone to stay with him or her. Normal activities that previously sustained them fall by the wayside. After their partner's passing, it's sometimes tough to resume their old friendships because they've isolated themselves from others for so long.

Many caregivers may feel as though their mate has already died because his or her "personality" is gone or changed beyond recognition. They mourn the loss of the partner that was and the life they lived before the illness. They worry about the financial toll the illness takes. They hate seeing their spouse suffer, and they're not sure how much of the caregiving burden they can continue to bear. They may wish the ordeal were over. Even though these thoughts are normal, the spouse can feel guilty, as if he or she is a bad person and not a loving mate.

As horrible as this period is in a marriage, for many, it can still be a time of beauty and love. Neither spouse takes each other for granted. They know their time together is short, and they appreciate each day. They cherish each other and speak of their love. They share memories and spend time talking about what is important to them. And they, as much as possible, try to prepare for one spouse to die and the surviving spouse to live on.

Gina talked with me about her life with her husband, Jerry, in the time prior to his death from cancer. "It was the best year of our marriage," she said. "We were forced to slow down, reevaluate our lives, and pay attention to what was really important. We had in-depth, spiritual talks, and we loved each other so much. The memory of that time has sustained me after Jerry's death."

It's important for caregivers to make time for self-care. Ask friends if they are willing to visit with your spouse for an hour or two while you take a nap or go for a walk. Join a support group for caregivers. The government, as well as philanthropic organizations, have services that provide relief for caregivers. Ask your doctor, minister, someone from hospice, or go online for information. Also see the Resources appendix for suggestions.

## Young Widow or Widower

A life-threatening illness or a sudden death usually takes a young couple by surprise. They may have little or no previous experience with grief and adversity. Coping with the illness and subsequent death of a partner is the last thing they expect at this stage of their lives. They're full of dreams and plans for the future and believe they have their whole lives ahead of them.

It's difficult for young spouses to believe that they've become a widow or widower. For example, when Stephanie's 28-year-old husband died of a heart attack after playing a game of basketball, she walked around in a daze for months, unable to believe he was really gone. The first time someone labeled her a widow, she stared at the woman blankly, thinking, "I'm a widow? I can't be a widow. They have gray hair."

There are few people the bereaved spouse can lean on who understand. While young couples often have friends who are divorced, few have friends whose husband or wife has died. Their friends usually don't know how to support the bereaved partner. The uniqueness of the situation is isolating.

In addition to the traditional grief platitudes, young spouses are told things that, while meant to be well-meaning, are actually hurtful. "You're young. You'll marry again," is one example. Another is, "You are so blessed that you had him for a few years. You had a good marriage. That's more than most people have in a lifetime."

The bereaved spouses can also experience difficulties with their in-laws. If there are no children, the in-laws might pull away after a time, not feeling as if they have any real connection with their son- or daughter-in-law. Or even if there are children, the in-laws may detach from them because it's too painful to talk to or see the grandchildren without the presence of their son or daughter. On the opposite spectrum, the in-laws might immerse themselves in the surviving family, interacting with their grandchildren as a way to forget their own pain. The parents and spouse can bond over their mutual grief. While the grandparent's involvement with the family can be helpful to the spouse and children, it can also be intrusive and burdening. It is important to work out some sort of arrangement that will benefit all concerned.

| survival strategies | If you have children, you'll need to forge stronger bonds and find new ways to communicate with your in-laws. Because their child isn't around to be the primary communicator and to smooth out rough patches, you'll have to take on that role. Be direct with them. Let them know they are important in the children's lives, and tell them what they can do to help. |
| --- | --- |

## Losing Your Longtime Spouse

The older the spouse, and the longer the marriage, the harder it is for the surviving mate to pick up the pieces of life and go on. It's been a long time since they lived alone. Or perhaps they never have because they might have married during a time when it was more common to remain at home, rather than move out on their own. Their lives are so intertwined that they don't know how to function well by themselves.

The elderly who have lost a mate are particularly vulnerable. By the time a couple is old, they have usually experienced multiple losses as their friends and family members die. Gradually, their support system whittles away. Grief becomes a familiar feeling, and they're often in a state of mourning.

An older widow or widower may have other factors in their lives that become exacerbated by their grief over the loss of their mate. They might have their own health issues. They might live on a fixed income and have fewer financial resources for coping. Plus, they may have diminished mental and/or physical capacity to handle the challenges they now face alone.

Often after the death of a spouse, the relationship with the adult children changes. The surviving parent may become more emotionally and physically dependent on the adult children, both to help the parent cope with his loneliness as well as meet the day-to-day challenges of living without his spouse. The adult children might now step in with caretaking responsibilities, providing company, meals, and housekeeping; taking the parent to the doctor; or making sure the bills are paid. Sometimes this help is welcome. Other times the surviving parent may feel guilty about being a burden or resent the need to be taken care of.

**Widows and Widowers**

MISC.

In 2008, according to the Administration on Aging, widows accounted for 42 percent of the 65-or-older U.S. population. Widowers accounted for 14 percent.

# Living Without Your Spouse

After your mate dies, you mark time differently. Your life falls into two halves—a pre-death-of-your-spouse half and a post-death-of-your-spouse half. You'll first count the days, then the months, and finally the years since your husband or wife died. Even though your life may be full with the actual business of living, you know exactly how long ago the death occurred.

## Struggling to Adjust at Home

When a spouse dies, the reminders of her are all around you. You can't escape. All your senses are affected—sight, hearing, smell, taste, and touch. You see the empty chair at the table, find yourself listening for familiar noises like the sound of the car pulling into the garage, touch the empty place in the bed next to you, or feel the absence of her presence.

You become familiar with the smell of your partner's skin, soap, shampoo, perfume or cologne, cigarettes or cigars. Catching a whiff of a familiar scent can immediately remind you of your spouse. When a spouse dies, his scent lingers on the clothing he's worn or on his pillow. It's not uncommon for the bereaved to cherish some clothing or a pillowcase and use it when they need to feel connected with their loved one. They'll clasp a pillow to their chest, or hug a group of clothes hanging in the closet. Sometimes they'll cry or have a conversation with the deceased while they hold the article of clothing. Women may take comfort from wearing a husband's sweater, coat, shirt, robe, or pajamas. After a while the husband's smell will fade, replaced by hers or disappear through washing, but the idea of being wrapped in his clothes is still important. Men might keep a handkerchief or scarf with her perfume on it or sleep with her nightgown nearby.

Nighttime is often a private time for sorrow and tears. Those who grieve often have problems sleeping. Spouses have an even more difficult situation because the empty space in the bed is a reminder that their loved one will never again sleep next to them. No snuggles, pillow talk, or intimacy. Some women can even feel fearful without their husband. Noises in the dark can sound ominous, causing them to sleep lightly or startle awake.

| MISC. | **Create a Personal Retreat** |
|---|---|
| | Because of the barrage of memories in your home, you might choose one room (or part of a room) in the house to paint and redecorate. Or you can replant a corner of your yard or change your patio. This can give you a place to escape the constant reminders of your loss, where you can nap, read, watch TV, work, or do hobbies. That doesn't mean you won't think of your loved one or grieve in that space, but you've created a personal retreat. |

## Learning Your Partner's Tasks

Learning to live alone after the death is an arduous process. Usually, spouses divide household and parenting duties, with one person taking on the majority of a certain task, while the other might have little knowledge of how to do the job. For example, in a traditional household, a wife shops for groceries and cooks, and the husband is in charge of their finances or mowing the lawn.

After the death, bereaved spouses may struggle to master survival and other skills at a time when they can be weighed down by sadness and fatigue. In addition, their mental abilities might seem foggy, making it hard to learn new things or make difficult choices. Consequently, they might neglect these unfamiliar areas, and their health and financial well-being can suffer.

Bill had this happen when his wife, Doreen, passed away. Bill could grill a mean hamburger or steak, but that was the extent of his cooking skills. Doreen did everything else. After her death, his daughter and the neighbors left meals for him, but he didn't want to rely on them. Yet going into the kitchen—the place of so many happy memories of his wife—was so painful that he avoided the room as much as possible. He lost so much weight that his doctor scolded him. Alarmed, his daughter took him to a cooking class so he could learn in a neutral environment. After several months in the class, Bill felt ready to tackle making meals in his own kitchen and became proficient enough that he regained some weight, and his daughter stopped worrying about his eating habits.

Many bereaved spouses welcome the diversion from their grief that extra work provides, even though they may feel overwhelmed. They bustle from one task to another, trying to keep their mind empty while their hands stay busy. They (and others) think staying busy is helpful. But busyness, per se, doesn't usually aid the spouse because it can block the grieving process.

The need to do double duty can also take a toll on the bereaved spouse. They're tired and may feel they don't have the energy or space in their lives to grieve. Claire experienced this when her husband passed away. A friend inquired how she was doing. "I'm keeping busy," Claire replied. "That's good," the friend said. "No," Claire told her. "It's not good. I'm doing the things my husband used to do *and* my things, and I don't have time to grieve, and I need it. It's *not* good that I'm busy."

A surviving spouse who is feeling overwhelmed should not be afraid to ask for help. Most people are willing to help, but don't know what to do or are too busy with their own lives to think of what someone might need. Don't assume they don't care. Often, if asked, they're happy to lend a hand.

## Difficult Choices

Part of the grieving experience involves making complicated decisions during a time that you're grieving, stressed, exhausted, and not thinking straight. People in the throes of grief are in a highly emotional state, which can affect clear thinking and make them susceptible to the input of others. Be wary of making any significant decisions during the grieving process.

Surround yourself with family and friends whom you trust because you know they have your best interests at heart. They can help you take care of some of the tasks that are difficult.

## Financial Decisions

From the day of the death, decisions are thrown at you, starting with what mortuary to use. You are confronted with a bewildering array of forms to fill out and financial decisions to make, often accompanied by a sharp drop in income. For many bereaved spouses, the scramble to take care of financial concerns feels intrusive to their grief. While they might realize the necessity, they wish they could be left to their grieving, instead of being forced to deal with practical concerns.

The people at the mortuary should be helpful in guiding you through initial steps to take for the funeral and beyond. But keep in mind that mortuaries and cemeteries are a business, and the people who work there may try to pressure you into choosing a more expensive funeral package than you want or need. Take one or more trusted friends and family members with you who can support you emotionally as well as aid you in making sensible choices. There are also guidelines and inventories online that list financial steps for you to consider. In addition to friends and family, you may need direction from your estate-planning attorney, tax advisor, and financial advisor.

In addition, the death of the spouse may seriously affect the surviving partner's income. Pension plans and social security benefits can be affected. Be sure to plan ahead whenever possible. In some states, jointly held assets such as a checking or savings account may be frozen as soon as the bank becomes aware that one of the joint owners has died. It may take a court order to release them. Therefore, you may find yourself without funds at a very vulnerable stage in your life. Be sure to know the laws in your state.

**survival strategies**

Get at least 10 copies of the death certificate because you will need them for a variety of situations, such as life insurance, bank accounts, and investment accounts. The more accounts you have, the more copies you'll require.

Take the time you need to make important financial decisions, even though family, and others, like an insurance company representative, might try to pressure you into making immediate choices. You want to be fully informed and give careful consideration to your decisions, not make them because you were lonely, grieving, and suggestible.

## Personal Possessions

The way people grieve the loss of their husband or wife will differ when it comes to possessions. Some need to immediately empty shared rooms, such as the bedroom, of all their spouse's belongings, and maybe paint and redecorate. Others cling to their mates' possessions for years, perhaps never letting go of anything. Sometimes, they hope that their spouse might return and use the stuff, even though they know their spouse is dead.

Personal tokens can also be used for comfort. For example, a wife might wear her husband's watch, or a husband might carry a love note from his wife in his wallet. When they look at the token, they can feel as if their spouse is with them. The bereaved spouse might also take some satisfaction in distributing possessions to friends and family, believing that the recipient will think of the deceased whenever they use it.

There's no one right way for anyone to deal with their loved ones' "stuff." Give yourself time to figure out what you want to do. Acting on impulse can backfire. As you recover, you'll find yourself naturally cleaning out and letting go, although you'll probably always keep some personal mementos.

## Moving

People who are bereaved often make a move when they don't have to. They might want to flee their home with so many painful reminders, or they may impulsively relocate to live closer to their adult children or other family members. However, this isn't always the wisest choice. You will take your memories and your grieving wherever you go. If you give up your friends, your routine, your activities, or a job, it might be harder to start again in a new location. You'll be grieving the loss of your home and lifestyle as well as your spouse. Plus, your children might not spend the amount of time with you that you think they will.

If possible, don't make a physical move right away. Take some time to see what support you have from those around you, and give yourself the opportunity to engage with the previous activities you might have given up when you first lost your spouse or had to become a caregiver. If you make a decision that's well thought out, you'll have more success, regardless of whether you stay or go.

**cautions and concerns**

If you move to live near your kids, make sure you discuss your expectations with them beforehand. Just because you imagine having family dinners every Sunday doesn't mean your child and his or her family will be able (or want) to do so.

## Helping Your Children Cope

Children who've lost a father or a mother have to cope with a radical shift in their life. Their childhood will be far more painful and difficult than if their parent hadn't died. They will struggle with their grief, plus miss all of the benefits of having two parents throughout their childhood. For the rest of their lives, they will regret not growing up with both their mother and father.

If your spouse is dying, involve your children in the process as much as possible. Don't keep the fact that he or she is dying a secret. The children will have lots of questions. Answer them as honestly as you can, using simple, age-appropriate language. Children also need time to emotionally prepare for the death of the parent and say good-bye to their mom or dad.

The best way you can help your children cope with the dying and death of a parent is by being aware of your own feelings and actions. How you process your feelings, and the way you treat your children, will make a big difference in enabling them to feel secure. They are already trying to cope with their grief. If they feel you are overwhelmed to the point of neglecting them, acting angry or tearful, they will feel unsettled and probably act out in ways that will be even more difficult for you to handle, for example, becoming cranky, angry, or belligerent.

Recognize that you might feel impatient and irritable. Try as much as possible not to take it out on your children, and apologize if you do so. Let them know your feelings, especially if they see you in tears: "Mommy is sad that Daddy has died. I'm okay. I'm just missing Daddy." As much as possible, keep to a normal routine. Children will need a familiar structure to their lives because so much else has changed for them. Prepare them ahead of time for any necessary life changes, such as a move. It may also help your children cope when you bring the deceased parent into conversations. For example, "Daddy would be so proud of the A you got on your math test."

Keep the lines of communication open and watch for any attitude and personality changes. Stay involved in their lives, both by quietly being with them and interacting in their activities. How they do in school is another important indicator of their coping ability. Enlist the help and support of their teachers, the principal, and the school counselor.

| survival strategies | One way to help your children deal with their grief is by drawing pictures and cards and writing stories, songs, poetry, and journaling. The drawing and writing can be about their feelings, stories about their family, or letters to the deceased parent. Music is also helpful. Learning a musical instrument and playing music that reflects their feelings can help them cope with their loss. |
| --- | --- |

## Coping with Your Spouse's Death

Experiencing your grief is critical to working through your mourning. Often, spouses are so busy that they don't take the time to grieve. Planning a funeral, making financial arrangements, and trying to juggle household and parenting tasks by yourself can leave little opportunity to process feelings. Your focus is on learning to adjust and survive. You can end up distracted and numb. Or, as you worry about your basic survival needs, your primary feelings can be fear and anxiety. After you solve problems, finalize your decisions, and stabilize your financial situation, you are free to more fully process your sadness and pain.

It's important to set aside some time to grieve. Hold a favorite picture and talk to your mate. Take a walk and find a place to sit in solitude where you can remember him or her. Write down your thoughts and feelings in a journal. Seek out others, especially those who have lost a spouse, to talk with. Here are some other coping tips.

- Take baby steps. Some days, all you'll want to do is stay in bed weeping or sit frozen in a chair. On those days, give yourself permission to take small steps. Break down self-care and necessary tasks into small chunks.

- Set up a place of remembrance. Many families find comfort in creating an area with pictures, meaningful keepsakes, and maybe a candle and vase for flowers.

- Play soft music or audio CDs at bedtime to soothe your mind and help you sleep.

- Join bereavement groups for spouses. Many widows and widowers find it helpful to attend a bereavement group. They take comfort from sharing their feelings with others who understand. (See Chapter 18 and the Resources appendix for more information on bereavement groups.)

- Be gentle with yourself. Don't beat yourself up for continuing to grieve, or fault yourself for what you can't do. Criticism will only make your grief journey harder.

| survival strategies | You don't need to have had a perfect marriage in order to mourn the loss of your husband or wife. Your partner was an important part of your life, and you'll still grieve his or her loss. |

Even though it may seem like the pain of your spouse's death will never end, it will. That doesn't mean you won't have times of sadness. Recovery is a long-term goal. When a few days or weeks pass without major grief episodes, you may think you're okay, only to have grief hit you again, perhaps even harder, and you realize that you only had a temporary reprieve. With time, these episodes will become farther apart.

Kenny talked about the death of his wife, Lois, from cancer, six years ago. From outward appearances, Kenny didn't seem to be grieving. He was a jovial man who'd had a live-in girlfriend for five years and a successful business and social life. But in private moments, Kenny admitted how excruciating it had been to watch his wife deteriorate. He told me he'd been there every step of the way with Lois, and a part of him died when she did. No one understood what it was like for him. The memories of the experience gave rise to the feeling of grief even six years later.

As you move toward recovery, you'll take on the challenge of a new life, despite your grief. You'll become more independent, learn new skills, make some important life changes, try other activities, and make new friends. Your life may become very different from the one you led before the death of your mate. Although you may continue to miss your partner, you can come to take pride in forging on independently.

## Essential Takeaways

- Experiencing the pain from the loss of your spouse is critical to working through your grief.
- Caring for a dying spouse takes an emotional, mental, and physical toll on a husband or wife.
- Rely on and communicate more with other family members and friends, especially about important life decisions.
- The surviving spouse has a painful adjustment to living alone because the reminders of the loss are everywhere.
- Recognize that your children will need support to have an ongoing relationship with their deceased parent. Share photos and movies and tell stories about their mom or dad.
- Although it will take time, most spouses return to their previous level of physical and emotional functioning.

# chapter 9

# Death of a Child

The depths of pain

How others may react

Losing a child at different ages

The effect on the rest of the family

How helping other parents helps you cope

Surviving your child

The death of a child is the most painful kind of loss. Our children represent our future. In them, we invest our hopes and dreams, love, time, energy, and money. We wish for them a happy childhood, a productive adulthood, and a contented old age. We want (and expect) to outlive them.

The relationship of parent to child is different from all others. The love of a parent for a child is instinctive, powerful, and enduring. For loving parents, their children are the light of their lives. When death extinguishes that light, they are plunged into a deep, dark, and unbearable abyss.

## The Sharpest Pain

The death of a child throws a family completely off balance, like a car that's lost a wheel. There's not only the loss of the son or daughter, but also the former stability of the family unit. The family feels incomplete. There's emptiness now where before there was a person.

The family will never feel "normal" again because someone will always be missing.

No matter how old your child, the heart-wrenching pain of losing him or her stays with you always. The passing of the child doesn't sever the parental bond. In fact, death can intensify it. The connection continues on, even though the object of those emotions has died.

Most people experience grieving for their children in similar ways. They are overwhelmed with complex, intense, and self-absorbing emotions. Their life undergoes a shift, where their priorities change. They often struggle to function on two levels—the outer one, where they try to cope in their work and family lives, and the inner one, where they are engrossed in their grief. Theirs is an ordeal that no one who hasn't been there before quite understands.

Even answering the common social question, "How many children do you have?" can cause confusion and concern to bereaved parents. They come to dread the question because there is no easy or comfortable response, and they never know if it will make them emotional. Where before a mother or father could take pride in stating, "I have (number) children," now the answer only gives them pain, no matter what they say. Even though 30 years have passed since Harold's third child died as a baby, he still struggles with telling people how many children he has. "My tongue gets tangled," Harold said. "If I say four, I have to explain, and I don't want to. I've learned that saying three is best."

## Wanting to Die

Often, bereaved parents think of dying. They are in emotional and mental agony, and they long to be with their dead child. They don't want to live the rest of their lives without their son or daughter. It's not that they are actively suicidal. For them the idea of dying means that they will be released from their pain. Those thoughts are appealing when you're in the depths of despair.

After 2-year-old Max's death, his mother prayed to die. She knew she couldn't commit suicide because of how that act would devastate her husband and parents, but she wanted God to release her from her pain and reunite her with her son. These feelings stayed with her, even through her second pregnancy. It was only when she went into labor, and was on the way to the hospital, that she said to herself, "I'd better stop praying to die."

Many parents cling to the idea that they will someday reunite with their child in an afterlife. Whether or not they had strong religious beliefs before their child's death, the idea of being with their child again gives them hope for the future. Sometimes holding on to that hope will help them get through the dark times.

> **cautions and concerns**  While depression and wishing to die are often a common reaction for parents whose child has died, if you start having suicidal fantasies, and you've figured out a way to kill yourself and have the means to do so, then it's important to see a psychiatrist or a mental-health professional who specializes in bereavement right away.

## Guilt

Parents are supposed to protect their children. Even if the parents didn't cause their child's death, they may still feel guilty, as if they somehow broke a primary rule of parenting—keeping their child safe. If one or both parents had a part in the death, through negligence or an accident, the guilt and regret becomes a prison sentence they will live with every day for the rest of their lives.

Nancy struggled with guilt for a long time after her 5-week-old son died of *Sudden Infant Death Syndrome* (*SIDS*) while Nancy was sleeping. "I blamed myself for taking a nap," she said. "Maybe he wouldn't have died if I'd been awake. It was harder to bear, to not feel guilty, because there wasn't a reason for the death. He was an apparently healthy baby, and then he was gone."

> **definition**  **Sudden Infant Death Syndrome (SIDS)** is the sudden, unexpected death of an apparently healthy infant, usually when sleeping (or thought to be asleep). SIDS is the leading cause of death of infants between 1 week and 1 year of age. Approximately 7,000 babies die of SIDS each year.

Parents can feel guilty about their parenting, especially wishing they'd spent more time with their child. It's not uncommon for parents to work hard, then, when they're home, focus on the tasks needing to be done, rather than actually spending quality time with their child. They assume that there will be plenty of opportunities in the future. When parents look back, they wish they'd stopped to play more and work less.

As I mentioned in Chapter 2, parents (and other family members) often have regrets about the death. They wish they had taken different steps to protect the child. They wonder if (or even believe) the child would still be alive if they'd done (or not done) something differently. Regret can intertwine with guilt. Parents feel guilty for many of the things they regret. With time, some parents are able to move past their regrets by realizing that their child was loved and brought up in the best way the parents knew how.

You can take control of your guilty thoughts, although it requires mental self-discipline. Visualize your child standing in front of you. (You might need to make your child older in order to be able to communicate.) As you look at your beloved child, ask yourself if he or she would want you to beat yourself up. Of course, the answer is no. Then imagine the loving and forgiving things your child would say to you, and try your best to let them in. It will take time for the guilty feelings to pass. Repeat the exercise as often as you need.

## Vulnerability

After one of their children dies, parents lose their sense of security about life. They feel vulnerable and know how vulnerable their children are. They also realize there are families who've lost more than one child and become horrified and frightened by the idea of that happening to them. Parents become more protective of their remaining children, all the while knowing they're powerless to safeguard every aspect of their children's lives.

Your intuition is one of your best parenting tools, although it's the least obvious. Most parents have a story or two of when they followed their intuition and prevented problems with their children. Many parents disregard their instincts, especially if someone else, such as a doctor, reassures or overrides them. If your intuition tells you something is wrong, or to do or not do something with your child, follow through.

# Reactions of Others

The innocence of children touches people's hearts. Almost everyone understands the close bond between parent and child. Even strangers, when learning of the loss of someone's son or daughter, stop to mentally commiserate with the bereaved family. If they're religious, they may send a prayer of support.

## Shock and Survivor Guilt

Nothing knots the stomachs of parents like the thought of losing one (or more) of their children. It's every loving parent's greatest fear. The loss of a child they know sends a shockwave of fear through parents. When a child dies, all the parents who know that family put themselves in those parents' shoes, imagining losing their own child. The idea is so painful, a parent can't conceive what the reality must be like. They are heartsick for the deceased and their family. Yet at the same time, the parents may feel some survivor guilt because their own children are alive and healthy.

Recently a company asked me to lead a grief-counseling group. One of their employees had just lost her 10-month-old daughter, and all of her co-workers were upset. Her supervisor cried and told me, "I cannot even fathom what she must be going through. Even though my children are grown, the thought of having lost one when he was a baby ... of losing him now ...." Her response is typical of what other parents think at such times.

If someone in your community loses a child, reach out to the family. Send a card or contribute to a fund for them. There are places online, such as a memorial website or Facebook page, where you can leave a message of condolence. The support of others, even strangers, means a lot to the family.

Make sure you stop and take a few minutes to appreciate your own family. Give everyone hugs and tell them you love them. Make calls or send e-mails and texts to others whom you love. Expressing your caring for others, and feeling theirs in return, will bring comfort to you.

## Withdrawal

While it may seem unbelievable to those who haven't experienced it, many people avoid families whose child has died. They often experience a subconscious (and irrational) fear that the tragedy is contagious and might spread to their family. Or they don't know what to say, so they avoid making the attempt, although they first might make a token call, send a card, or attend the funeral before disappearing. Others don't even make an effort.

Sometimes the avoidance is blatant. Friends will be in the vicinity of the bereaved parent(s) but pretend they didn't see them. If they do speak with them, they'll talk about everything under the sun except the death of the child. Or they'll change the subject when the topic of the child's death comes up.

The first time this happened to Lori, whose 14-year-old daughter, Megan, died of a previously unknown heart condition, she was in the grocery store. She saw the mother of one of Megan's classmates. The woman pretended not to see her and ducked down another aisle. Then she must have hurried out of the store because Lori didn't see her again. At first, Lori felt hurt, but after a few more similar occurrences, she realized some people just weren't able to deal with her.

When you lose a child, you don't feel normal; few, if any, of your peers have lost a child. Your family is now different from all others you know. You feel the distinction, and you often see the difference reflected in the stilted words and distancing behaviors of people. As family members, friends, and acquaintances avoid you, you're left isolated in your agony.

Parents are lonely in their grief. They miss their child dearly. Their friends may not understand their feelings. Social activities become unimportant, and they have people (some whom they care about) pulling away because those people don't want to see their grief. Friends also may be unsure whether to continue their regular topics of conversation, many of which involve their children.

**survival strategies**    It's easy to feel hurt by the avoidance of others. Try not to take it personally. People are not deliberately trying to hurt you. They just don't know what to say or do.

Other friends, acquaintances, or even strangers can step forward, offering the family much-needed support. Existing friendships can deepen. New friends, especially those who've lost a child, can become a lifeline. Long after the death, parents tell stories of how people helped them. The kindness of others benefits the family during the time of raw grieving, and it lives on in their memories.

# The Loss of Children at Different Life Stages

As children grow, their relationship with their family also changes, gaining a greater intensity as they age. For most parents, the longer they know their children, the more deeply they love them. Interactions at each developmental stage bring both challenges and pleasures to the parents. Parents whose children die not only lose the physical relationship, but also their role with that child, and a chance for that role to grow as the child matures.

Saying a permanent goodbye to their child is one of the hardest things parents will ever do. Most are completely unprepared for the level of grief they feel. The child's passing leaves a huge hole in their heart, one that will never be entirely filled. Many parents feel they've lost a part of themselves because of the death of their child. They're forever changed by the experience.

## Miscarriage

A miscarriage is an unexpected and devastating event. One day, you're planning to become a parent to a special baby, and then the next day, you're mourning the loss. It doesn't matter how soon into the pregnancy it happens. A pregnant woman feels the fetus growing inside her and forms an intimate connection with the baby early on. She begins to imagine her baby, seeing herself holding her infant. She dreams about being a mother to this child, no matter how many other kids she has.

Fathers, too, experience prenatal attachment to their babies. A man will place his hands on the mother's stomach and feel the child kick. He will talk to his baby, and think about playing with it someday. Even though a man doesn't feel the baby within his body like a woman does, he has a relationship with it.

Following the loss of a fetus, a woman has to cope with the affects of both a birth and a death. Her body reacts physically. Her emotions fluctuate due to hormones and sadness. She might be numb or in shock, until a wave of grief hits her. For many young mothers, this might be their first experience with loss, and they don't understand their feelings.

After a miscarriage, it's normal for mothers to blame themselves. Even if the doctor reassures her, it's hard not to feel guilty. Dozens of questions arise to haunt her. "Did I do something to lose my baby? Maybe I didn't eat right or get enough sleep. Maybe I should have exercised more (or less). Maybe I was under too much stress." So in addition to her grief, a mother experiences guilt.

It's not uncommon for others to invalidate the loss of a baby because of miscarrying. Parents are told things like, "Maybe it's for the best." Or "You'll have another one." Although family, friends, and co-workers mean well when they make these statements, the message that comes across is: This event wasn't a big deal. You need to get over it and move on.

"I hate it when people trivialize the loss of a child due to early miscarriage. To me, that baby was real, and her death still hurts."

—Anne, about her miscarriage in 1996

In addition to the grief parents feel about their loss, they have fears for the future. "Will we be able to have a healthy baby? What if it happens again?" Most women who miscarry, however, go on to have successful pregnancies. By understanding the waves of emotion that can hit you after a miscarriage, you can help yourself heal.

It may aid your recovery to find a ritual to bring some feelings of closure. Write in a journal. Plant a tree in your baby's memory. Write a poem about your baby or about the loss. Paint a picture that represents your feelings. Write a goodbye letter to the baby.

## Death of a Child, 0–12

For most parents, a baby is a dream turned into a reality. The birth of the first child propels a man or a woman into the position of father or mother, experiencing a previously unknown depth of intimate, protective love. It's a bond they believe will last all their lives.

After the death of a baby or little child, sometimes parents have a longing for another one to fill their empty arms. This is especially true when the deceased child is little because the parents are younger and the baby will be closer in age to his or her siblings. But children are not replaceable. Each child is different, in looks, personality, talents, and interests. A new baby will not take away the family's pain, although the infant can bring joy and a new source of love. However, parents first need to give themselves time to grieve before they try to conceive.

After Nancy's baby died, she and her husband tried to have another one right away. But she had two painful miscarriages. Finally her doctor told her she needed to rest her body. They waited a year before trying again, and then their son was conceived and born healthy. "Looking back," Nancy said, "I can also see I needed that time to heal my heart as well as my body."

## Death of an Adolescent

The death of adolescents places an additional level of grief on family members. Teens are at a stage in life where they are showing promise of who they will become—the contribution they might make to the world. With their death, those around them must mourn their passing, as well as the loss of their potential.

Teenagers and young adults are often at loggerheads with their families. If the death happened during one of these times, parental guilt can increase. Or, if the young person has outgrown this difficult stage, parents can feel like they've put all this energy into navigating their child through adolescent problems, only to lose her or him.

Adolescents think they're indestructible. This attitude is due to lack of life experience and the incomplete development of their brains. At this stage in their lives, they venture out on their own, without the parental protection they had as a child. Many teenage deaths from accidents happen because of incautious risk-taking, unwise choices, or influence of peer pressure.

**The Teen Brain**

MISC.

According to the National Institutes of Health, the prefrontal cortex area—the region of the brain that governs judgment, decision-making, and impulse control (which inhibits risky behavior)—is not fully formed until age 23 to 26.

Although it may be painful to be around your son or daughter's friends, you might also find them a source of comfort. It's not uncommon for the friends to want to hang around the bereaved family, especially if you make them feel welcome. They have suffered a loss, too. As the years pass, they may still stop by and give you opportunities to reminisce about your child.

## Death of an Adult Child

When children become adults, the relationship with their parents changes. Many times, parents have developed pride in and respect for their adult child. An adult child can become a friend, perhaps even a close friend. Still, the grief of parents who've lost an adult child is often discounted, as if the pain is somehow less because the child is grown. But actually, it's usually the opposite. You have raised your children to adulthood and seen them develop lives of their own. You expect them to provide you with grand-children (or perhaps they already have), then live to raise them. You think they'll take care of you in your old age.

If the child was troubled (for example, they had a long-time drug habit), or the relationship wasn't close, the parents can still hope that their son or daughter will turn around and live a happy, productive life, which will include a close connection with the family. With the death, that hope ends. The parents must mourn the actual death of their child, as well as the loss of hope for change.

When I was called to a company to counsel employees about the loss of one of their colleagues, Rhonda came to see me. She told me her co-worker's death had brought up feelings about her son's passing, and she wasn't sure what to do about it. I asked her how long her son had been gone, expecting she'd give me an answer in years. Instead, she said, "October." I counted back. "Four months ago?" Rhonda nodded and began to cry. She told me her 35-year-old son had been physically fit, but had died suddenly of a stroke. Then she asked me if something was wrong with her. Gently I asked her why she had that idea. She said that her husband (not her son's father) kept telling her she needed to "get over it." Although it probably wasn't his intention, by trying to hurry her into recovery, he'd convinced her that her grief was wrong. When I asked her what she did with her feelings, Rhonda said she hid them from him.

I validated Rhonda's feelings and let her know nothing was wrong with her. As she shared with me about her son, I saw her unwind. I told her she would mourn the loss of her son for the rest of her life, and needed to give herself permission to do so. I gave her some resources she could turn to for support. After our talk, she sat up straighter, confidence in her face. I'd provided her with the reassurance she had needed. Her feelings were normal, and she could take as long as she needed to grieve her son's passing.

Like Rhonda, it's important for parents of the deceased adult child to allow themselves all the time and space they need to grieve. If others, no matter how well meaning, try to invalidate or push you out of your grief, you need to set boundaries with them. Let them know that your feelings are normal, and there is no timetable for your grief.

| Expressions of Grief | "I lost my son and best buddy. We loved to go to baseball games together. We had season tickets. I can't even watch baseball anymore without hurting. Sometimes I go to a game just because I know he'd want me to. But it's hard." |

—Len

## Effects on the Family Unit

A family is a community made up of people who are bonded emotionally. If something happens to one member of the family, the others are going to also be affected. Relationships and roles can change because of the death. For example, a parent who has lost an adult son may now take on childcare responsibilities so the daughter-in-law can go to work. Or the daughter-in-law may move away with the grandchildren, leaving the parents to grieve the death of their child as well as the loss of closeness with their grandchildren.

## Marital Problems

A child's death can strain a relationship to the breaking point. If a marriage is troubled before the death, it is particularly vulnerable. However, divorce is not an inevitable outcome. When a child dies, both parents are overwhelmed with pain and struggle to survive. However, as I said in Chapter 3, men and women often grieve differently. This can lead to misunderstandings that can cause fights and distance in the relationship at the very time a couple needs their bond to be strong.

Harold talked to me about the long-ago death of his baby son and how it affected his marriage. "The bad part of it was that I couldn't help my wife," he said. "I couldn't handle my own emotions, and I withdrew. We never really did talk about his death. It was something that was always there, but we didn't talk about it."

Some of the ways a couple has always bonded may fall by the wayside. It's not uncommon for one or both of the couple to stop engaging in activities that formerly brought them pleasure. In addition, a husband or wife (or both) may lose desire for sex due to the lack of an intimate connection, fatigue, or deep sadness. This can be especially difficult if one partner desires sex and the other doesn't.

Often, there's (spoken or unspoken) blame involved, which creates a rift between the couple. One parent can blame the other. They both fault each other, and/or one or both blame themselves. The feelings can be corrosive to an individual's physical and emotional health, especially when the negativity turns to bitterness.

Partners can turn away from each other's grief, instead of turning toward each other. Each one doesn't know what to say to comfort the other. Hugging, without words or with few words, is often the best way to be supportive. Saying, "I understand," "I know," or, "I feel that way, too," is often all that's needed to establish closeness.

## Sibling Grief

Children may have to process the loss of a sibling alone. Their parents are often too grief-stricken initially to be able to help them. Extended family members may also be incapacitated by grief. Sometimes, children try to escape to the homes of friends and neighbors, just to be away from their pain-filled houses.

However, children who've lost a brother or sister often don't have a lot of understanding from their peers. They no longer feel "normal" because the death makes them different. Their friends and classmates (after the funeral) go back to a regular life, so the bereaved siblings may feel isolated. Their friends may not know what to say or do to support them.

| survival strategies | Your children need to know it's okay to talk to you, even if you become emotional. Tell them: "You aren't making me cry. The sadness is always there. Even if I cry, it feels good that we are talking about (the deceased). It helps me when you talk to me because then I know what's going on with you, and I can hopefully help you, too." |
| --- | --- |

## Extended Family Members

When a child dies, the focus is on the immediate family. But members of the extended family suffer as well, often without the support shown to the parents. Grandparents can be very close with their grandchildren. The child might hold a special place in his or her aunt's or uncle's heart. Cousins might be good friends of the deceased. But relatives are often left to grieve alone.

Extended family members don't just have grief from their own loss; the suffering of other relatives torments them. For example, a grandmother can grieve the loss of her grandchild, and feel pain for her adult child who is the parent. She might also suffer because she sees the sadness of her spouse, son- or daughter-in-law, her other adult children (the aunts and uncles), and grandchildren (siblings and cousins). The pain of each family member compounds her own.

It's important for family members to draw together and rely on each other for support. At the same time, each one needs to understand everyone is in mourning and will be for many years. Some people's grief might manifest in irritability, anger, or withdrawal, difficult reactions for the rest of the family to deal with. Try (as much as possible) to not take others' behavior personally, but set limits if anyone is hurtful. Keep reminding each other that the reactions might be caused by grief.

## Coping by Helping Other Parents

Most parents who lost a child report that the people who helped them the most were other bereaved parents. They felt only those who'd been through the ordeal truly understood them. Involvement in bereavement groups for families who lost children can become a lifeline. Parents help parents in an unending chain. When a child dies, other bereaved parents step forward. Then eventually, those parents reach out to others in the same situation. Often, someone who knows both families, such as a minister, matches up bereaved parents. Or one family might be acquainted with the other, and they offer help. Sometimes strangers extend a helping hand, knowing how important it is for newly bereaved families to receive support from those who've been there. (See the Resources appendix for support groups.)

Gail, whose 14-year-old daughter passed away from a sudden heart condition, described the drawing together of bereaved parents as "a club you don't want to belong to." Another mother in the community, whose teenage daughter died 15 months earlier from a similar condition, contacted her. Gail thought. "If she's survived a year and a half of this, I bet I can."

## Life Goes On Without Your Child

As much as parents might want to die or disengage from reality, life goes on. For many parents, the fact that the "world" didn't stop when their child died was a shock. For many months or even years, parents just struggled to survive the loss. At some point, which is different for each person, they gradually began engaging more in life. (Chapters 20 and 21 discuss more ways to help yourself heal.)

"The world gets older but he's still two,
And we dream of things he'll never do."

—From "The Garden of Stone," a poem about Max, by Michael Kaner

Having other children doesn't ease the pain of losing one. However, the presence of other children helps anchor parents. They know they must survive and make a semblance of living for their other kids. And their other children provide a source of pride and joy for them.

Children stay alive in their parents' memory. Birthdays and the anniversary of the death are common times for parents to think of their deceased child. Many parents use rituals to mark the sad occasion. For example, they might visit the grave site on a birthday or light a candle in church on the anniversary.

**survival strategies** Many times parents are able to use thoughts of their child to comfort and support themselves. A mother of a 9-year-old who died in an accident said, "I've been through the worst. Nothing else can break me down now. She's my angel. I use her as an inspiration every day."

While parents never "get over" the death of their child, they learn to accept the fact of the death and come to terms with their altered lives. They find ways to integrate the child within themselves. Often parents talk about that their child has become an internalized part of them, and they find that comforting. Eventually parents can come to a place in their lives where they aren't in pain anymore—at least most of the time. There will still be sadness when they think of their child, especially for what might have been. However, the grief, fear, regret, and uncertainty can (for the most part) pass.

## Essential Takeaways

- Grieving the loss of a child is unique and more powerful than other losses.
- Other people have a hard time being around families who have lost a child, so they may avoid them.
- Losing a child is always an intensely painful experience, yet parental grief can differ due to the age of the child.
- Siblings often feel alone, unable to rely on comfort from grieving parents.
- Grieving parents often cope with their loss by helping other bereaved parents.
- Many bereaved families find they receive the most helpful support from bereavement groups.

# chapter 10

# Death of Extended Family and Friends

Losing the older generation

Losing members of your generation

The death of friends

Losing pets

An extended family is a group of people woven together by bonds of blood, love, and history. Some families are more tightly knit than others. With a caring, extended family, we have more people to love us and more for us to love. We have a sense of being part of a greater whole. We have a place in the tapestry of our "clan." When someone dies, a hole is ripped in the fabric of the family. Almost every member is affected in some way.

Our extended family provides living links to our past, present, and future. They are part of our cherished memories, and we hope to make more with them. Depending on the closeness of your relationship with them, when a relative dies, it can be a major loss. However, the loss of a relative may not be recognized by society as the profound loss it often is. People grieving the death of a relative may not receive much, if any, support. They may even have their grief discounted by others. Friends and pets are often considered part of our family as well. Their death can greatly impact us.

# Grandparents

Grandparents can have an important and lasting influence on their grandchildren. Research shows that children who spend time with their grandparents have cognitive, behavioral, and social benefits, as well as higher self-esteem, fewer behavioral problems, and better social skills.

More children are taken care of by their grandparents than by daycare and nursery schools combined. Grandparents who offer childcare for their grandchild provide a trusted resource for their family. Parents know that their children have a safe and loving environment, which is inexpensive, or even free. Grandparents, whether or not they do childcare, also ...

- Provide unconditional love and acceptance.

- Are a welcoming refuge away from parents.

- Teach skills and do activities related to their jobs and interests, which busy parents may not know or have time for.

- Pass down values and skills from earlier generations.

- Help resolve problems between their adult children and grandchildren or between the grandchildren and other family members.

- Serve as confidants.

- Provide a feeling of warmth and emotional security.

- Strengthen family values.

- Pass on the family history.

With the modern trend for men and women to delay becoming parents until later in life, it's more common for children to have elderly grandparents, or to lose them early. In addition, families are more mobile than in the past and are often scattered across different cities, states, or even countries. Therefore, many children miss some of the benefits of having youthful grandparents, or those whom they see frequently.

A nice part of being grandparents is that the burden of discipline doesn't usually fall on them. They can get away with spoiling their grandchildren. They can wind them up with sweets and excitement, then send them home to their parents. Consequently, their grandchildren frequently adore them. They look forward to spending time with grandma and grandpa. That close relationship can continue until the death of the grandparents, and the memory of it can last a lifetime.

<table>
<tr><td>**Expressions of Grief**</td><td>"I loved my grandma *so* much. I know I'm lucky to have had her for so long, but maybe that makes me miss her more. She gave me so much time and attention. She loved hearing about my life. We both looked forward to our visits. I can't imagine how it's going to be without her."</td></tr>
</table>

—30-year-old Elena

Grandparents are often children's first loss experience. It's common to lose one or more of your grandparents when you're still in childhood. Sometimes the child's grief gets lost among the pain of the adults. No one may take the time to explain much of what's happened. Children need ways to talk about and process their feelings. Chapter 19 goes into how to help children cope.

Children may be too young to remember their deceased grandparents. Or perhaps one or more died before their birth. They may hear stories about and see pictures of their grandmother or grandfather. It's not uncommon for children to grow up wishing they'd known their grandparents.

Grandparents are often the glue that binds families together. Relatives will gather to celebrate special occasions with them. They may keep squabbling factions of the family together. When the family matriarch and patriarch pass away, sometimes families drift apart.

## Siblings

As you grow up, you expect to eventually lose grandparents, aunts and uncles, and, at some point, your parents. But you don't expect to lose a sibling, at least not until the far distant future when you will all be old and may be ailing. But even then, you expect to have advance notice. Therefore, the death of a brother or sister can come as a painful shock. Even if you're prepared, you can suffer from their passing. The person who's been there for part or most of your whole life is no longer there.

For many siblings, the death of a brother or sister is frequently a huge, and often unrecognized, loss. Society doesn't acknowledge sibling grief. Siblings are often pushed aside, as if their pain is less than other family members. Supporters focus on parents, spouses, and children of the sibling, believing they have the more legitimate grief.

When others don't appreciate your grief, it can make you feel confused or guilty. If you have difficulty in recovering from the death of your sibling, you may be made to feel something is wrong with you. You may feel isolated in your mourning. There are few people to talk to who understand and are able to provide validation for your feelings.

There are no support groups for siblings. When you attend a regular bereavement group, the facilitator or the other members can contribute to your feelings of isolation. They may subtly or overtly make you feel your loss isn't as important as the losses of other members'. However, many bereavement groups will welcome a sibling griever with open arms.

When we're grieving, a part of us can revert to our inner child. Our inner child looks for comfort from the familiar source—our parents. Yet when a sibling dies, the parents (if they're alive) are so devastated that there's little or no comfort to be had from them. Instead, we may have to comfort them. Or our parents may have passed away. While we might feel grateful they are spared the pain of the loss, we can still miss having them to console us.

"How could my brother be dead! He's been a part of my whole life. A part of myself."

—Ben

## Squabbles and Best Friends

Siblings have a complex relationship. Their childhoods are woven together. Brothers and sisters run the gamut from best of friends to bitter enemies. You may have played, fought, and competed with your siblings. Growing up, at times you love your siblings and other times you hate them. Older siblings may feel protective of younger ones. Younger ones may look up to an older brother or sister.

Your siblings know your weaknesses better than anyone, and they may not hesitate to jab you in those areas. But the best of siblings fiercely love you. They'll have your back and be there when you need them. They are people you can feel envious of and, yet, also extremely proud of their accomplishments. Their passing can leave a huge rift in our hearts and lives.

## Facing Your Own Mortality Issues

No one triggers your own mortality issues like the death of a brother or sister. You are usually not far apart in age. You also share the same genes, and you were also raised in the same environment. Therefore, it makes sense that when a sibling passes away, you start to think about your own death. Sometimes you start to fear dying and death. Hopefully, you use your sibling's death to do some thinking about what you want out of life, and how you can contribute to the world in some way (no matter how old you are). You may also decide to make healthy changes in your lifestyle, to enhance your quality of life (and maybe extend it).

# Aunts and Uncles

Because we have aunts and uncles from both our mother and father's sides of the family, some people have several of each. When an aunt or uncle dies, you can feel concern for your grandparents (if they're still alive) because they've lost a son or daughter. Your mother or father is grieving the death of a sibling. His or her spouse (who's also become your aunt or uncle) is in mourning, and your cousins have lost a parent. You may try to set aside your grief to comfort your relatives. But it's important that you give some attention to yourself, too.

While writing this chapter, I had a dream that an aunt and uncle of mine had died. I felt desolate. They weren't supposed to go yet. Emptiness started seeping in where their place in the family was. I started feeling guilty about not having spent much time with them lately. I was struck by the enormous source of love they'd been to me that now was gone. I was so grateful to wake up and realize it was just a dream. That time will come, but not yet. The dream made me realize that I still have opportunities to interact with and appreciate them.

## Loving Parental Figures

Sometimes an aunt and uncle can be a source of unconditional love without the complications you might have with your parents. When you're a child, you might feel closer to your aunt and uncle and spend a lot of time with them. As you grow up, you can drift away. Or you might not be close, barely even know them. You can also remain very close all your life, perhaps feeling as if he or she is a second parent, thus grieving the death as much as you might your mom or dad. Or, as I felt in my dream, you can regret that you didn't spend much time with your aunt or uncle. Perhaps you wish you had expressed appreciation and love to him or her. This kind of loss can cause you to renew your relationships with other family members.

## Parental Mortality Issues

When we lose an aunt or uncle, that death can be a harbinger for the eventual deaths of our parents. Or if your parents have already passed away, the death of an aunt or uncle may mean that an entire generation is passing away or is completely gone. You don't just mourn your aunt and uncle; you can grieve again for the other family members you've lost. You can feel the absence of the whole generation before you. A part of your history is gone. You, your siblings, and your cousins are now the older generation.

# Cousins, Nieces, and Nephews

As children, cousins are people to play and fight with, and cause mischief together. As adults, they can be a source of friendship and support. Some people have only a few cousins; some people have many. Some are as close as siblings; some you barely know. Or perhaps you were close as children, and still retain that childhood bond, but you seldom see them. As with siblings, when your cousins start to die, it can bring up your own mortality issues.

If you have nieces and nephews, you may love them as if they were your own children. They've been a special part of your life. You've watched them grow up. You've spent time with them and have a lot of influence on them. You take pride in their accomplishments.

When a niece or a nephew dies, you have your own grief about the loss. Yet you also worry about and grieve for your sibling who's devastated at the death of his or her child, as well as your parents grieving a grandchild, and other nieces and nephews who've lost a sibling or a cousin. The whole family is rocked with grief. You might be so focused on taking care of everyone else that your own pain is overshadowed.

Holidays and special occasions after the death of any relative can bring sadness. But it may feel especially poignant when you've lost a niece or nephew. You can't help but remember earlier times with them. You grieve their loss, yet also know how much sorrow their parents and siblings are carrying. Holidays can reflect and magnify the pain of the whole family. They may also be a time to share and enjoy memories. (Chapter 6 covers how to cope with the holidays after a death.)

## Death of a Friend

We are born into a family and unless we sever ourselves from them, we're pretty much stuck with them. But friendships are a choice. We've decided that something about a certain person appeals to us. We've taken that person into our life and heart.

Most people have all kinds of friends. The bonds of friendship run the gamut from those who are friendly acquaintances to those who are closer than blood relatives. Friends can range from those that begin in childhood and last for a lifetime, to ones that are only a few months old, showing promise of deepening into true friendship. You may have a friendship with an individual, or you could have a group of friends who are tight—a brotherhood or a sisterhood. Perhaps you've been companions for many years.

Expressions of Grief

"I can't tell you how much sorrow and loneliness I feel. How can I explain what's it like to be the last of a tight group of women? We had friendships that lasted for 65 years."

—80-year-old Carol

Your friend might be one you do certain activities with. For example, she may be your movie-going friend or fishing buddy. In addition to missing your friend, you now miss doing that activity with her. It no longer feels the same. You may even lose your enjoyment of that activity.

Friendships usually develop from propinquity, for example, work, neighbors, church or temple. After the death, when you're in those situations, you also miss them. However, you may have the comfort of grieving with others in your organization or neighborhood. You can band together to help the family in some way.

You might have a mentor or confidant whom you consider a friend. This person supports and coaches you to be a better, more successful person. You look to him for advice as well as support. When he dies, you don't know what you will do without your mentor in your life.

There is a well-known concept in the book and script-writing world. In a plot, there comes a time when the character who is the mentor must leave or die. Although that "death" is painful for the hero or heroine, it's also necessary. Without the mentor, the hero or heroine is forced to go on alone. She must grow into her potential in order to meet the goal of the story. The movie *Star Wars* is an example, when Obi-Wan Kenobi dies.

However, just as Obi-Wan's voice stayed in Luke Skywalker's head, so, too, does the memory of your friend remain in your heart and mind. Their wisdom, zest for life, kindness—or whatever qualities they possessed and shared with you—are not lost. Part of your grief journey involves the acceptance that you can go on without them. You're a better person because of their friendship.

## When You're Not Close

Often your youth or physical or emotional distance from your family keeps you from bonding with some relatives. When they die, you might not feel any grief. You may have some concern for other family members, or you may have some regret that you didn't really get to know them, but you're not really that impacted.

However, sometimes you have a relative (or more than one) who is difficult or even abusive in some way. A grandparent or an aunt or uncle may have tormented or emotionally damaged your parent, which affects the way you were raised (giving you your own problems). This abuse can also directly impact you if your parent didn't protect you from the "bad" relatives, and they emotionally and/or physically hurt you, too.

Because of this difficult person (or people), you may avoid family gatherings, or at least that part of the family. You may feel the need to protect your children from them. If you do go to family get-togethers, you may dread dealing with those relatives. You may become very quiet in their vicinity or engage in arguments with them. Consequently you may not enjoy family holidays.

When difficult family members die, you may feel conflicted about the death. You may still have loved them, even though you might feel hurt or angry, too. Or you may not grieve their loss. In fact, you may be glad or relieved they're gone (although you may feel some guilt about having those thoughts). After their death, you may feel safer with your family. The death can free you to be around the rest of your relatives again.

**survival strategies**
If you've lost a difficult relative, a good way to process your feelings is to write the deceased a letter, telling him or her how you feel. Include how you wished the deceased could have treated you. Mention any emotional damage he or she caused you. Talk about how you intend to heal yourself. Then tear up the letter and throw it away.

## Coping with the Death of Loved Ones

The death of our relatives makes us remember our shared past. We return to our childhood, reliving times with them. We think of memories we haven't thought of in years. We can feel a sense of nostalgia for our youth, and grieve for a time gone by. We also wander through other points in our life, seeking out memories of the deceased family member. As relatives gather for the funeral, we interact with them, telling stories of the deceased. The stories can provoke laughter and tears, but in the togetherness of sharing, we can briefly return to a time when life with that relative was good. We can realize how blessed we are to have had that person in our life.

As I've previously noted in this chapter, because the death of relatives may be an overlooked area of grief, others can minimize your loss, which can feel hurtful or shaming. Try not to take their comments to heart. Keep in mind that people may make dismissive remarks for a couple of reasons:

- They haven't experienced that type of death, so they don't know what the grief is like.

- They didn't have the bond with their relatives that you do with yours, so they won't understand the depths of your loss.

- They're just plain insensitive.

When you receive remarks that try to play down your grief, respond with a simple comment such as: "He was important to me. I loved him dearly, and I'll miss him for a long time." After you say this, most people who care about you will try to understand your grief. If someone continues to criticize you for your feelings, avoid him or set boundaries about what he can and can't say to you.

The death of an older relative can be seen as the passing of a torch to you. You might decide to take on some of the traditions of the relative who died. You can gather memories and stories of family history from the remaining family members and write them down or record them. You can construct a family scrapbook or make a family website or Facebook page. Making sure the family history stays alive can give you comfort.

With relatives who don't live with you, it can be hard to believe they've passed away. Even though you know they are gone, you can fantasize that they're still alive. You can imagine them still living in their house (even if it's been sold). As you come to realize that your loved ones remain alive in your memory, you can value the idea that you're forever connected to family members.

# Death of a Pet

There's a difference between people who are pet lovers and those who aren't. If you've never had a beloved pet, then you'll have a hard time understanding the grief of someone who's just lost one. Those who love their animals make them part of the family. As David Whiting, a columnist for the *Orange County Register,* put it: "Forget pet. Think furkid." Therefore, the loss of a fur/feathered/scaled child causes deep pain.

## Companionship and Unconditional Love

Pets are one of the best and healthiest stress relievers we have. Research shows that simply petting a cat, dog, hamster, bunny, or other pet gives us tactile comfort and relieves stress. When you have a pet, they become part of your daily life. The special thing about pets is they are a nonjudgmental source of unconditional love. They greet you when you come home, perhaps giving you a warmer welcome than your family members do. They often stay in your vicinity, curling up next to your chair or on your lap. They can make you laugh at their antics. Animals accept you for who you are. They bond with you and become loyal and protective companions.

---

**People and Pets**

Misc.

Studies show that in 2010, Americans spent $47.7 billion on pets. More than 45 million households in the United States have at least one dog, and more than 38 million households have at least one cat.

---

That doesn't mean animals don't have opinions. Pets can let you know when they're upset with you. But they'll forgive you, and they won't stop loving you. Sometimes pets seem to understand your mood. When you're sad, they may try to comfort you. Sometimes the love of your pet, and responsibility you feel to take care of your animal, is all that gets you through difficult times.

## When Pets Die

One of the unfair parts of life is that pets have a shorter lifespan than their human owners. As pet lovers, we know we'll most likely outlive our "fur children." Most people have a series of one or more animals. Therefore, over a lifetime, we lose many beloved pets, and grieve their loss over and over again.

Sometimes you can prepare for the loss of your pet. You can tell that your animal is growing old and feeble. Just knowing you'll not have him around much longer can make you sad. Yet at some point, you know the quality of life of your pet isn't good, and you need to let him go. It's time to euthanize your pet.

Other times, the death of your pet is unexpected, for example, your dog gets run over by a car, or she has a serious illness you didn't know about. You take her to the vet, and then learn the bad news. You may not bring your pet home again, or if you do, you only have a few days or weeks with her.

When the death of your pet is sudden, you're unprepared for the loss. The death leaves you shocked and grieving. A pet loss can also be traumatizing, especially if you witnessed the death; for example, a car hits your dog or cat or you were present when she was euthanized (see Chapter 4 for my story of Angel).

It's also not uncommon for pets to stray and get lost. You can have agonized fantasies about what may be happening to them. You may wonder if you'll ever see them again. You don't know whether to grieve or give up hope. The more time passes, the more you lose hope and the more you grieve. After weeks pass, you begin to grieve their loss.

Many pet owners will say the death of a beloved pet is among the most painful losses they have experienced. They may grieve their pet more than they do the loss of some relatives and friends. People who may not show much emotion about other losses may cry over the death of a dog or cat. It hurts to come home and not have your dog, cat, or other animal there to greet you. You have to brace yourself to walk into your own home. You miss the presence and companionship of your pet.

**survival strategies**

Children can bond deeply with their pets and feel devastated by the death. Losing an animal may be the child's first experience with death, or at least that of "someone" they love and live with. If parents handle the children's loss appropriately, the death of a pet can offer valuable lessons about death and grief. Parents need to honor their children's grief and encourage them to share their feelings. Parents might feel tempted to distract children from their grief and rush to replace the pet. That only gives children the wrong message for how to grieve—attempting to "fix" feelings instead of processing them.

Sometimes people are surprised by the grief they feel about the loss. Perhaps they didn't realize how much the pet meant to them. They took his presence for granted. After the death, they might have regrets about how they treated their pet and/or that they didn't appreciate him more when they had him.

## Coping with the Loss of Your Pet

Some people feel ashamed about the depths of their feelings about their pet's death, as if they are supposed to reserve intense emotions only for humans. They know how much they loved their pet, but think something's wrong with them for grieving. And society doesn't provide much support. There's no ritualized mourning for pets. Upon hearing the news, friends, family, and neighbors don't descend on you with condolences and food. There's no funeral to help you formally grieve your loss. No one sends sympathy cards.

Because the world is divided into pet lovers and others, those who are "others" don't understand the bond between people and their furred and feathered children. Therefore, when you lose a beloved pet, the "others" won't be sympathetic. They might even belittle your loss. An "other" might say, "It was only a dog. Why are you so upset?" The "others" also don't realize that each pet has his or her own personality. No two are alike. For example, they might say things like, "Just get another one." They don't understand that pets are not replaceable.

| Expressions of Grief | "Our beautiful brown Lab, Tank, passed away on Saturday evening. We enjoyed every day with him and gave him a life we believe every pet should receive. He loved every person he knew and was never aggressive a day in his life. We are going to miss him for the rest of our lives." |
|---|---|

—Tom, about the loss of his dog

Over your lifetime, you may have had many pets that you've loved, enjoyed, and grieved for when they died. But there are a few that are even more special. They may seem like the children of your soul. Their loss breaks your heart. As much as you might bond with your other animals, both the ones you currently have and the ones you'll have in the future, it's not the same. The grief over the loss of your special pet is even deeper, and on some level, you may always miss that special animal.

Because people grieving the loss of a pet may feel embarrassed by the depth of their grief, they may avoid sharing their feelings with others. Or, if they do try to talk to friends and family, they may be criticized for their feelings. Thus, they feel alone in their grief. You have the right to grieve the death of your pet. Don't let anyone belittle you for mourning your loss.

Pets are not interchangeable. As lonely as you may feel when you come home to a house without your beloved animal, don't rush to adopt a new pet. While a new animal will be fun and distracting, it won't make up for the one you've lost. Give yourself time to grieve. When you're ready, the right animal will come into your life.

Just because you've "only" lost an animal, doesn't mean you won't experience a grief journey. Your pet might often be in your thoughts. You can imagine you feel its presence. You may hear it barking or meowing. You may have dreams of your pet. When you lose a beloved pet, you can experience any of the emotions and reactions discussed in Chapter 3.

**survival strategies**

You don't have to grieve alone. Find others who have loved and lost their pets. They'll understand what you're going through. They won't try to diminish your pain, although you might find yourself jockeying for conversation space because they'll want to tell you their pet death stories, too. There are online bereavement resources and groups for people who have lost their pets (see the Resources appendix).

As time goes by, your grief will fade. That doesn't mean it won't be triggered at times. It's not uncommon for people to remember a beloved pet years later and say, "I still miss (pet)." No matter how many pets you have, special pets remain in your heart.

## Essential Takeaways

- The death of a beloved grandparent or other relative can be a major loss; the more you love your relative, the more grief you'll feel about his or her death.
- The loss of a friend can hurt as much as the death of a family member.
- The death of a family member you've had issues with can cause conflicted feelings.
- Allow yourself to grieve the deaths of relatives, friends, and pets, regardless of what others think about the loss.
- For some people, losing a pet can feel as painful as losing a close friend or family member.

# chapter 11

# Death in the Workplace

| When someone you work with dies |
| Constant reminders |
| Different employees, different reactions |
| The role management plays |
| Ways to cope |

Many people spend more time at their job, and with their co-workers, than they do with their families (at least when they're awake). People who work together can form close bonds of friendship and community. Often, employers and employees describe themselves as a "family." Therefore when a co-worker dies, the loss can have a profound impact on the other employees because they've lost one of their own.

## A Work "Family"

Employees don't have to be close to be impacted. People who work at the same business usually have their work lives intertwined. They work in departments or teams. This person depends on that person who depends on that person, and so on. The death of an employee means there's a gap in the process, and the loss can affect the co-workers, even if they weren't emotionally connected to the deceased. Even if people's jobs don't overlap, they meet at breaks or in the lunchroom, at the coffee pot, copy machine, or the restroom and at company outings. Just knowing a fellow employee has died can make others sad.

Matt had transferred to Angie's department a few weeks before Christmas. Angie loved candy canes, and saw some on Matt's desk. Even though she didn't know him, she asked if she could have one. After she finished it, she went back to him, introduced herself, told him about her love for candy canes, and asked if she could have another. He flashed her a big grin and said, "Take them all." When Matt died suddenly a few weeks later, Angie was in tears, grieving for a man she didn't really know, but whom she thought had a wonderful smile and generous heart. Some employees may think they shouldn't grieve for a co-worker, especially if they weren't close, but it's important to respect how you feel.

**Grief in the Workplace**

MISC.

In the United States, workplace grief can cost businesses over $75 billion per year. Employees who are grieving (both from personal problems and losses at work) can have reduced productivity and increased errors, accidents, and absenteeism.

## Disbelief

At work, the presence of the deceased is still vivid, even though the person has passed. Employees keep expecting the deceased to walk through the door or see him in some of the regular places. If the death was sudden, co-workers have a hard time believing the news. In their minds, the employees see their co-worker as alive. "I just saw him yesterday," is a common comment. Even though they logically know he has passed, emotionally they have a hard time believing the truth.

If the employee died suddenly, co-workers think of the last conversation they had with the deceased. They might even go back in time, pondering every contact with her over the last weeks or months. They replay what was said and how the person looked. They search for clues that might have foretold the death. If they find them (or think they do), they wonder if they could have done something to help.

## Employees Helping Each Other

Employees may dread going to work the next day after the death and in some of the days following. Yet at the same time, most want to be at their job. They need to grieve with their colleagues. They want to support others who are more affected. Most want to help with the extra work and make sure everything is handled.

Interacting with your co-workers can feel comforting. As much as your spouse or friends might be sympathetic about your grief, they don't have the relationship with your co-worker that you do. At work, your co-workers know what you're going through because they're going through similar emotions. You don't feel alone because you can exchange information, tell stories about the deceased, give each other hugs or pats on the shoulder, and validate each other's feelings.

| | |
|---|---|
| Expressions of Grief | "We try to act like it's normal, but it's not."<br>—Randy, after his co-worker died suddenly |

## Management Escalates or Eases Tensions

Some employers, managers, and HR recognize the need for employees to take some time to grieve. They may close the business for the day and send people home. Or, if the work continues, they may allow the most impacted employees to leave. Most managers also recognize that employees won't be very productive for a few days. The best managers do what they can to represent the company in providing an empathetic reaction that best supports their employees.

The difficulty comes when owners or managers aren't sympathetic and understanding, nor do they modify their expectations of the workload in the first week following the death. When this happens, in addition to interfering with the employees' grieving process, management comes across as cold and uncaring. As a consequence, employees may feel angry and resentful, and morale suffers in the affected department and perhaps in the whole company. The impact of this inconsiderate treatment can cause resentment that lasts for years.

People crave details of a death. The details help a person fit the fact of the death into his or her mind. So when a co-worker dies, it's important for fellow employees to know what happened. Yet HR is constrained by law from asking the deceased's family too many personal questions. Unless the family members volunteer the information, the employees may be left with the uncertainty and frustration caused by the lack of knowledge.

Sometimes families may share the information with management or HR, but request that the information isn't distributed to the rest of the employees. This is especially true when the family feels some shame about the circumstances of the death—for example, suicide or death from drunk driving. However, this can cause employees to speculate about what happened. They may correctly guess at the cause, or they can come up with other reasons that may be hurtful to other employees, the family, or the reputation of the deceased.

Manny had a serious medical condition, but continued to come to work. He cared about his co-workers, joking with them and bringing them gifts of food. He and his co-workers also socialized outside of work. Manny never complained about his health and maintained his sense of humor. Most employees weren't even aware he was very ill.

Manny's supervisor, Robert, was an analytical man who lacked people skills. The way Robert interacted with Manny and other employees caused them a lot of stress. Robert's intensity with Manny about his illness incensed his close friends. When Manny died after leaving work early, his co-workers blamed Robert, feeling the work stress had contributed to their friend's demise. The team's sadness over Manny's death was exacerbated by their anger with Robert, who continued his distancing behavior, even though he quietly grieved Manny's death.

## Reminders All Around

Most employees don't have much, if any, experience with losing a co-worker, especially if the company employs a lot of younger people. Because employees may lack the experience in the death of a co-worker, their reactions may take them by surprise. In addition, they're impacted by others' emotions and the changes the death will make (at least temporarily) in their job.

## Memory Slaps

Your job is usually the place where you can often forget your other problems. Yet when the problem is at work, it's hard to forget because you have memories all around you. The death of a co-worker is different from losing a friend or relative (one you don't live with) because of these constant reminders.

There are places and circumstances at work where you expect to feel sad (and perhaps brace yourself beforehand) like when you walk past the deceased's workstation. Other times, you have memory slaps—unexpected reminders of the deceased. For example, you walk into the conference room for a meeting and see the deceased's empty seat. These memory slaps can keep employees on edge and in a state of grieving.

The following are some of the other ways you're reminded of the loss of the co-workers:

- You see co-workers with red eyes and know they've been crying. Sometimes their emotion makes you cry, too.

- You miss the deceased greeting you in the morning (or at other times of the day) and saying good-bye at night.

- If you had common interests, you remember you can't share them with your co-worker anymore. For example, you're both sports fans and rooted for the same team.

- You might still have e-mails and other documents from him, or meetings with him scheduled on your calendar.

- The deceased is the one you went to for help or when you had questions, or you depended on her in some way.

- Vendors, customers, and employees from other branches of the company might call, asking for the deceased, and you need to break the news to them.

- You don't see the deceased's car, truck, or motorcycle parked in the normal space in the morning. Or, if he died at work, his vehicle may still be there for a few days.

- The deceased would bring in treats or share food with co-workers, and you miss her thoughtfulness.

**cautions and concerns**

Don't rush to clear out the deceased's workspace. Employees perceive this as uncaring. Instead, make it a temporary area of remembrance. Put out a picture of the deceased, a vase of flowers, a candle (if permitted), and cards or a journal for employees to write condolences, stories, and what the deceased meant to them. The cards or journal can later be given to the family.

## Circumstances Contributing to Grief

While a close relationship to the deceased is the most obvious reason for co-workers to grieve, other circumstances can cause (or add to) their reactions. You can't prejudge who will be affected, why they are emotional, and the ways they will grieve.

Here are some other reasons employees may be more strongly affected:

- If the death occurred at the workplace, especially if employees witnessed it.

- If the deceased employee had been out of work due to illness, and the co-workers had adjusted to her absence, but they may not have expected her to die.

- If the deceased employee had young or teenage children. Co-workers will be even more upset thinking of children who must grow up without a mom or dad.

- The type of personality the grieving employee has. For example, a sensitive person might be more emotional, while an analytical one might not feel a lot of grief.

- If the grieving employee has also lost a family member(s) or close friend(s) in the past few years.

- If the employee has a lot of experience with death, they can feel more impacted, or they might be accustomed to loss and feel less affected.

# Reactions at Work

Employees may feel angry with certain supervisors, believing that job stress, a heavy workload, or poor management contributed to the employee's death. Existing problems in the workplace can contribute to the way the death is handled by the company and how employees respond. If people already view management as harsh and uncaring, then the way they manage the death can cause their already existing resentment to flare up, or can go a long way toward making the employees feel cared about. The death provides an opportunity for the company to heal old wounds, help employees to bond through their grief, and smooth out twisted lines of communication.

Employees can feel confused about what they should do and how they should grieve. They talk about the deceased, compare what they know, or share stories. They try to find out how the family is doing. They try to comfort each other and wonder whether they should (or can) do something for the family.

One of the most prevalent changes in the workplace is the silence in the business or in the department where the deceased worked. Any usual loud talking and joking is absent. What conversation there is, whether in person or on the phone, is muted. There's a hush that's often commented on by employees. Their sadness is almost palpable. Just walking into the room and hearing the quiet is enough to remind people of the loss. The hush usually lasts for the first few days.

**survival strategies**

Remember that your colleagues are grieving in their own way. Don't take any signs of irritability, anger, or isolation personally. Do your best to show understanding to your co-workers. It's not uncommon for co-workers to feel numb and wonder if something's wrong with them because they're not grieving like everyone else. Numbness is a normal reaction and will wear off after a while. Other employees may never become very emotional. Everyone is different.

## Repressed Feelings

The workplace is considered a place where you act professional. That means you don't show your feelings, or at least not any emotions that aren't positive. Therefore, employees may feel they must restrain their grief reactions. They don't want to expose their feelings and perhaps risk being judged for appearing emotional; yet at the same time, it's difficult (and for some impossible) to hold back. Employees who cry can feel ashamed about their inability to control their emotions. Many employees feel they need permission to grieve at work. Give yourself permission to grieve for a co-worker instead of trying to suppress your feelings.

## Lack of Focus and Concentration

It's common for bereaved co-workers to struggle with their focus and concentration, especially the first few days. They may feel they are not entirely "present." Their thoughts are with the deceased. It doesn't help that they may feel emotionally exhausted from lack of sleep the first night or two, thinking about the deceased and his or her family. Co-workers may seem distracted. Some leave their work areas and roam through the building talking to others. They make mistakes, and must redo their work. Or they read the same paragraph over and over because they aren't absorbing the material.

This happened to Annelise, who worked for a call center. When a popular co-worker died, even though she didn't know him well, she was sad and distracted. When she spoke with customers, she'd repeat herself. The customer would say, "You already said that." Annelise apologized, realizing she had no memory of what she'd previously said.

Some people use their work as a way to avoid thinking and feeling about the loss. They ignore everyone and focus on their job. If they stay busy enough, they can mostly disconnect from their feelings (and those of others) and what's happening around them. Other employees float between the two extremes. They'll focus on their work, then something will again remind them of the death, and they will lose their concentration.

| cautions and concerns | Be careful if you have a job that involves safety. Slow down. Monitor your thoughts and feelings and stop what you're doing if you're distracted or emotional. Take a break, but don't just disappear. Make sure your supervisor knows what's going on with you. |

## The Job Must Go On

Even though employees are grieving, the needs of the business continue. That means employees must do their own work even though it may be difficult for them. Someone must fill in for the deceased co-worker, at least temporarily. There might be confusion and disorganization as people try to figure out the deceased's job, as well as knowledge gaps of things the employee took to the grave. The extra workload adds to the stress, and can impede the grieving process of employees because they have too much to do.

Although employees intellectually know the importance of keeping production up, they may also feel guilt and resentment because continuing to work feels disrespectful to the deceased and to their own emotions. They may feel as if the workplace should stop and mourn for a few days. It helps if managers acknowledge the difficulty employees may have in mourning and having to work at the same time.

# Management's Responsibility

After the death, owners, managers, and HR have a complicated role to play. The notice of the death drops on them when they already have a full workload. They must notify other employees, both those above them in the management chain and those below them. They may try to contact (or go see) the family to express their condolences. They try to anticipate how the loss will affect their people and set supportive actions into play.

They have to deal with their own feelings about the death of the employee and cope with the reactions of their staff. In addition, they have to focus on getting the work of the company done, and juggle assigning people to take over the duties of the deceased. If the death occurred because of an accident at work, they might have to deal with the company lawyers, OSHA, and maybe the media. They might also have to notify customers and vendors. They may have to figure out how to get coverage for employees attending the funeral. They try to guide the family through the final steps and make sure they receive the last paycheck and vacation pay, plus help with the paperwork for life insurance.

Owners, managers, and HR often feel they have to be "strong" for their employees. That means not showing their feelings. Instead, they focus on being there for their people. However, for some, this can be difficult, especially if they were close to the employee or are otherwise affected by the death. It's important for managers to show their feelings, especially tears, for three reasons:

- Your emotions show that you're a feeling human being.

- Your emotions demonstrate that you care about your staff.

- You act as a role model for other employees by showing them that it's all right to express their emotions.

If possible, offer grief counseling to your affected employees. If your company has an Employee Assistance Program (EAP), contact them. Most EAPs have access to grief/crisis counselors. If not, try to locate a local counselor who specializes in grief and crisis counseling. The counselor can coach management and Human Resources in the best ways to help employees as well as offer solace and support to upset employees.

## Coping with a Co-Worker's Death

Your grief will be strongest in the first week, although you may miss your co-worker for a long time. Your feelings will likely come in waves. You might feel numb or emotional and have a hard time being at work. When the weekend comes, employees often spend time with their families and process the death. When they return to work, they can feel more balanced.

The funeral can provide an opportunity to mourn with others, say goodbye, and feel a sense of closure. Sometimes employees feel they don't want to intrude on a "family and friends" event. Unless the family has requested a private ceremony, it's good to attend. Having their loved one's co-workers show up to mourn the loss is comforting to the family.

Recognize that you might be distracted, which can lead to mistakes. If you are doing work where mixing up some numbers, words, or other tasks can lead to considerable consequences, make sure you double-check your work or have a co-worker check for you. Do the same for her. Keep a list of things that need to be done so you don't forget them.

Take advantage of grief counseling that your company offers. (You can also request that the company bring in a grief counselor if they haven't thought of it.) The counselor may provide grief groups as well as individual counseling. From the grief counseling, employees learn that they're not alone in their feelings and reactions. They have a chance to share stories about the deceased and learn more about her. They'll also learn some coping skills. In a way, the group is like a mini-memorial, and the employees bond through the experience. Afterward, even though they're still sad, they often report feeling better.

| survival strategies | Even if you don't think you "need" counseling, go to the grief group to support your co-workers. You'll be surprised how much you'll gain from the experience. |
|---|---|

After one group for a popular young manager who'd died in a motorcycle accident, an older man took me aside. "It just goes to show you," he said. "You *can* teach an old dog new tricks." I must have looked puzzled, because he continued, "Before, when I'd hear on the news that grief counselors were going to a school or a company after a tragedy, I'd say, 'If they (the children or employees) weren't screwed up before, they *sure* will be now.'" His tone turned serious. "I was wrong. This was a helpful experience. Not just for me, but I saw the effect on the others, as well. I feel so much better. More at peace. Thank you for that. From now on, I'm going to encourage, not discourage, grief counseling."

Some other do's and don'ts for owners, managers, and HR:

- Do send out a company-wide notice of the death. If you have a smaller business, gather the employees together and tell them the sad news.

- Don't discuss the co-worker's death and performance goals or other work topics in the same conversation or e-mail.

- Do have managers check in with each of their team members to see how they are doing.

- Do ask specific questions, such as, "How did you sleep last night?" or "How did it feel to come to work today?" rather than just saying, "How are you?" or "Are you okay?"

- Do encourage employees to take care of themselves.

- Don't stop employees from attending the funeral.

- Allow employees to take some time off if they need it. However, encouraging them (in a supportive manner) to return to their normal routine is also important.

- Do appreciate and acknowledge the employees for how hard it is to work and grieve at the same time.

Although the death of an employee may hit co-workers hard, most people are able to return to their normal level of functioning after the funeral. They might still have stabs of sadness from missing the deceased or feel some frustration that he is not here to lend his expertise to the work situation, but they're no longer distracted and grieving.

## Essential Takeaways

- People who work together often form a sort of "family," but you don't have to be close to a co-worker to be affected by her death. Give yourself permission to grieve.

- A death in the workplace can be especially hard because reminders of the deceased are all around.

- Respect how your co-workers react differently. Some may need to talk, while others may isolate. Don't take co-workers' reactions (such as irritability) personally.

- How a manager handles the death of an employee makes a difference in the morale of the company.

- Corporate grief counseling can benefit employees.

# chapter 12

# Death at School

- When someone at school dies
- Grief reactions of students
- Dealing with a student's suicide
- How to cope

We like to think of schools as safe harbors for our children, where they're insulated from death. The reality is that students die, and so do their teachers, coaches, and well-liked staff members. Often this is a child's first experience with death, or at least a death of someone he sees five days a week. When someone passes away at school, the impact on students can be quite strong.

## Death Visits the School

A school is a close-knit community made up of students, teachers, coaches, support staff, parents, and volunteers. When someone at the school dies, the impact is felt by almost everyone. The death of a student or faculty member sends a shock wave throughout the school. Often the local paper reports the death of the teacher or student, and the larger community mourns the loss as well.

### Death of a Teacher or Coach

Teachers have a huge impact on their students. Most people can think back to their school days and still remember the name of their most influential teachers. Children spend hours with their teachers. At the grammar school level, they can spend more time with their teachers than they do with their parents. The loss of a faculty member, especially if it's the child's own teacher or coach, can cause bewilderment and grief.

Coach Paul collapsed and died of a heart attack during his high school team's basketball practice. His team, and everyone else who witnessed his death, was traumatized by the experience. Paul was a popular teacher and coach, only 40 years old. His family, wife Heather, and three young daughters came to all the games. Both Paul and Heather frequently had his players over to his house after games. He also mentored students who needed extra guidance. His death shocked the school, sending a wave of grief through the campus. There wasn't anyone who didn't know and like Coach Paul.

As much as people grieved over his death, they also worried about his wife and daughters. The school had several grief counselors work with the students, especially those who were traumatized. The students, faculty, parents, and administration soon channeled their grief into several fundraisers to benefit the family. They also made a calendar that covered the six months left in the school year. Parents signed up to deliver meals to the family three times a week.

Paul's basketball team had the hardest time recovering. The boys desperately wanted to win their next games to honor Coach Paul. Yet their grief and trauma caused a lack of focus. They actually played worse than before, which made them feel ashamed and guilty. Some were in tears after a game. Finally, Heather invited them over to her house. She gave them a chance to talk about their feelings in an understanding, familiar environment. She cried, and the boys cried. By the end of the day, she'd helped them work through their guilt. The next week, the team started feeling more optimistic and it showed on the court. For the first time since Coach Paul's death, they won. This time they were in tears again, but of joy, not of shame.

## Affected Faculty, Staff, and Parents

It's not just the students who are affected by the loss of a teacher. The faculty is connected, often having taught together for years. When they lose one of their own, they have to cope with their feelings, as well as try to comfort the students and help them process their emotions. At the same time, they try to keep an eye on the whole student body—for example, noticing if a child is crying. Not all teachers feel capable of facilitating the students' grieving, especially if they, themselves, are mourning the loss, and they don't know what to say and do to help others.

Teachers and students aren't the only ones who mourn the loss of a popular faculty member. It's not uncommon for some parents to become very involved in school programs such as sports or clubs. They might also volunteer at the school. In lower grades, they meet the teachers at Back to School nights, conferences, school programs, and other activities. Parents might get to know a certain teacher well, and/or appreciate how he interacts with, inspires, and educates their child. They may feel grateful to the teacher for taking a special interest in their child or stimulating her educational experience. Some parents may grieve the loss of the teacher as much as the students do.

Sometimes a teacher is very popular and students may take a lot of her classes throughout their high school or college years. They may spend one or more semesters or years with this instructor. Aside from what the students learn, the teacher may influence their thinking and worldview. They become a mentor whose teachings may last a lifetime.

**survival strategies**   If the instructor and/or the school has a Facebook or other type of webpage, current and former students may be able to express their grief through posting a message.

After Lauren graduated from college, she heard about the death of one of her high school teachers. He'd taught Advanced Placement classes, and she'd taken as many of his classes as she could. He'd been her instructor for two years. After his death, she felt sad for days. "I didn't even feel this sad when some of our relatives died," Lauren told her mom. "That's because you knew him better," her mom replied. "You spent more time with him than you have with some of our relatives. He made a big impact on you. I'm sad about his death, too."

Most students don't thank their teachers. Sometimes, when they're in school, they may not even like their instructor because of the rigorous standards held by him. It's only later, after they've had upper educational and/or life experience that they realize the impact the teacher made on them. They have fond memories of the teacher and belatedly appreciate what they learned, even if it seemed tough at the time.

When the teacher dies, they can feel grief and regret that they never expressed their appreciation to her. They might not be able to attend the funeral because it takes place in another town or state. Or they've heard the news too late to attend. Therefore, they have no chance to formally mourn with others who share their feelings, and they might feel isolated with their feelings.

## Death of a Classmate

The death of a classmate is going to cause differing reactions, depending on the age of a child. Younger children might have difficulty understanding what happened, or they may have some misconceptions about the death. They can have a lot of questions about death and what happens afterward. They can become fearful of dying or of their family members dying. They might act out in school or become fearful about going to school. Their fear may manifest in clinginess, headaches, and upset stomachs.

"I don't have a best friend anymore. We were supposed to be BFFs (best friends forever). When will I stop crying? I cry every day."

—16-year-old Amanda about Tiffany, who died in a car accident

Most tweens and teens have a more mature understanding that death happens to everyone, and you don't come back to life after you've died. Yet at this age, adolescents can think they are invulnerable. They don't really believe they can die. The death of a peer gives them a jolt of reality about their own mortality and can cause some uncertainty about life.

Often the deceased has siblings and/or cousins who attend the school. They might also have close friends in different classes. The classmates of siblings, cousins, and good friends can also be emotionally impacted. These classes may need extra support.

## The Impact on the School Community

Although most people in the school community are impacted by the death, not all people will grieve in the same manner. A teacher might have to deal with his or her own feelings, plus manage a classroom full of grieving kids. Some of the kids may be apathetic, some obviously sad, some distracted, and others acting out. These are all different ways the students might be manifesting their feelings.

The members of the school community can feel sad even if they don't have a personal relationship with the deceased. Being around others who are grieving can cause you to experience the feelings as well. You can feel sorry for the loss and the impact that loss has on the students and on the deceased's family. You can worry about how the students will cope.

If a student has a terminal illness such as cancer, but is still able to attend school, educate his or her classmates about the illness. This helps them understand what the ill student may be going through and how to interact with him. Students can ask questions and express concerns. This kind of education also has the effect of increasing empathy and giving them the opportunity to be of service and friendship to the ill child.

## Circumstances Impacting the Death

The impact of the death differs depending on the circumstances involved. It's important for administrators to determine how and why the students and faculty may be impacted. These are some considerations:

- Type of death—accident, suicide, sudden illness, chronic or terminal illness, or violent death.
- Size of the school. In a smaller school, almost everyone knows everyone.
- Whether students or faculty witnessed the death.
- Size of the community. In a small town, the inhabitants have more interactions and closer ties with each other.
- Popularity of the deceased student or faculty member and how long he or she attended the school or taught there.

- Any other traumas or crises the school has been through in the last few years.

- The time of year of the death—summer, end of the school year, holiday season.

- Type of community—inner city with frequent gang violence or suburban community with a low crime rate.

- Other community involvement that intersects with the school, which would cause families to know each other, such as involvement with sports teams, church, or clubs.

## Reactions of Grieving Students

A student's grief can manifest at school and at home. With some students, you might see the effects in both places. Other students might only demonstrate them in one or the other.

Some grief reactions include the following:

- Withdrawing

- Becoming angry, irritable, argumentative, or bullying

- Becoming tearful

- Acting out or exhibiting regressive behavior

- Having nightmares

- Pain and sadness

- Guilt (even if there's no logical reason to feel guilty)

- Difficulty concentrating, which can lead to a decline in academic performance

- Substance abuse or increased risk-taking behaviors

survival strategies

Parents should encourage their children to talk to them about the death and ask questions. Answer the questions as honestly as you can.

# Suicide of a Student

After the well-publicized shootings at Columbine, Virginia Tech, and other schools, parents and school officials can have nightmare visions of such a thing happening at their school. Most schools have implemented emergency plans with teachers, parents, and students about what they should do in case of a violent incident.

However, shooting sprees at schools are rare. We might think they're more common because every time it happens in the United States, national media picks up the story. It's splashed across television and computer screens and the newspaper. Plus, traumatic situations like this are memorable, so they stick in our minds.

Administrators, teachers, and parents need to be far more aware of potential suicides, which, unfortunately, are not rare for students. While the highest percentage of teenage deaths is caused by car accidents, suicide is the third leading cause of death in ages 10 to 24. Sometimes the student gives no indication that he or she is unhappy, and the death may come as a complete shock to parents, friends, students, and teachers. Other times, there were signs the student was depressed, but not that he or she had thought of committing suicide.

## Bullycide

More and more children and teens are taking their lives because they're bullied at school. They and their parents might try to stop the bullying, but sometimes schools are not responsive. Other times, the student suffers in silence. His or her family might not know about the problem. "Bullycide" is a term coined to label a suicide caused by unhappiness and despair due to bullying.

Marty was a shy young man who gravitated toward computers and online games and avoided sports. He had a small circle of male friends who shared the same interests. They were all used to being called "geeks." But in tenth grade, some of the jocks started teasing Marty about being gay, which he wasn't. They began to roughhouse with him, often punching him in the shoulder or arm. His friends didn't come to his aid because they were afraid of coming under attack themselves.

Although Marty didn't say a word to his parents, his mother saw a bruise on his arm and wormed the story out of him. Outraged, she stormed into the principal's office. The principal promised her that he would "look into it," but nothing changed. Two weeks later, Marty couldn't take any more. After school, he went into his bedroom and hanged himself.

## Handling the Suicide

As painful and emotional as a suicide is, it's important to minimize the notice given to the student who committed suicide to avoid copycat deaths. Teenagers may glamorize the idea of suicide because they see the deceased receiving a lot of attention, and that may appeal to them. (It doesn't seem to matter that he or she is dead and unable to enjoy what's happening.) Other students who are depressed or in need of attention may choose to follow in the deceased's footsteps.

Some do's and don'ts for school administrators and teachers:

- Don't send students home, but do provide grief counseling to help them process their feelings.
- Rather than hold a memorial assembly, do schedule an event to talk to the student body about bullying and the tragic effects it can have.
- Do communicate the facts honestly.
- Do offer group and individual grief counseling.
- Do teach signs of depression and suicide.
- Do provide resources for depressed students.
- If bullying contributed to the suicide, do discipline the offenders and educate the student body about bullying. Institute a zero-tolerance policy for bullying behavior.
- Do help students communicate their thoughts and process their feelings of sadness, guilt, anger, and blame.
- Do send materials home for the parents, explaining what happened, and educating them about warning signs of suicide.
- Don't hold a fund-raiser for the family, or dedicate a memorial to the deceased.

If you're a student and one of your friends talks about hurting (or killing) himself, it's important to act on that information, even if you've promised to keep it a secret. Your friend's life is at stake. Tell your parents, the school principal or counselor, or your friend's parents.

# Helping Students Cope

How the school administration responds to the death is important to healing the faculty and student body. The goal of the administration should be to restore the emotional and mental balance of students, faculty members, staff, and (perhaps) parents and to reestablish regular school functions and routines as efficiently as possible. To do that, the administration must act quickly to offer support services to the whole school.

Administration must distribute the news, aid students and faculty in processing their feelings, oversee the education of faculty and students about grief (including reactions that might be misconstrued as misbehavior), assess at-risk students and give them extra support, and help the school community cope and recover. If the administration provides the right support, then faculty and students can process the death in a healthy manner. But if they don't, such as ignoring the death, faculty and students can be adversely affected.

## Handling the News

Often the death is already known because the news quickly spreads throughout the campus as students communicate with each other. Other times, only the administration knows about the death and releases the news. As word gets out, parents become anxious about what the school will do to support their children.

The best way to break the news of the death is for each teacher to talk to his or her students or for a counselor to visit each classroom. However, the teachers need to have a faculty meeting beforehand so they can confer about what to do. This gives them a chance to process their feelings together. In addition, they need to receive education about grieving, instruction in handling the grief of their students, and some suggestions for tasks the students can do to facilitate their grieving.

A school assembly isn't the best way to break the news or discuss the death. It's too big for individuals to share their feelings or for teachers to monitor the reactions of the students.

## Learning and Sharing

The death provides an opportunity to teach students about loss and grief. The knowledge will not only benefit them now, but also help them cope with future losses. Through talking about their feelings, the students can process their emotions.

What teachers can do:

- Give the facts that are known, using clear language. Younger children may have a hard time understanding euphemisms or metaphors like "passed away" or "went to heaven."

- Educate students about grief reactions and help them understand the thoughts and feelings they're experiencing. Encourage them to share their feelings.

- When a child expresses feelings, validate them by saying things like, "I understand you're sad about (name's) death." Or, "It's hard to accept that (name) has died."

- Encourage the students to talk about their memories of the deceased. This can help them focus on happier times and realize that their teacher or friend can always stay with them in their hearts and minds.

It's important for teachers and counselors to offer a variety of support activities. Besides class discussions and group and individual counseling, students can process their grief through writing and drawing pictures. Drawing is especially effective for younger children; however, some older students might prefer to draw or paint a picture about how they feel rather than write about it. Teachers can encourage students to make cards for the family, or musical students might compose a song.

After a general class discussion, allow the children to talk in a small group with a teacher or counselor or talk to teachers and counselors individually. However, after they have a day or two of small group and individual sessions, then the school can have a larger memorial assembly.

## Students at Risk

Some students are more vulnerable than others, and their grief may make them more at risk for withdrawing, slacking off at school, acting out at home or in school, abusing substances, becoming anxious or depressed, or feeling suicidal. It's important to refer students for extra help if their symptoms impair their functioning or last beyond two months. These students will need more extensive support. Administrators, teachers, and counselors need to monitor them, counsel them, interact with their parents, and refer them to community resources such as bereavement groups for children. Chapter 19 gives more information on helping children cope with grief.

At-risk students include the following:

- Those who are friends with (or emotionally close to) the deceased
- Those who witnessed the trauma
- Any who've suffered a previous loss or trauma
- Those who lack social support
- Anyone with a history of mental illness

One way to help these students is to have the school counselor (if the counselor is familiar with grief counseling) meet with them on a regular basis. Or the school can bring in a grief counselor. A group can provide the vulnerable students with a place to talk about their grief, normalize their feelings, and learn coping strategies. If the school doesn't have grief counselors, administrators or teachers should speak with the parents and give referrals to community resources.

## Aids to Recovery

One way to help students process their grief is by planning a memorial activity. They can organize a memorial service, or raise money for the family, for a philanthropic cause, or for something that will benefit the school. They can also make a more permanent memorial on the school campus, for example, plant a tree, put up a plaque, or build a bench with the deceased's name on it. They might also create an online memorial page or website. Or they can construct a memory book to give to the family with pictures and stories about the deceased from the students and faculty.

When a drunk driver killed 17-year-old Andrew, the whole school community was shocked, angered, and grieving. The students and faculty channeled their grief into arranging a memorial service to be held at the school. With the help of the teachers and administration, Andrew's classmates were allowed to plan and implement the service, and they invited Andrew's parents and sister, as well as the community at large, to attend. During the ceremony in the gym, there wasn't a dry eye in the building, and afterward, the students reported feeling better. They still grieved for Andrew, but they felt they'd come to some acceptance of his death and that their emotions were more balanced than before the ceremony.

survival strategies

The school should send a letter home to parents, keeping them updated on what is being done to help the children cope with a death at the school. The letter can also include tips on what parents can do at home to help.

Most students are resilient. They're buried in homework, plus many have extracurricular and social activities, which keep them busy. Older students may have jobs. While they might still miss their teacher or friend, school life goes on, and they become focused on other things. While they never forget the loss, with the proper support, they can set it aside and move on.

## Essential Takeaways

- The death of a student, teacher, coach, or other school personnel can affect the whole school community.

- Students may withdraw or feel angry or depressed about the death.

- Unhappy, depressed students may be at risk for suicide, especially those who are being bullied.

- Organizing a memorial service is one activity that can help grieving students and school personnel feel better.

# chapter 13

# How to Support the Bereaved

Avoid giving negative messages

Handling the funeral

What to say (and what *not* to say)

Offering support right after the death—and beyond

Specific ways you can help someone who's grieving

We feel so powerless when those we care about grieve. It's a natural human desire to try and "fix" the griever's feelings or painful situation and/or make the person feel better. Yet we also feel helpless. Most of the time, we can't replace the loss, especially of a loved one.

Most people are uncomfortable with those who are grieving. We have no formal education about grief to make it easier to interact with the bereaved. We don't understand how to be there for them. Many people make the mistake of staying away because they don't know what to say or are afraid they'll say the wrong thing. Or they want to hurry the grievers into "feeling better." They don't realize how, by listening and caring, they sustain the bereaved as they mourn.

## Negative Messages

Usually, when people give negative messages, they don't intend to come across as critical or hurtful. It's just the opposite. People mostly have good intentions. They want to console, support, or direct the bereaved. They often have little or no personal experience with bereavement and what's really comforting as opposed to what they think is helpful. Because they don't know what to say, they fall back on clichés. Or they're so uncomfortable that they say something, anything, to fill the silence. They might also have a personal belief that it's better to remain stoic than to express emotion. As I've mentioned in previous chapters, attempting to suppress your feelings isn't a healthy way to handle grief. It can lead to other problems.

## "Be Strong"

As I discussed in Chapter 6, after a death, a pervasive message that's often given to the bereaved is that he or she must be strong. Other people feel better if they think the bereaved is strong or appears to be doing okay. They don't feel so helpless to fix the unfixable. Sometimes the bereaved are told to be or stay strong. Or they're admired for how they are handling the death—for being "so strong" or "so brave."

However, this can lock a mourner into acting strong because everyone else believes it's an admirable response to the death. Therefore, you can be trapped into a show of strength because others admire you for "being strong." This reinforces the belief that's how you "should" be. You don't feel strong inside, but because people are admiring you for it, it must be right. In addition, it's hard to admit to someone who's commented on your strength that you're not so strong after all. You might even feel ashamed because you think breaking down makes you weak. Or you might be afraid that others will judge you as weak.

> **survival strategies**
>
> It *is* important to be strong for your young children and adolescents because they need to know they can depend on you. However, being strong doesn't mean withholding your feelings. You can let them know when you're sad, and they can see you cry. Just make sure you talk about it, and reassure them that you're there for them. Say, "I'll be okay. I'm sad because I'm missing (name)."

Other mourners may feel that they, too, must be strong to support the bereaved. So they try to suppress their feelings so they can "be there" for anyone who might be more emotional. Everyone is so busy being strong, there's no place for grieving. When there's little space for expressions of grief and pain and tears, mourners are denied the comfort and healing that come from sharing their feelings with sympathetic others.

During a funeral, it would be helpful if priests, ministers, and rabbis would give permission for those attending to cry. They could say something like: "Grieving is a normal response to the death of (name) and your tears honor him by showing how much you cared about him. It's also okay not to cry if you don't feel the need. That doesn't mean something is wrong with you or you didn't care about (name)."

I'm often asked if something's wrong because a person doesn't feel like crying. She cared for the deceased, yet isn't outwardly grieving like everyone else. Usually this person is either numb or she has a less sensitive or emotional personality. It's okay not to cry when everyone else is. You may cry later, or you may never cry.

## "Get Over It"

One of the most harmful things to say to someone who is bereaved is "You should get over it" or "You have to move on." Usually this means the speaker has a judgment about how long mourning should last, and he or she is uncomfortable because the bereaved continues to grieve. The problem is that grievers can start believing they are deficient or weak because they haven't recovered from the loss. Grief isn't something that can be rushed—there are no shortcuts. Everyone must work through his or her grief, not get over it.

# Funeral Behavior

From the time of ancient humans, we have had some form of ceremony to mark the passing of loved ones and ritualize the grief of the bereaved. While the rituals differ depending on religion or culture, they serve the same purpose. They bring people together to acknowledge the passing of someone they knew and cared about.

## Attending the Funeral

Attending a funeral is uncomfortable for many people. They don't want to feel sad or see others cry. They may not know what's expected of them during the service, but attending the funeral is an important experience. It provides an opportunity to do the following:

- Say goodbye

- Grieve with others

- Face the reality of the death

- Be there for the family

- Get to know the deceased better through hearing stories and eulogies

- Begin to feel a sense of closure

survival
strategies

Many people avoid funerals because they don't want to view the body in an open casket. You can still attend the funeral without viewing the body. When other people line up to walk past the casket, remain in your seat or step outside.

The number of people attending the funeral is often comforting to the family. Numbers seem to reflect the caring and respect others have for the deceased and for her family. The larger the attendance, the more the family sees the larger impact the deceased has had on her community. Having people attend who knew the deceased from various areas of her life is also important. This helps the family see how respected and/or important she was in those other places, such as at her jobsite. They might make statements such as, "She had 30 people show up from her work!"

## What Not to Say at a Funeral

The basic fact to remember when someone is grieving is *presence*, not *words*. In the beginning, there really isn't a lot you can say that will offer comfort to the bereaved anyway. They may feel shocked and overwhelmed, especially if the death was sudden. Much of what's said to them doesn't sink in. However, saying the wrong thing may make an impact—a bad one. What's important is attending the funeral, demonstrating that you care, showing your sorrow, and spending time with the bereaved during their grief journey.

Don't use clichés or platitudes, quote religious verses or share religious beliefs, volunteer your own grief stories, or state your expectations that the griever will get over the loss. These may come across as condescending and unfeeling. It can also stifle expressions of emotion, and could cause someone to question the legitimacy of his own grief. Later on in the grief journey, you can share about your losses, or quote poems or Bible verses that helped you through your time of grief. Now's not the time.

**cautions and concerns**    If you can put it on a bumper sticker, don't say it.

The worst thing you can say to a griever is, "I know how you feel." Even if you've suffered a similar loss, everyone is different. Therefore you don't know just how he or she feels. People who are bereaved, especially if it's a unique loss such as the death of a child, may feel offended or hurt by that statement. Instead, using an empathetic tone, you can say:

- "I can't even imagine what you must be feeling. I just want you to know I'm here for you if you want to talk."

- "I've been there, so I know what you're going through. If you'd like my support, please contact me."

- "I've lost my husband, too, so I've been through what you're going through. If you need to talk to someone who understands, I'll be there for you."

Religious platitudes or sayings are often uttered at funerals and afterward. The most common religious cliché is, "He is in a better place." Even though you may have that belief, the family may not share your religious faith. Or they may believe as you do, but don't want their loved one to be in that better place just yet. Here are some other religious platitudes to avoid saying:

- "God knows best."
- "It's God's will."
- "Don't be sad; she is in heaven."
- "God doesn't give you more than you can bear."
- "He's an angel now."
- "God must have needed (name) more than you."
- "With faith, you don't need to grieve."

Other comments or clichés to avoid are ones that tell the bereaved how to grieve:

- "Suck it up."
- "Keep a stiff upper lip."
- "Just get over it."
- "Be brave."
- "You should be grateful you had him/her for so long."
- "Keep your chin up."

Well-meaning platitudes are often intended to console, but they can come across as just the opposite. They can sound trite or unfeeling:

- "Good things come from bad."
- "What doesn't kill you makes you stronger."
- "At least (name) had a good life before he died."
- "It was (name's) time to go."
- "I'm sure you'll feel better soon."
- "It was for the best."

- "What's done is done."

- "At least you had her for (amount of time)."

If the bereaved volunteers statements, like, "He's in a better place," or "She's no longer suffering," you can agree with them. Just don't be the first to say it. They are using these statements to comfort themselves, and it's safe to echo them.

If you feel uncomfortable, or don't know what to say to the bereaved, it's okay to acknowledge that. For example, "I don't really know what to say. I just want you to know that I'm thinking of you." Or, "I can't put into words how sorry I feel about (name's) death."

Expressions of Grief

"Don't ever ask to take away someone's pain; just walk with him or her."

—Maryanne, who lost her husband

## Do's and Don'ts for the Funeral and Reception

There are some things you *can* say to family members at the funeral and reception that will feel comforting. Family members want to know how their loved one made an impact on others. They want to hear stories about the deceased and know people will remember him or her. Here are some other do's and don'ts:

- Don't offer your own grief stories.

- Do give a hug, handclasp, or shoulder squeeze, where appropriate.

- Don't try to "cheer up" the bereaved.

- Don't say, "Call me." Instead, reach out to him or her.

- Do talk about what you learned from the deceased.

- Do say how you'll miss the deceased.

- Don't assume you know how they feel and put words in their mouths: "You must be so sad," or "You must feel terrible."

- Do say, "My thoughts (and prayers) are with you."

Stephanie, a woman with Down's Syndrome who attended my church, passed away in her sleep. I didn't find out until several weeks after the funeral. I didn't really know her family, except to say "hi" to them, although we usually attended the same service. The Sunday after I learned Stephanie had passed away, I went up to her parents and told them I had just recently heard the news, and said how sorry I was. Her mom grabbed my hand and started crying.

I had a strong urge to say, "She's in a better place," which shocked me. I *know* better than to say that. I held back by reminding myself that they already knew Stephanie was in a better place. Instead, I talked about how I loved Stephanie's enthusiasm for church—how her face would light up when she sang (using words and sign language) a familiar hymn. I shared my admiration for the way the whole family loved and cared for her. Their love had always been so obvious; it was a joy to see. Stephanie's mother continued to cry and clutch my hand. She told me how hard it was to come to church and have Stephanie's seat remain empty. I could see by the look on her face that she appreciated my sharing with her. The whole conversation took about five minutes, but I know we were all touched by it.

# Helping the Mourner

There is a saying, "Laugh, and the world laughs with you. Cry, and you cry alone." When it comes to crying, in the beginning, the bereaved have plenty of company in their tears. It's only as the journey goes on that others' tears dry up. The grievers often continue on their sorrowful journey alone.

Right after the death, the family may be inundated with calls and people dropping by, often bringing food. Sometimes all the attention is welcome; sometimes it's overwhelming and may feel intrusive. Usually, family members aren't really hungry and have more food than they can fit in their refrigerator. If bringing food is important to you, think of something that doesn't need refrigeration.

## Right After the Death

If you do talk with family members, it's normal to want the details about the death. Sometimes, however, they've told the story over and over and they're sick of relating it. Instead of asking about details, ask, "Would it be too painful for you to tell me what happened, or are you tired of talking about it?" Then respect the answer.

Many times, offering your silent presence is the best way to comfort the bereaved. You can listen if they want to talk, and talk if they want to listen. There may be periods where not a lot is said. Sitting or standing next to them, offering hugs or handholding, giving them tissues if they're crying, are all quiet gestures of support.

| Expressions of Grief | "It's better to talk to the griever than to avoid them and pretend they're not there." |
| | —Barbara, whose 2-year-old son died |

Family members might not feel hungry. But at some point, you can encourage them to eat. You might offer to prepare something for them. Grieving people may have a "lump" in their throat or a "knot" in their stomachs. It helps to have foods that they don't have to chew much or won't have trouble swallowing. Bring over soup, protein drinks, yogurt, or smoothies. You might have an easier time coaxing someone to drink something nutritional rather than to eat.

After a death, you may want to call or drop by the house. Some families appreciate the attention and personal condolences. Having others grieve with them is meaningful. Other times, families retreat from the world and mourn in private. Or an individual in the family may shut herself away and not talk to the visitors. It's important to respect the needs and wishes of the family. They may not directly tell you what they need, so watch for cues that show whether they desire company or not.

The family may have someone monitoring the phone and the door. Don't try to force your way past this person. Just leave your name and a message. If no one answers the phone, leave a condolence message. Grieving families usually appreciate receiving cards. Add your own note to the card to make it more personal. You can also add a note to an online condolence website, which the family can read when they're ready.

In the beginning, it's common for others to tell the bereaved their own grief stories. People share these because they want the bereaved to know they understand how they're feeling. They might not realize this isn't a good way to convey empathy, at least in the first weeks of the grief journey. Allow the focus and attention to be on the bereaved's grief story, not yours.

The day of my father's death, I shared the news with two of my friends in separate conversations. Before I got far in telling my story, they interrupted me by saying, "I know how you feel. I lost my ...." For one, it was his grandmother, and another, it was her father. They then proceeded to tell me about the loss of their loved ones. I know they meant well. They were both desperately trying to convey to me they understood my grief because they'd experienced it, too. Yet, in so doing, they took the conversational ball away from me. I was aware of it, and I wanted to say, "I don't want to talk about your death story because my dad died today, and I need to share *my* feelings." I didn't say anything because I recognized how hard they were trying and appreciated their efforts. Yet I made a mental note to never do this to anyone. Now in similar situations (after the person has told me of a recent loss or when I'm at a funeral) I say, "I know what it's like to lose a father (or a parent). If you ever want to talk to someone who's been there, I'll listen."

What could my friends have said or done that would have worked better? One thing would have been to listen without telling me their grief story. The other would have been to draw me out. By asking caring questions, they could have gotten me to talk more and helped me process my feelings. Following are some questions they could have asked:

- "How are you feeling?"

- "How did you feel about that?"

- "What was your father like?"

- "What was your relationship with your dad like?"

- "How is your family doing?"

You can use a few snippets of your experience with death as a way to relate and open the conversation, but make sure the other person doesn't feel as if he must have the same experience. For example, "When my dad died, I felt numb for the first hour. How did you feel when you heard the news?"

## In the Weeks, Months, and Years Following

After a few weeks, support from others drops off considerably. Relatives return home. Friends and neighbors become involved in their own lives. The loss (for the most part) can disappear off their radar.

The best thing you can do for those grieving is to remember your friend, relative, neighbor, or co-worker is on a journey that may last a long time. They will need your involvement more than just after the death. Touch base with them throughout the next months and first couple of years. Even as years go by, give them a call when you know he might feel sad, like around the deceased's birthday or the anniversary of the death.

**survival strategies** | When you call the bereaved, don't pressure her to respond. She might not be up to talking. Leave a message that says: "I wanted to call and see how you're doing. You may not feel like talking, and I understand if you don't get back to me for a while. I just wanted you to know I was thinking of you."

# Specific Ways to Help

When there's a death in the family, many people want to help, but they don't know what to do. They may say something like, "If there's anything I can do to help, let me know." This offer, while kind and (maybe) heartfelt, is basically useless. Can you imagine a bereaved spouse calling you and saying, "I'm overwhelmed and can barely function. My yard looks like a forest. Could you please come over and mow my lawn?" Or, "My kids are as sad as I am. We all need a break from each other's pain. Can you please have them over for a play date with your kids?" *You* are going to have to make specific offers to spend time together, talk, do activities, or help with tasks.

## Listening, Not Talking

As I've mentioned, one of the best things you can do for someone who is grieving is be there to listen. The bereaved have their departed loved ones on their minds, and often long to talk about them. They want their loved one to be remembered. They want to share about them, and they want to talk about what they're going through without them. After a while, this can wear on others, so the bereaved don't have a lot of chances to talk about the deceased.

When I talked with a mother whose teenage daughter died three years previously, at one point, she broke into tears. At the end, I thanked her for sharing with me, mentioning that I knew the interview had been painful. She told me that anytime she gets to talk about her daughter, it's good. She just wished she had more opportunities to do so.

What most people don't understand is that you can aid (although not fix) the bereaved by listening and drawing them out, then validating how they feel. Show patience and respect for their process. Acknowledge the tough time they might be going through. These are some other do's and don'ts:

- Don't ask, "How are you?" We're conditioned to say, "fine" or "okay" or "I'm all right," no matter how we really feel.

- Do ask, "How is it for you since (name) died?" Don't just accept an "I'm fine" response.

- Do say, "I understand you're feeling (whatever emotion they've shared about their feelings)."

- Don't badmouth the deceased. This may cause the griever to have to defend him.

## Lending a Helping Hand

It's okay to feel uncomfortable yet still do something that you know is right or good. Don't let your discomfort stop you from reaching out to the bereaved. If you don't know what to offer, the best thing you can do is ask what they might need. People have differing needs when it comes to space, privacy, intimate sharing, and solitude versus a crowd. Ask them what's helpful. For example, "Do you prefer silence or talking?" Or, "Would you rather be alone or with people?"

Expressions of Grief

"One really nice gift I received in a sympathy card was booklets of stamps (to be used for thank-you notes)."

—Linda, after her father's death

Here are some other ways to help:

- Offer to store some of the excess food that people have dropped off in your refrigerator or freezer.

- Offer to help with yard or housework, pick up groceries, and run other errands.

- Encourage the bereaved individual to feel included and wanted.

- Encourage (nag, if necessary) the griever to eat healthy, rest, exercise, and seek any necessary medical attention. Offer to go on a walk with her or cook a meal together.

Many people don't want to be a burden, as if it's shameful to need help. So they will suffer in silence as things around them deteriorate. A general offer of "Let me know if you need anything," is often not accepted. But if you offer something specific, especially if it's something you're already doing, they might be more inclined to accept. "I'm going to the store and can pick up some groceries for you. What do you need?" Or, "I'm dropping off clothes at the dry cleaners. Why don't I swing by and take yours, too."

If you do offer help with a specific task, many may still turn you down, even if they need the help. Sometimes it works to tell them, "If the situation were reversed, I know you'd do this for me, and you'd want me to say yes. And maybe you will have to help me in the future. So allow me to do this for you now." For people who are concerned about being a burden or accepting favors, it may help to let them know that accepting your offer doesn't mean they are indebted to you. Rather it's the other way around. You need to get them to understand that by your helping them, they help you—they do *you* the favor. These are some examples:

- "Your husband, Henry, and I used to talk about gardening, something we both enjoy. Since he died, I haven't enjoyed working in my yard because I feel bad that he's not here in his. I know you have your hands full. Please let me come over in the next week or two and mow your lawn and do some trimming. I'll feel much better if I can do this for Henry and for you."

- "I'm going to take my kids to the park on Saturday, and I'd love to swing by and get yours. The children all play so nicely together, which my two *don't* do by themselves. I'll be able to sit on the bench, watch them and knit instead of playing referee."

## Avoid Giving "Should" Advice

The bereaved are often inundated with unsolicited advice, both right after the death and all along their grief journey. Advice when it's prefaced with a "should" or "shouldn't" comes across as critical, even if that's not your intention. No one needs negative feedback at any time, but especially when they're grieving. Some common comments are these:

- "You shouldn't dwell on it."
- "You shouldn't feel sad."
- "Your loved one is in heaven now, and you should be happy."
- "You shouldn't cry so much. It's not good for you."
- "You should accept it as God's will."
- "You shouldn't keep her photos out."
- "You should keep busy so you don't think about it."
- "You should accept his death."
- "You should go back to work."

Although sometimes a bereaved individual may lash out at a comment like this, it's more common for someone who's bereaved not to say anything. He may have a reaction, but doesn't share it. Instead, he feels hurt or angry and pulls away from the critical person. Rather than letting a "should" remark fester, here are some possible responses to this type of feedback:

- "Please don't tell me what I should or shouldn't do."
- "I know you mean well. You may not realize your advice is coming across as critical (or insensitive)."

- "Rather than advice, I'd like (what you want or need)."

- "It's more helpful for you to do/say (what you need) than tell me what to do."

- "I know you're trying to help me, and because you haven't lost a (relationship) you can't really know what it's like and what I need to do."

In the last example, notice I used "and" as a transition word, rather than "but" or "however." "But" tends to negate a positive first sentence. This causes people to focus on the second sentence, which is often negative. "And" is a milder way to link the sentences.

> **survival strategies**
>
> If the family posts about their loss on Facebook, feel free to respond (although leave out any details you may know about the death). However, respect their privacy if they haven't posted. Send a personal e-mail or card instead.

Don't make the purpose of a visit or outing to "cheer up" the grieving individual. This may force her to pretend to feel okay. If she shows or expresses sadness, you may feel hurt or offended that your company or activity didn't "fix" them. Do make it safe for her to spend time with you and feel sad and cry.

Patience is the key. At first your efforts at getting together may be declined. Don't take it personally, and don't stop asking. Sometimes it takes a while before someone is ready for company or outings. If he keeps turning down your suggestions for activities, ask him what he'd like to do instead.

## Helping Others Help You

If you are the one who is grieving, most of your friends may have concerns about saying the wrong thing. So you need to help them help you. Because others might not know what to say or do to support you, you need to be direct. Tell them you like talking about your loved one (if you do). Let them know it's okay if you cry. Tell them they don't have to fix your pain; all they need to do is listen. Your friends will probably feel relieved by the information. Many of them can handle spending time with you and just listening.

> cautions and concerns
>
> Don't be concerned or take it personally if you don't hear from the grieving person. Grieving people may need to temporarily withdraw from others. This gives them the time and space to process their emotions, reflect on what happened, and recharge. When they return to normal life, they have renewed energy and increased ability to cope with the changes in their life.

Bereaved individuals won't emotionally move on before they're ready. You can't force them, no matter how well meaning your intentions. However, by supporting them in their grief process—where they are right now—you help give them solace. That, in turn, helps them slowly move on.

## Essential Takeaways

- Negative messages such as "be strong" may be well intentioned, but can come across as insensitive.
- Offer your support at the funeral with your presence; words are not always necessary.
- Help the mourner right after the death—but don't forget about him or her in the weeks, months, or even years following the loss.
- Do make an effort to see and talk to those who are grieving, and make specific offers of help.

# Part 3

# Loss in Other Life Circumstances

Although we tend to think of grief as stemming from bereavement, that isn't always the case. In this part, we explore additional losses that can cause you to feel grief and other emotions. There are some losses in our lives that we expect (even when we try to deny them), such as aging or the death of grandparents. But we may be less prepared for a job loss or divorce. Human relations can bring us the most joy in life and also cause us the most pain. We look at the grief from separations and divorces, as well as loss of a job or a home.

We can also grieve for what happens to our bodies as we age and/or become seriously ill. Our struggle with growing old or becoming disabled can feel very painful. These types of losses can also make us confront our own mortality, which can be a scary process.

# chapter 14

# Painful Partings

When friends part

Closure with friends

When romance ends

Taking responsibility and moving on

As humans, we derive much of our happiness from social interactions. Healthy relationships with people enhance our emotional and physical well-being. Over the course of our lifetimes, we'll form many friendships. We'll also develop romantic relationships. We allow friends and lovers into our hearts. We invest a lot of ourselves with them, and when we lose friends and lovers we can lose a piece of ourselves. It hurts, and sometimes we grieve for them more than we do a death of someone close to us.

The breakup of friendships and romantic relationships makes us feel powerless. Unlike death, which is final, we believe we should be able to work things out with people we love. We hold out hope for a renewal of the relationship. When we have to accept that a friend or lover no longer cares about us in the way we care about him or her—when that person leaves us and that relationship dies—we must undergo a grief journey.

## The Loss of a Friendship

Most of us have a variety of friendships, from superficial to extremely close. Some of our friendships start when we're young and last a lifetime. Others are newer, but just as special. Best friends stick together through thick and thin. Friends can carry us through the darkest of times and celebrate our achievements and special events.

An ideal friendship is a balanced one. There's a give and take that evens out over weeks, months, and even years. If one friend goes through a crisis, the other friend is there for that person, and vice versa. Both people understand and support each other. They enjoy one or more of the same activities. Even though they may become busy with their lives, they remain friends in their hearts.

Some friends know all our business—they know our true selves. Others only know us from work or other activities. And many friends are in between. Friends provide companionship, entertainment, challenges, support, and solace. Many times, we expect a friendship to last all our lives. Sometimes they do, but when they don't, we can suffer from the loss.

When a friendship ends, you may not know it. Often there isn't a final event that tells you it's over. Your friend has changed, distanced herself (perhaps denying anything's wrong, when something obviously is). Sometimes two friends just drift apart. Or you may have one or more arguments, or he suddenly drops you. You may not allow yourself to grieve until you realize the friendship is over.

Those who grieve the loss of a good friendship don't often receive much recognition for their feelings or support for what they're going through. One of the reasons they don't get much empathy is because there are always plenty more potential friends. Almost anyone can be a friend. Lose one, grab another person and make him or her your new friend. Yet friendships don't work that way. There's a connection you make with a friend that's more meaningful than what you have with the average person. As you spend time together, open up, have fun, and help each other, the friendship deepens. You develop a tight bond.

**Expressions of Grief**

"I can't understand why she would just stop talking to me. We did so much together. I feel the grieving is lopsided. She doesn't seem to care."

—Amanda, about her year-long friendship with Amy

When friendships end, they're often unresolved losses because the other person doesn't usually sit down with you and say, "This is my problem with you. We need to find a way to work it out, or we won't be able to be friends." Instead, they tend to back off or disappear entirely. Nor do they say something like, "We need to accept things have changed, and we're no longer the friends we were. We can wish each other well, be grateful for the past times together, and acknowledge we are heading in a different direction." As painful as these discussions would feel, there would also be a sense of closure, something that's usually missing when friendships end.

## Gradual Change Versus Sudden Endings

Sometimes long friendships change, and the two people head in different directions. These usually happen because of the following:

- You bonded when you were in a certain place or involved in a specific activity that now has ended.

- One or both of you has gone away to school, moved, married, gotten a new job, had a child, or changed other circumstances, and have became so involved in the new life that there's little contact between you.

- Your friend changed in a way you don't like or behaves in a way you don't approve of.

- You changed and no longer "fit" with your friend.

As painful as it might be to leave behind a friend you care about, and have to grieve the relationship that was, it's harder still to be the one who is left behind. You might try to communicate and work things out, but have little success. Or you might stoically accept the ending without making any attempt to prevent it, although you still grieve.

Rosalie had a 40-year friendship break up literally overnight. She and Jean had been so close and shared so much, and suddenly, when Rosalie couldn't make it to Jean's father's funeral, Jean told Rosalie to get out of her life. Rosalie went through a long period wondering how she could make it right with Jean, and spent time with her trying to piece the relationship back together. Rosalie came to realize that the friendship had died, and she'd been unable to accept the outcome. Rosalie stills thinks of Jean, wondering how she's doing, but says, "I'm all right with her not being part of my life because what we started with, the good and the bad, became mostly bad."

 Pay attention to people's patterns. If they've cut off others before, it's possible you will end up on the dump list the moment you displease them (whether or not you actually did something wrong or hurtful). Sometimes the slight can be in their imagination.

## It's Over, But They're Not Really Gone

You can become stuck in the grief process if you're forced to see or perhaps interact with your former friend through work, participation in an organization, because you're neighbors, your kids go to school together, or other situations. Because you no longer have your old friendship, and the other person continues to ignore or avoid you, treat you with polite distance, or has turned mean, you can continuously feel hurt or angry. You can dread having to see the person. You don't have a chance to heal from your grief because your former friend is there in person, but not in the same spirit.

For two years, Mac and Jeff were buddies at their job. They took lunch together, often went out for a beer after work, and socialized with each other's families. Both men were fond of sports and loved to joke and play pranks on each other. Then Mac was promoted to supervisor, and everything changed. Jeff could understand most of the changes, but not Mac's complete about-face. He turned down social invitations, became distant with Jeff, and started to ride him harder than the other team members. Not only did Jeff lose a good friend, but the job he'd enjoyed so much, partly because of the relationship with Mac, soon became something he dreaded going to. Jeff didn't feel he had a chance to grieve because he was so stressed out about work.

## Are *You* the Problem?

You may have a pattern of friendship losses. Often these end with the other person no longer talking to you. After multiple losses, you may become tired of grieving the loss of friends. If this happens, it's good to step back and evaluate yourself and your friendships. First look at the type of people you are trying to befriend. You just might not fit in with them. Try developing friendships with different people. However, the hard work comes when *you* are the problem. You might be seen as a "too" person—you're too …

- Needy.

- Much of a partier.

- Political.

- Religious.

- Busy to be a good friend.

- Self-important.

There's nothing wrong with having religious or political convictions. The problem comes when you demand that your friends think and believe the same way you do. If you can't allow tolerance in your relationships, people tend to leave you. If you want friends, you need to find individuals who believe as you do, or allow them to be who they are. Don't talk about politics or religion. Instead, value their other qualities.

If you're a busy person, you need to realize you may be sacrificing your friendships to your lifestyle. Yes, good friends are going to understand. Just try to keep in touch—sending e-mails or texts, calling and making plans when you can. Otherwise, you might find you don't have your friends when you need or want them.

Needy people often have the hardest time recognizing how they can drain others. They tend to have a lot of problems in their lives, and their constant drama can burn their friends out. When a friend leaves, needy individuals feel hurt and abandoned. They deeply grieve the loss and may not understand why the other person doesn't. Usually friends who pull away don't know how to tell the other person "you're too needy" because it sounds so hurtful. And they may have already seen the needy individual's inability to accept personal feedback. They want to avoid an argument, so they don't say anything.

## Grieving the Loss of Groups of Friends

Many people have a group of friends. They are bonded to the individuals and to the group as a whole. Sometimes the group develops from work, where we often spend more time with co-workers than with our families. We can bond through other types of proximity—the same school or living in the same neighborhood. You may develop mutual friends through your romantic partner. Or the group can develop through a favorite activity or interest. People can become close because they're in the same life stage, such as new motherhood. When the group disbands, you may or may not maintain individual friendships, but still must grieve the loss of the whole. In addition, you have to grieve the loss of the activities you shared and what the group provided you, which you no longer have or may have to find elsewhere.

When Jessica's writers' group of more than a decade disbanded, she felt set adrift. She'd built processes and a good portion of her confidence from their feedback and support, and then it was gone. Because the group members had worked so long together on something that was such an important part of her life, she felt like she'd lost friends, co-workers, and fellow dreamers, all at the same time.

## Loss at Different Life Stages

Although you will always mourn a good friend, no matter what your age, the loss of a friend can hit you in different ways at different life stages. Youth and the elderly may be the most vulnerable. When you're a teen, you're very attached to and dependent on your friends, sometimes more than your family. When a friend deserts you, or worse, becomes an enemy, the pain deeply hurts. It can also affect your self-esteem, and make you miserable at school.

The elderly may lose friendships that have lasted many years. In their old age, they've had far more friends die than at any other time in their lives. They may have continuous grief as one friend after another passes away. They may lack the number of friends they once had, so every loss eats away at their support system. Elderly people also lose friends due to physical and/or mental deterioration that makes one or both unable to meet the needs of regular friendships. Or one or both move from their homes (and perhaps communities) to be closer to family members, and/or to stay in some form of assisted living.

**cautions and concerns** The grief of the elderly is likely to manifest in physical problems. Physical problems can also cause grief. Chapter 17 explains this in detail.

# Coping with the Loss of a Friend

Even if you have hope the friendship will resume, you need to grieve the loss of the relationship that was, and, at some point, you may have to declare closure on the actual relationship. You deserve friends who are there for you, communicate with you about problems and issues in the relationship, and are willing to work things out with you. Once it's apparent that your former friend is not this type of person, you need to let go and allow yourself to grieve.

One of the best ways to process your grief and provide closure is to write two (or perhaps three) letters to your former friend. The first letter is the one you *don't* send. In it, you tell her exactly what you think and feel. You want to get the intense feelings out of your body, and say any snarky thing you want. Then tear it up when you're finished.

The next letter is the one you send to your friend. This simply states how you felt about the friendship and that you miss her. Say you wish things could have been worked out. State that you are writing to put closure to the relationship, and you wish her well. This letter is not to share your hurt or anger. Your friend doesn't care, or at least not in the way you want. You are only stating a few facts.

Review your letter before you send it. If you find negativity, criticism, or blame seeping into the second letter, tear it up and write another one. Sometimes it takes a third attempt to hit the right tone.

# The Loss of a Romantic Relationship

Unless you marry your first boyfriend or girlfriend, you can cycle through anywhere from a few to many romantic relationships. (Chapter 15 discusses divorce.) Most people have fallen in love and had their hearts broken on one or more occasions. Grief is a normal feeling when someone you care about leaves. Even if the relationship wasn't one in which you were madly in love, it can still hurt when your partner breaks up with you. It's important to process and heal your grief and other feelings from the previous relationship. Otherwise, you may carry the damage into a new one, and risk sabotaging it, thus starting the grief cycle all over again.

Hopefully if your lover decides to leave, he sits down with you and discusses the problems and why the relationship needs to end. Your lover takes responsibility for his part in things going wrong and he says goodbye. However, all too frequently, your partner disengages, hoping you'll get the idea, acts out in a way to force you to be the one to break up, or severs the relationship with a hasty phone call, e-mail, text, or change of status on Facebook. Your pain and grief are compounded by this kind of treatment.

## Slow Death of the Relationship

Sometimes relationships fizzle out. Either they are on again, off again, or you gradually fall out of love or realize you're not a good fit. It may be hard to leave because you do care about the other person. There are enough good parts in her and in your relationship to keep you in it. But one or both of you know it's not right, and it's time to leave. With this type of relationship you can do a lot of your grieving beforehand when you know the end is coming. Or, if the other person leaves and you didn't know she was unhappy, the grief can hit you at that point.

After the relationship has ended, you can grieve the good aspects of it. You can miss your companion. You can miss having sex. You might even second-guess yourself and wonder if you really did love her. You may try again, only to come back around to the same realization—you don't belong together.

> **survival strategies**
>
> When you're having trouble in your relationship or are thinking about leaving, write down how you feel, what you don't like, and what you want in a relationship. Then when you break up, you can refer to your writing to remind yourself why the relationship wasn't working.

After Kevin's girlfriend of three years broke up with him, he initially had mixed feelings. Their relationship had its ups and downs, and somehow had died out. But after a few months, he became lonely. His girlfriend started seeing someone else. He felt abandoned and hurt and had trouble sleeping and eating. He decided his girlfriend had been perfect for him after all.

Like Kevin, when you idealize someone after your breakup, it's often from loneliness and unresolved grief. You can dwell on the good things about the relationship. You think about everything you miss. By blocking out the difficult attributes of your partner, you can stay stuck in your grief. It's important to remind yourself that if he or she had been the right person for you, the relationship would have worked out.

## Sudden Breakup

With a sudden breakup, couples can have a big fight and break up in the heat of the argument. With some couples, the fight can come out of nowhere. For most, however, they have had a history of disagreements, often on the same subjects. The final fight is the last in a series of battles.

If the couple wasn't fighting before, the topic you two are arguing about can be compounded by the *way* your lover is fighting—for example, screaming, name-calling, or using profanity. The fight feels so damaging. You don't want to be with someone like that, no matter how remorseful he or she might be afterward.

The other reason for a sudden breakup is that one partner wants out. The lover hasn't communicated any dissatisfaction, so the partner has no idea what just happened and may be left with unanswered questions. The lover who left often isn't willing to talk about the relationship. The shock of the breakup can compound the grief.

Although Rick had been thinking he needed to date more women before he settled down with Julie, his high-school sweetheart of six years, he hadn't communicated anything to her about his state of mind. Then one day, she pointed at a picture of a wedding dress in a magazine and commented that it was pretty. Alarm bells rang in Rick's head. That night he told Julie he wanted out of the relationship. His decision shocked her. Julie felt betrayed by Rick's lack of communication, especially when she thought everything was good. She had to grieve the loss of a relationship she thought was headed for marriage.

# How to Move On

Having your heart broken is one of life's most painful experiences. Sometimes the breakup is accompanied by hurtful, mean words and behavior on the part of one or both people. If this happens to you, you don't just have to heal from the loss of the relationship, but from how it ended and what your former lover may be doing with someone new. The wise griever takes time to heal. Depending on the depth of your feelings, it can be a few weeks to many years before you feel recovered.

## Disenfranchised Grief

Sometimes the loss of a relationship isn't given the credibility for the intense grief it can cause. People may think, "Well it wasn't a marriage, so the grief isn't as strong." Yet you still could have been head-over-heels in love. Your breakup can cause more hurt than you've ever felt in your life. You want and need support from loved ones. Here are other reasons people might discount your grief:

- You're young. (You'll get over it. There are always more fish in the sea.)

- Your friends and/or family didn't like your partner.

- Your partner was already married or in a romantic relationship.

- You're attractive and/or successful. (You'll quickly find someone new.)

- Your lover was from a different race, culture, or religion.

| cautions and concerns | Don't jump back into dating to try to "fix" your feelings or take away the pain. Besides the fact that it probably won't work, dating will only mask your pain. You can hurt the men or women you date because they think you're emotionally available, when in fact you're still grieving for the past relationship. |
|---|---|

Family, especially, may discount the grief because they usually have high standards for the kind of partner they want you to have. No one may be able to live up to their demands. They may have made things difficult for your partner, instead of welcoming him or her into the family. Friends tend to be more supportive.

## Guilt and Blame

Both guilt and blame are often felt after a breakup. Guilt and blame are two sides of the someone-did-something-wrong coin. When you review what you said and did or what you failed to say or do in the relationship, you may be filled with remorse. You might believe that if only you had acted differently, you would still have your relationship. You can beat yourself up, causing yourself more hurt.

It's common to blame the other person, coming up with a litany of how he or she "did you wrong." While this reaction is normal when the breakup is fresh and the pain is intense, it's not a good place to stay in emotionally. If you focus on all the things the other person did to ruin the relationship and hurt you, you won't be able to see your own part in what went wrong between the two of you. If you don't look at how you're responsible, how can you learn and grow? How can you avoid making the same mistakes again? Even if you did little to contribute to the demise of the relationship, you picked the person. Therefore you need to look at why you chose that person.

How well we respond to our grief and the challenges from our loss makes a difference in how we'll recover and move on to new lives and new relationships. Although you can't change the past, you can change your future. Part of the successful conclusion of your grief journey is learning the lessons from your past relationship. When you do, you can feel stronger and more in control of your future dating life.

## Essential Takeaways

- Friendships may be some of the closest relationships we have, and their loss can deeply hurt.

- The pain of losing a friend often isn't recognized and supported by others.

- The loss of a relationship can break your heart. Proper grieving is an important part of healing.

- Learning from the demise of the relationship helps you make better future choices.

# chapter 15

# Death of a Marriage

Grief from divorce

Emotional reactions

Affected family members

Recovering from divorce

Grieving over a divorce is different in some ways than grieving over the breakup of a romantic relationship. In a marriage, you take vows to stay together for the rest of your lives. On your wedding day, you feel totally in love with your partner and believe your love will last forever. You have a dream of how your future will look, including an idealized relationship with your husband or wife.

The two of you build on those vows, creating a life together, which may involve children. A divorce shatters that life. You have to grieve the loss of your marriage, your life as it was, the shared plans and commitments, and the future you dreamed about. Everyone else who's involved with the two of you—family and friends—may grieve as well.

## Separation and Divorce

A separation and divorce causes a mass of emotional, physical, and logistical problems and complications. While you're in the midst of grieving the loss of your marriage, you might have a legal battle over property, possessions, and income. You might also have a custody battle (which can get really ugly) over your children. You may need to divide up the household possessions, move, change legal and financial paperwork, deal with your children's reactions to the divorce, and many other things. Unless you have full custody of your children, you have to deal with not seeing them every day, or even what you consider very often. Losing out on being with your children every day is one of the hardest parts of a divorce. It can take you a while to even get settled enough to allow yourself to process the intense emotions you may feel.

## Breakdown of Communication

Good communication involves talking in a way your partner can absorb and understand, not in a way that's critical, belittling, blaming, or condescending. When there are issues in a marriage, about half of the time the problem is unhealthy or ineffective communication. The more frustrated, hurt, angry, resentful, and upset the couple becomes, the more their communication worsens.

This happened in Shelly's marriage. After her divorce, she realized the biggest issue with the marriage was that she and her husband had stopped talking about the important stuff. Their love never went away, but it became buried under too many other things.

When communication breaks down in a marriage, it can severely damage the relationship and is often one of the leading causes of divorce. People tend to equate communication with talking, and that is one way to communicate. Yet there are plenty of marriages where one or both people talk a lot, yet nothing is ever resolved.

## Broken Trust

Trust covers many areas in a relationship. Some kinds of trust, like fidelity, are common to most marriages, and provide the structure for the whole relationship. In addition, you may trust your partner to love you, treat you well, keep her word, be a good parent to your children, and many other things, big and small. In a relationship there also may be ways you don't trust your partner, for example, to be on time. These issues tend to be more annoying and perhaps hurtful than deal-breakers like an affair, but they can still wear away at a marriage.

A divorce often involves broken trust. Most people would agree that the greatest breach of trust comes from infidelity. Even couples who stay together after a spouse cheats suffer from the act of unfaithfulness. After the infidelity, the couple may take a long time to repair their marriage.

For many couples, cheating is a deathblow to the relationship. The trust is shattered, never to return. The betrayed spouse can feel profoundly hurt and bitterly angry. His self-esteem and self-confidence takes a hit. He can grieve the loss of the faithful spouse he thought he had.

When Tara's husband had a fling with a co-worker while on a business trip, she was devastated and wanted to die. In the beginning, she curled up in a ball and wept for hours. She didn't eat or sleep for two days. Although her husband was remorseful, he continued to work at his job, interacting with the co-worker every day. Tara was unable to rebuild her trust in him, and ended up leaving the marriage.

| survival strategies | Even though a piece of paper says that you're now single, you may not feel that way, especially if you didn't want your marriage to end. You may still feel emotionally, mentally, and spiritually married. Give yourself permission to grieve as you go through the difficult, and maybe agonizing, process of separating your *self* from the marriage. |
| --- | --- |

## Secondary Losses

The end of a relationship usually involves multiple losses, many of which can feel painful. These losses may be tangible or intangible. Some of these are the loss of ...

- Your home.

- Your financial status.

- Living with your children.

- Your normal routine.

- Your relationships with extended family and friends.

- A shared identity.

- Your role as a husband or a wife.

- Companionship.

- A sexual relationship.

- Support.

- The meaning of the experiences you shared.

# Struggling with Emotions

The breakup of a marriage can be excruciatingly painful, especially if children are involved. What started out as a bright, shiny marriage is tarnished and dark—a place of sadness and grief. You may feel as if you're on a roller-coaster of emotions that go up and down and twist around. You wonder if the ride will ever slow down and come to an end.

If you don't have children, a divorce can be a complete severing of the relationship. From the moment you know the relationship is ending, you can begin to grieve. The problems and grief can linger if you have children because you can't make a clean break with your spouse. You are forced to put up with him or her for the rest of your lives. You have to find a way to be co-parents, no matter how you feel about the idea. The interactions with your ex can enhance or prolong your grieving.

## Shame and Failure

Divorce often brings a crushing feeling of shame. You've failed at one of the most fundamental and important human relationships. It's hard not to feel something's wrong with you when you can't make a marriage work. In some religious beliefs, you're committing a sin by divorcing. You've broken the vows you made before God. You may be shamed and ostracized by fellow believers.

## Negativity and Bitterness

Some people are dealt cruel blows by their spouse—the very person who was supposed to cherish them. Then during the separation and divorce, the ex continues his or her manipulative, hurtful, or distancing treatment. If this happens, there's no doubt your spouse caused you profound pain and grief, and it's easy to focus on everything your ex did to you (and perhaps to your children). The list might be quite long.

While you do need to spend some time processing your feelings about how you were (and continue to be) treated, dwelling on your ex's wrongdoing for an extended amount of time may cause you to become stuck in negativity, bitterness, and even hate. Some people can remain in that place, never getting through their grief journey, for the rest of their lives. They cause themselves great unhappiness and make the lives of others around them miserable. In fact, their unpleasant attitude drives most others away and can keep them from finding love and happiness again.

Financial issues such as alimony and/or child support are also a major sort of frustration, resentment, and bitterness. It may seem unfair when you have to fight for what you believe you deserve. Or you may feel your ex is trying to take advantage of you, and you have to defend your financial position. You can be angry if your ex never does or buys anything for the children, or isn't willing to split the cost of extras such as music lessons or sports clubs.

| survival strategies | When you can't have closure from the other person, you have to find it within yourself. Writing about your feelings helps you work through them. |
| --- | --- |

# Family Issues

A divorce isn't just about two people. Families, both immediate and extended, are also caught in the rift and the chaos that may follow. They, too, may grieve. They can also choose sides and can inflame the relationship between the ex-partners.

## Grieving for Your Children

When you have children, you know they are impacted by the divorce. You want to do all you can to keep them safe and help them get through it. Because of the divorce, there may be times you grieve for what your children are experiencing. You grieve that:

- They are grieving.

- They now come from a broken home.

- Their co-parent might not be as involved and caring as he or she should.

- You don't get to see them every day.

- You don't always see them for holidays or special occasions.

- Finances constrain what you can do with and for them.

- Their parents can't get along.

The more you help your children cope, the more you ease their grief (and yours). Schedule holidays and special events well in advance so you and your children can prepare for them. Be flexible with your ex when it comes to visitation. For example, if his mother's birthday falls on your weekend, allow him to take the kids to their grandmother's celebration. Start new traditions that the children will look forward to and remember. Chapter 19 goes more into helping your children deal with a divorce.

## Your Ex's Family

When you divorce, you can lose a whole part of "your" family—the side that belongs to your spouse. For some people, this isn't a problem, but others may love their in-laws, brothers- and sisters-in-law, and nieces and nephews. For most families, divorce means giving up much, if not all, of your interaction, with the ex's family. It might hurt if they take sides (or your ex forces them to take sides) or if they see you as the one to blame for the breakup of the relationship.

Even if you grieve the family relationships as they used to be, as much as possible try to maintain them, if only for the sake of your children. (Hopefully your in-laws care about you, too, and are also grieving the loss.) Invite them to attend birthday parties and holiday get-togethers. Send them pictures of the children, with and without you in them. Mail them cards on their birthdays and anniversaries. Take your mother- or sister-in-law out to lunch. After the initial turmoil and withdrawal due to the breakup, they may connect with you again. Be patient. Sometimes it takes months, or even years, for it to happen.

Monty was divorced and had custody of his son. The boy's mother had moved to a different part of the country and was estranged from her parents. Monty knew how important it was for his son to stay connected with his ex-wife's parents. He sent them regular e-mails, updating them on their grandson, including things like pictures and report cards. He allowed them to come see his son and spend the weekend in his house. Every spring break, he drove four hours to the state border and handed his son off to his grandparents, who then drove another four hours to their home. At the end of the week, they reversed the process.

## Extended Family Grief

You aren't the only one who grieves when you get divorced. Your family may also love your spouse. They've usually known him or her almost as long as you have. They've seen the two of you through major milestones in your life. They had dreams for your future and that of their grandchildren. They may grieve the loss of the grandchildren you didn't have, but they wanted. In addition to their grief, they worry about you (and about their grandchildren). They want you to cope emotionally and financially.

**Expressions of Grief**

"One thing I found early on was that I needed to make sure that I spoke to people who listened, but who did not take sides, and who did not overly sympathize. I didn't need to be made into a victim, and I didn't want [my ex] made into a bad person. I needed support, but not someone who'd let me wallow in emotions. That was critical for me. Staying in the grief can get to be too comfortable a place. That's where doing things helped."

—Marty

# Coping with Divorce

The intensity of the pain from the divorce usually happens within the first six months and may last two or more years. Your grief can be complicated by the following:

- How your ex treats you and/or your children
- Separation from your children
- Secondary losses such as lack of financial resources
- Your support system (or lack of one)
- If your ex is moving on and dating or is in a relationship
- If you've allowed yourself time to process your emotions

## Self-Doubt

Self-doubt is often a part of the grief journey after a divorce especially if you …

- Were married young.
- Were married a long time.
- Were emotionally and/or financially dependent on your spouse.
- Had your self-esteem ripped to shreds by your spouse.
- Never had much self-esteem in the first place.
- Are left to work and raise your kids alone.
- Lose custody of your children (for whatever reason).

Self-doubt can be crippling if you allow it to take over. Keep telling yourself, "I can do this." Surround yourself with "cheerleaders" who will encourage you. Take classes to enhance your knowledge and skill level. Seek counseling to help you process and heal. Don't let self-doubt stop your grief journey.

## When Your Ex Moves On

Even though you might feel you have recovered from your divorce, when you learn your ex is moving on, you may grieve anew because he or she is dating again, getting remarried, or having a child with a new partner. Your grief may be about nostalgia for what you once had, but now your ex has with someone new. You can still feel connected to him or her, and it hurts to see your ex move on. Or you may not feel connected, but you can feel hurt, angry, or resentful that you don't also have someone to love. You can worry how the new relationship may affect your children, especially that he or she might take over your role as a parent. You can also feel envious of or sorry for the new partner.

**survival strategies**   You can't do much, if anything, about your ex's behavior. You can only change yourself. Changing yourself—how you feel, think, and react— might have a side effect of causing your ex to change, but don't have any expectations.

## Processing the Pain

A divorce can be just as painful—although in a different way—as a death. However, you may not receive the same support as those who suffer a bereavement. You may feel emotions you've never experienced before such as despair, terror, betrayal, or rage. Or your emotions may be more intense than ever before. You can fear you'll never be happy again.

If you don't process the pain and learn from your divorce, you can repeat your mistakes. Allow yourself to feel your emotions. Write about them as well, especially the ones that feel ugly, dark, mean, or petty. Talk about your feelings with those who support you. You might need to tell your story (and its variations) over and over. That's part of healing.

After Michelle was divorced from her husband, there were times she lost it—crying jags that seemed to last forever. Her mother and a few other close friends helped her through it. And she also attended counseling. "Talking, talking, talking!" Michelle said. "There really is a lot to be said for venting!"

## Moving On

At some point in your recovery, you realize that you need to start moving on with your life. That doesn't mean you have to get out and date. That might still be too scary at this point. Instead you have to engage in activities that you enjoy, that stimulate you, cause you to grow, and give you new meaning in your life.

Form new friendships. Your new friends won't know you as half of a "couple." They'll know you as who you are now. You don't have to talk about your divorce if you don't want to. You might choose to focus on different topics of conversation.

Engage in new activities. There must be something (or many somethings) you've always wanted to do, try, see, explore, or learn. Or you might take suggestions from friends and family members. Now's the time to try one or more different things, until you find the ones you enjoy.

Get in shape. Eating healthy and exercising is good for you. There's nothing like a fit and trim body to make you feel younger, attractive, and good about yourself. (Plus, there's the added satisfaction you receive from your ex seeing you look good.)

> **Expressions of Grief**
>
> "I took up belly dancing. It's very hard to be depressed with belly-dance music going. I also painted the house, and got back to my own roots. A lot of what led to the divorce was that I stopped putting myself first. If you don't have a self to put into a relationship, you're not going to be contributing much."
>
> —35-year-old Dina

After a breakup, one of the most common fears I hear from clients is: "Will someone ever love me again? Will I always be alone?" Often this fear keeps people in relationships far longer than they should stay. When you start dating again, you may feel discouraged by the selection of men or women you meet. Remember, all it takes is *one* person to fall in love with. He or she is out there, but you might not meet until you've done the necessary work to heal and are ready for a healthy relationship.

## Essential Takeaways

- Poor communication plays a big part in relationship problems.
- Divorce comes with more losses than just the marriage.
- Your family members can also experience their own grief journey from the divorce.
- It's important to allow yourself time to process the pain and heal from the divorce so you don't repeat the same mistakes.

# chapter 16

# Transitions and Grief

| Losing your job |
| Secondary effects of job loss |
| Coping with transitions |
| Losing your home to foreclosure or disaster |

Sometimes you anticipate and prepare for transitions that cause losses in your life. Other times transitions drop on you like a rock, causing turmoil, stress, and grief. Some losses, like a layoff or foreclosure on your home, can devastate you. It can feel like your life is changing for the worse, and you're powerless to do anything about it.

## Job Loss

Whether you lose your job due to being fired or laid off, a plant closure, downsizing, or a business failure, your reaction may surprise you. The transition and the loss involved may hit you far harder than you thought it could. You may feel some of these reactions:

- Numbness, disbelief, even denial
- Fear and anxiety
- Disappointment
- Loneliness

- Anger, irritability, bitterness, betrayal

- Overwhelmed, depression

- Frustration

- Helplessness, hopelessness

One of the reasons losing your job is so difficult is because you're dealing with the emotions caused by the loss as well as problems due to the loss, often ones of survival. A way of life has ended, and with it the security your work provided for you and your family. You have to make difficult decisions while you're struggling with powerful emotions. The loss can cause a personal, marital, and/or family crisis.

Grief is not usually associated with a job loss, yet it's often a prevalent emotion. The more you love your job, the more you'll grieve its loss. Because you're grieving, you can have any of the grief reactions mentioned in Chapter 3. When you lose a job there's a lot to mourn:

- Work you may love; meaningful work

- Steady income

- Benefits

- Co-workers you value

- A sense of accomplishment

Sometimes your business fails. Not only do you lose your job and income, but also a dream that you've worked extremely hard for. You've invested your time and money for (perhaps) many years. You also may have employees whom you cared about and who depended on you. Now they, too, are out of a job. The financial setback can last for years.

When Jack lost his job, his world collapsed. He'd worked for his company for 10 years, moving up through the ranks until he'd reached a level where he supervised 11 people on a project he felt personally responsible to complete. He spent long hours at the job and brought work home on the weekend, missing a lot of his son's baseball games and other activities.

After the successful conclusion of the project, his entire department was laid off. At first Jack was incredulous about the team's termination; then he felt betrayed. He also felt awful for his co-workers. Jack quickly turned bitter. He made some token efforts to find a new job, and then lapsed into depression after a few weeks. He camped on the couch and stared at the television. It took a serious "we're running out of money" talk from his wife to motivate Jack to get off the couch and back into a serious job search.

## Your Job, Your Identity

Our job is usually a descriptive term we use, both for ourselves and others. A common question that's asked upon first meeting someone is: "What do you do?" The other person usually answers, "I'm a (job title)" or "I do (job)." The answer gives you an immediate label for the person.

When you have a job, it starts to shape you. Many people, especially men, place a huge part of their ego and identity into their work. They may define themselves by their success, sacrificing years of personal and family time to devote themselves to their work. The job gives them meaning and purpose. When their work is taken from them, they may no longer know who they are. They may feel lost and have a struggle with their identity.

## A Sense of Shame

Subconsciously or consciously, we tend to associate the loss of a job with failure. Traditionally, it was the poor performers who were fired from jobs. Therefore, if you were unemployed, something must be wrong with you. After the economy changed in 2008 and so many companies went out of business, downsized, closed facilities, or laid off employees, most people understood that unemployment may have more to do with bad luck and less about you personally. Yet even though you might know on an intellectual level that you're in the same boat with millions of other people, emotionally you can still feel ashamed, as if you're a failure.

Your experience with shame starts with the way the layoff is handled. If you're given the news in a cold, unfeeling manner, and escorted out of the building by security as if you're a criminal, then you can feel humiliated.

Carrying your possessions in a box, you walk down the corridor of shame, as co-workers avoid catching your eye. Only a brave few may venture forward to give you a goodbye hug or handshake and wish you well. Although it's normal to resent the company (or certain people in the company), part of what you'll have to process on your grief journey is the way you were treated. Holding on to resentment is detrimental to your emotional and mental health.

Shame, like grief, is another important emotion that people may not be aware of feeling, often because they have so many other (more easily identifiable) emotions happening inside them. If you place your worth in your job, when you lose it, you can feel worthless. Worthlessness is another kind of shame. Just being unemployed can make you feel like a second-class citizen, which is also shameful.

Most people try to avoid their shame because it feels awful. However, some may go lengths to suppress their shame. For example, they may sleep too much or consume too much alcohol. They may avoid telling anyone about the job loss because they may feel like there's the stigma of "loser" on them. If they use their humiliation or embarrassment to avoid talking to others, they cut themselves off from an important source of support and healing.

Some people don't like their job or anything about it. When they lose it, they won't usually grieve. However, this loss may bring up prior shame from a previous termination from work that they did love. Because the earlier shame and grief was unresolved, it can emerge at this point, adding to the emotional burden people carry.

The longer you take to find a new job, the more you may feel ashamed, as if you are somehow inadequate. Or you might think (or know) others judge you as a failure. Some people give up at this point. Others force themselves to go on in spite of their shame and are eventually rewarded with finding a new job.

| Expressions of Grief | "Yes, there's shame. But I had to get over it because I was in survival mode. I had to find work."<br><br>—David, about his job loss |

# Secondary Losses

After a job termination, you can have many secondary losses. Aside from the obvious losses of income and benefits, without work, you can lose ...

- Your self-esteem.

- Your familiar routine.

- A purposeful activity.

- The predictability of your life.

- A sense of security.

- Respect from others.

Other secondary losses consist of material possessions. You might be forced to sell your house, a vacation home, a car, a recreational vehicle, or other things to help make ends meet. Or you may lose them to repossession or foreclosure. Whether or not you are grieving the loss of your job, if you have to part with possessions, give up vacations, or other activities you and your family enjoyed, you can grieve for the changes in your lifestyle.

## Family Problems

A parent's biggest fears about the job loss is how the reduced income is going to affect the family, especially when it comes to paying rent or a mortgage as well as other bills. Not only must you worry about financial survival, the extras you took pride in providing for your family now must be cut out. The parent fears that this situation is going to damage the family in some way. But while the unemployment of one (or both) breadwinner can put grave stress on the family, they can emerge stronger, and in some ways emotionally healthier, from the situation.

How you handle your emotions and interact with your family makes a difference with how you all will weather the situation. At the end of your period of unemployment, your family can be closer, and your children can have learned important values and skills such as the following.

- How to manage money

- Delayed gratification

- Doing away with an unrealistic sense of entitlement

- The benefits of earning their own money

- Increased creativity about finding ways to entertain themselves and get what they want

- Learning who their true friends are

- Knowing what's really important in life

There's a huge pressure on kids to own the latest toys and gadgets, and wear stylish, expensive clothing and accessories. It's normal for kids to want what they see on television and what their friends have. They, too, can grieve the family's lifestyle changes. Try to be sympathetic with their disappointment, frustration, resentment, or shame about the financial cuts, not receiving something they wanted, or not getting to do activities they enjoy or planned for. Educate your children about the emotions they may be experiencing. Some may be new to them, and they might not understand them.

**survival strategies**
It's normal for kids to want things and continue to ask for them even though they know money is tight. Instead of becoming frustrated with them, hold on to your patience. Calmly say, "I'm sorry you can't do that (or buy that) right now. We don't have the extra money."

Usually kids are good at finding ways to save and sacrifice if they're included in the decision-making and are praised for what they give up and change. Hold a family meeting where you break the news. Discuss the loss of income. Then allow the kids to contribute. They will feel better and gain self-esteem if they can say, "I don't need to have the new skateboard you promised me," rather than your saying, "You can't have that new skateboard." Or, "I can mow the neighbors' lawns or babysit for extra money," rather than your commanding, "You need to find a way to bring in money." Make sure you acknowledge them (and continue to do so) for their contributions.

Because you are stressed and fearful, you may also become angry or irritable. You may take your ire out on your family. Aside from making your spouse and children feel hurt, angry, or ashamed, this behavior leads to poor communication, misunderstandings, withdrawing or avoidance, and arguments. Do your best to remain even-tempered and supportive of your family members.

Your children will take their emotional and behavioral cue from you. Not only are they trying to cope with the changes in the family due to the job loss, they will also file away your attitude and behavior under the mental file, "How to cope with a job loss or other stressful events when you're an adult." If your kids see you handle the job loss with dignity and a positive attitude, that will reassure them, enhance their respect for you, and teach them how to handle life's difficult challenges. Therefore, you need to do whatever you can to keep a good attitude, even though you're stressed, fearful, and grieving. Communicate honestly with your children about what's going on, but also give them needed reassurance.

To keep your marriage intact, do your best to openly communicate with your partner. Limit criticism and blame. Your spouse is going to need to see you doing everything you can to find a job. Otherwise, he or she will become resentful, which will lead to marital distress. Make sure you help out around the house and do shopping and errands, even if those aren't your usual tasks. Pay attention to and allow yourself to feel your emotions on a regular basis to keep from having them build up and acting them out. Acknowledge to your spouse how tough this is and how much you appreciate his or her support. Keep reiterating to each other that, together, you can get through this.

## Financial Concerns

With the loss of a job comes financial as well as emotional distress. After you lose a job, you'll be busy trying to find new work, setting a budget, and finding other ways to earn money or spend less. You might also take advantage of your free time to catch up on other things you want or need to do. You might be so caught up with financial concerns that you don't have the time and space to grieve the loss of the job.

The more you need your job, the more you'll fear its loss. When I've worked for companies in the midst of layoffs and counseled upset employees, the ones in the most distress were usually the ones with heavy financial burdens. Not only did they live paycheck to paycheck, but they (or a family member) had medical conditions that they needed benefits for, or a spouse was unemployed, or children were in college, or they were also supporting extended family members, or they'd been laid off before and only recently started working again, or any number of additional problems. They weren't only fearful, but they also felt panicked by the idea of job loss.

Because of your financial fear, you might not initially feel grief. Only later, when things have calmed down, may the grief rise up. Sometimes, the grief doesn't hit until you have found a new job, especially if it's not as good as the old one. Here, too, you may not initially grieve because you're so busy trying to adjust to the new job and working again, that you're stressed, busy, and preoccupied. The grief remains buried inside. But once you settle in, you may mourn the job you lost.

It may be hard to return to the workplace feeling grief, anger, and resentment. Most people assume finding work will banish their old emotions. However, it doesn't always work that way. A new job doesn't automatically fix it for you.

## Coping with Job Loss

When you first have news that you will lose your job or you actually do lose it, take a few days to sort through your feelings. Allow yourself to recharge your energy and reassess your priorities. Talk to loved ones. Go for walks. Be nice to yourself. After the initial wave of emotions has passed, then you can plunge into budgeting, updating your resumé, networking, and hunting for a job.

When you go to outplacement services or other job-training organizations, you'll learn how to write a resumé, network, apply for jobs, and interview. There may be little or no attention paid to your feelings. You probably won't receive training in how to recognize your grief, much less process it.

One of the best ways you can process your emotions is to write about them. Some studies have shown that people who journal about their emotions are more successful at coping with the job loss and the transition to new work. Also, people who journal may find new jobs more quickly than those who don't, possibly because they're coming across in an interview in a calm, centered way. (Chapter 20 goes more into the positive aspects of journaling.)

It's vital that you take care of yourself during this time. Yes, you need to focus on finding work. However, you also have time that you can put to good use in other ways. You can …

- Seek support from others.

- Spend quality family time.

- Volunteer, especially at your child's school and activities.

- Tackle house and yard projects.

- Exercise (especially if you haven't had time because of your job).

- Do creative endeavors that you usually don't have time for. (Maybe you can make some money from them.)

- Reward yourself. For example, after several hours of job searching and filling out applications, take a walk, take a nap, have a bubble bath, or read a book for a while.

- Set boundaries with (or avoid) negative or critical people.

- Keep reminding yourself that this will pass.

- Speak and act in a positive, hopeful manner.

- Keep to your routine.

- Find other activities that give you meaning and satisfaction, so your job isn't the only source of your self-worth.

**Cautions and concerns**

Just like with a death, friends, family, and co-workers may not know what to say, so they distance themselves. You might feel lonely and isolated.

Let others know what happened to you. A lot of other people have gone (or are going) through the same thing. They can provide understanding and validation. They can also offer you coping and job-search tips.

Between the media and the horror stories of friends, family, and co-workers, it's easy to get sucked into the pervasive fear caused by a bad economy. As you scurry to find a new job, you may box away your grief. Yet it can underlie your actions and perhaps sabotage you. For example, you can tear up at inappropriate moments such as a job interview. You need to make time and space to process your feelings.

Seek help if you find yourself doing the following:

- Taking drugs and/or using alcohol to numb your emotions

- Sleeping far too much, or not being able to sleep

- Feeling hopeless (for more than a couple of days)

- Feeling suicidal

- Doing little or nothing all day

Even after people return to work, they can still fear possible job loss and financial insecurity. Future preparation makes a difference in how your loss will hit you. If you go through another termination, being prepared won't take away all of your painful emotions, but it can reduce your anxiety and help you better cope with the circumstances caused by the transition.

In counseling people during layoffs, I found the most resilient people were ones who lived below their means. They kept their expenses down, stayed out of debt as much as possible, and built up their savings and investments. When they lost their jobs, even though they were upset, they told me, "I'll be okay. I have enough saved to be out of work for a while."

During your time without a job, you (and your family) will (hopefully) discover a shift in your priorities. You'll have learned ways to save money and know from hard experience the importance of savings. Promise yourself that when you have a job and steady income again, you won't forget the lessons you've learned. Give yourself (and your family) the peace of mind that comes from making wise financial decisions. Then if a job termination happens to you or your spouse again, even though you may grieve the loss, you'll know that your family can get through it.

For many people, a job loss ultimately turns out to be the best thing that could have happened at the time because it forces them (or their spouse) in a new direction in life. Although at the time, the job loss is devastating, later when people look back, they feel grateful for the job loss because they ...

- Found a better job.

- Started a new business, or increased productivity of one they already had.

- Engaged in artistic pursuits or other activities that brought them pleasure, and they continued after starting a new job.

- Spent quality family time at an important period in their children's lives. Maybe they even decided to stay at home full or part time to raise their children.

It might take time to find work, but stay open to the idea of positive change leading you in new directions. Explore your options with trusted friends and mentors. Sometimes new opportunities are right under your nose, and your fear or other limitations might keep you from seeing them. Keep in mind your other talents that may have nothing to do with your job. Sometimes they are the key to new endeavors. And above all, don't give up hope.

## Loss of a Home

Our home is our own little spot on the planet, our safe haven. We may have worked and sacrificed for years in order to buy it. We often take the security we feel in our home for granted. It's not until it's threatened or taken away from us that we begin to grieve the loss of our shelter as well as our safe haven. Some people mourn for the house like they would a loved one. They may even grieve more than they would the death of a friend or family member.

If you lose your home, you are burdened by organizing, cleaning out, packing, finding a new place to live, saying goodbye to neighbors and friends, moving, then unpacking and assimilating into your new community. There might be little time to grieve. You might be numb throughout the process. Or you might pack and cry at the same time.

Unless you're single and you live alone, the loss of the house affects your whole family. Every family member old enough to understand and feel attached to the house and neighborhood may experience grief. Thus, parents have to deal with their own emotions, plus help their children with the transition and their grief.

cautions and concerns
It's important for parents to be aware that moving can be a major loss for children. Parents need to prepare their children as much as possible beforehand, and make efforts to help children to keep in touch with friends and family members left behind.

You don't have to own a house to lose your home. If you have financial difficulties, you might lose the house or apartment you rent. In addition to your fear from the financial problems, and stress from finding somewhere to live (even if it's transient) and packing and moving, you can grieve the loss of the place you've made your home. You can wonder if you'll find another one.

## What a Home Means

Most people put their heart into their homes. We sacrifice and invest time and money to make a nest for our family, including pets. Our home reflects our personal tastes. Every square inch might be carefully decorated. Or our home might be a work in progress with the improvements only in our heads, but they're ones we dream of making someday. Our house is our refuge. We (and our family) have made happy memories there. Our house is the source for family gatherings or activities with our (and our children's) friends.

The loss of a house can contribute to the breakup of the family. Sometimes various members have to stay with different friends or relatives. Some homeless shelters split men and women, so a father and son might stay in one area or place and a mother and daughter in another. Without the home, relatives might not have a place to gather, which may lessen family ties.

## Selling the Family/Childhood Home

Many people have a home where they spent a chunk of their childhood. This is the home of their "heart," where their memories of their youth reside. Sometimes this is their parents' home; other times it belongs to their grandparents or another relative. They go to this home for holidays and visits with parents and other family members. The house can symbolize family, warmth, security, fun, and love.

Although adult children may have moved out a long time ago, they can balk at selling the family home, even if they understand the necessity. Perhaps their parents want to downsize, or move to another location. Even worse, maybe one or both parents can no longer live alone because they need more care. Whether it's a positive or negative change for their parents, the adult children can grieve the loss of the family home.

It's not just adult children who may grieve the loss of the family home. The individual or couple who makes the decision to move may have grief at leaving their house, even if he or she is excited about the next place. Sometimes, however, it's not their choice. When a couple or individual becomes unable to care for themselves at home, they usually don't leave easily. They often put up a battle to stay in their home. In addition to the grief they feel at no longer living in their own home, they may feel resentful with their children who forced them to move.

# Coping with the Loss of Your Home

You can grieve when it's your choice to move from your house, but being forced out because you can't afford your home, due to foreclosure or some kind of disaster, is devastating. Many times you don't just lose a house, condo, or apartment. You can lose everything you've worked hard for, and may become financially destitute.

Usually the loss of a home involves high stress and anxiety as well as grief. Sometimes the stress and anxiety supersedes your awareness of grief. Part of coping involves realizing you have separate reactions, some of which may be more prevalent at any given time. Therefore, self-care involves trying (as much as possible) to reduce your stress and processing your differing emotions. Chapter 20 goes more into self-care.

## Foreclosure

Before a foreclosure happens, the homeowner usually has a long, downhill financial slide, lasting several months to several years. They may try unsuccessfully to work things out with the bank. This can cause strong feelings of frustration, anger, and bitterness. During the process, they can have trouble sleeping, stress headaches, difficulty eating or eating too much, and other physical signs of stress. As it becomes clear that they'll lose their house, they may begin to grieve.

Many people who've endured foreclosures have found there's a discrepancy in how their loss is treated by others. If the foreclosure was due to a family member suffering a serious illness or a job loss, then they receive compassion. If other people believe the loss happened because of "greed," then they judge or criticize the grievers.

By the time the foreclosure actually happens, you can feel emotionally, mentally, and physically exhausted. Yet you still have to face finding a place to live. Then you need to pack and move, another extremely stressful experience. Throughout the process, you might be aware of your grief, or it might not hit you until you're settled in.

Carol had scrimped for years to buy a home with a big yard. She put the majority of her life savings into the purchase. Carol loved her home. She enjoyed sitting on her back patio and listening to the birds. She'd planted flowers around the yard, and loved to watch her grandsons play on the grass. For the first time in years, her entire family had enough space to gather for holidays and special occasions. After she lost her job, she couldn't afford the mortgage payment. Although she tried to negotiate with the bank, they foreclosed. She moved into a small apartment, cramming her furniture in the rooms, and leaving the rest with her mother. Her life in the apartment kept her grief alive because she hated the space. She couldn't do her crafts or host family celebrations. Although she found another job, it didn't pay as much as her old one. She felt trapped and had no hope of ever saving up enough to afford another house.

## Disaster

Losing a home in a disaster is a frightening, traumatic experience. The disaster can have natural causes—fire, flood, earthquake, tornado, or hurricane—or it can have a human cause. Or like the damage to New Orleans from Hurricane Katrina, where the levees broke, both can contribute to the destruction of homes and property.

If you're in your home when the disaster strikes, you may fear for your life as well as for those of your family and pets. Even if you're not there when it happens, witnessing the aftermath is traumatic. Initially, you can feel shocked, numb, or dazed; grief and other emotions may not hit for a while. (Chapter 4 discusses reaction from trauma.)

In a disaster, you don't just lose your home; your personal possessions are also destroyed. You lose the necessities you need to live, along with objects you value—photos, family heirlooms, things your children made, records and documents, clothing, books, furniture, artwork. Some people have greater ties to possessions than others. Or people can value some possessions, such as a car, and grieve their loss, but not have a lot of emotional attachment toward other things.

The loss is overwhelming. We take for granted the things we use in our everyday lives. Stop and think through a normal day at your house. Go through your routine. Could you even imagine replacing everything?

When I did mental health relief work after Hurricane Katrina, I met with a group of women whose husbands worked for an oil company. The company had relocated them to a different city and into apartments. Two weeks after the event, grief had begun to seep into their awareness. However, they struggled to suppress their emotions because they knew so many other New Orleans residents were far worse off. Unlike many survivors, these women had intact families, their husbands still had work, and they had their cars.

Once the women understood that it was okay to grieve, they shared their feelings with me. They told me about their homes and listed what they missed the most. Many of the women blamed themselves for not packing more possessions when they evacuated before Katrina hit. They'd been used to leaving for a few days when a hurricane approached, and nothing had ever happened before. So they'd only taken a few days of clothes, their pets, and some things to keep their kids entertained because they thought they'd return home in a few days. "Why didn't I grab my jewelry? I had beautiful jewelry," one woman said. She placed her hand over the small gold pendant she wore. "This is all I have now."

Years afterward, people who've lost everything in disasters can cycle through moments where they still look for something of theirs that they lost. For example, they say, "I'll go look at my grandmother's photos." Then the memory returns that they no longer have Grandma's photos. They can grieve the loss all over again.

After your home is destroyed, you have to struggle to gather necessities and find a place to live, which may be difficult if your community is damaged. You have to deal with your insurance company, which may take a while to process your claim. You usually don't receive the complete value for your home and possessions, which is frustrating and can be a huge blow financially. It may take a long time to rebuild, and your neighborhood may never be the same.

Six months after Hurricane Katrina, I returned to Louisiana and visited New Orleans. As I drove through the abandoned Lakeview district, I saw block after block of ravaged homes, many of the brick ones mostly intact but lacking doors and windows. Some were boarded up. Some were left open. Weeds grew several feet high around the houses. Some cars and an occasional boat lay overturned in the yards. There was an emptiness—a lack of life to the whole area. Seeing the destroyed homes was an eerie experience. I could only equate it to scenes of war zones I'd seen on television. Here and there, families had parked a white FEMA trailer in a driveway. A few homeowners attempted to rebuild. I thought how those people must be both desperate and brave. I didn't know how they could bear looking out the windows and seeing the desolation around them. The sight must have been a constant reminder of their loss.

After a disaster, there is usually support (often free) from the Red Cross, FEMA, and other government programs, as well as private counselors. In the midst of trying to survive and cope after a disaster, it's important to take advantage of any support/counseling groups that are offered. Sharing with others who understand and can help you is an important part of your healing.

| cautions and concerns | Millions of pets have been abandoned due to homelessness. It's important for pet owners to find homes for their animals and not just leave them behind in the house. It may be weeks before anyone checks out the home, and pets often die from lack of water and food. |
|---|---|

After a disaster, survival is the foremost concern. People can't even think about their feelings as they try to reunite with loved ones and pets; find food, water, and shelter; and begin to put their life back in order. Grief may pop up at different times, sometimes unexpectedly, sometimes when they pause to think about it. Sometimes people won't grieve until years later. However, it's important that once they take care of survival needs, they do make time to process their emotions.

## Essential Takeaways

- A job loss can cause grief and shame.
- When you're terminated from a job, you also usually have emotional and actual secondary losses to grieve.
- Losing a home can be a devastating financial and emotional loss.
- Disasters can destroy almost everything a person owns, leaving them a lot of losses to grieve.

# chapter 17

# Grief Due to Physical Life Changes

The journey as we age

Living with a chronic condition

The effect on others

How to find acceptance

A common theme among the various physical life changes we can experience, such as aging, disability, permanent injury, or prolonged or terminal illness, is lack of control. Our physical selves are changing for the worse. Our bodies are not working, in pain, constantly fatigued, aging, or our mind is going, and there's little we can do. We see doctors, take medications, use expensive facial creams, maybe eat well and exercise. But ultimately, we can't wave a magic wand and restore our physical and mental health, or have it render us permanently youthful.

Grief is a pervasive part of physical loss, although many sufferers might not be aware of it. Having a chronic condition can disrupt life in many ways. Sufferers may have too much stress and need to process too many other emotions such as anxiety, frustration, anger, fear, or resentment. Their physical discomfort or pain might overwhelm their emotional pain. They might have to carefully control the energy they expend. They may be too busy trying to manage their lives, no matter how limited they are. Just accomplishing small tasks can take so much more preparation and energy for someone with a chronic condition than for other people.

## The Aging Journey

Age happens to everyone who's alive. Yet in our youth-oriented culture, we often don't value the elderly, and, in many cases, we denigrate them. In other cultures, the elderly are regarded as respected sources of wisdom and given preferential treatment. But not in America, where there's no apparent bonus to growing old (except, perhaps, retirement). We watch television and movies and see young, attractive actors, thin and toned, without wrinkles and sagging skin. They've become our standard of beauty, not our elders.

Gray hair or baldness, wrinkles, sagging skin, and age-related weight gain are seen as unappealing. Few people like the thought of growing old—of looking in the mirror and not seeing the face they're used to. So they (as much as possible) avoid the thought of aging. As people age, they can feel ashamed, as if something's wrong with them because they look older. For some people, growing old is disgusting. They don't want to see or think of themselves as old, nor do they want to be reminded that aging will happen to them. They may go to great (and expensive) lengths to prolong looking young.

"I feel ashamed. I can't hide illness and aging when I go out. I'm going to be exposed. I'm afraid people will see me as creepy because on some level, that's how I see myself. It's sad that older people get discounted so much. We're not the repository of knowledge we used to be, just dead brain cells. That's why I like the Internet. There, I don't have to expose myself as old. No one sees my wrinkles and weight gain."

—66-year-old Beth, who struggles with poor health

With aging (especially depending on how much we value our appearance and physical prowess), we can cycle through grief for the rest of our lives. We grieve some aspect of our body that has changed; for example, we grow our first gray hairs or develop lines around our eyes and don't like it. Some time passes, and we hit the next age-related loss: our hair grays more or falls out. We have lines in our foreheads to match the ones around our eyes. We grieve again, and the cycle continues.

Everyone is on the journey to aging, and they have to go through it. A lot of people don't know how (or want) to do that. Instead of mourning their youth, they close the door on their grief and try to stay young forever. But they can't go on like that. At some point, they're going to need to grieve, then accept what is happening. Otherwise, these individuals may end up with a frustrated and unhappy old age.

## Lack of Support

One of the difficult parts of aging is that you don't receive the support you want for your grief. Everyone older than you discounts your feelings because it's worse for them, and they think you should be grateful for what you have. Everyone younger doesn't understand because it hasn't happened to them, and they want to avoid thinking that someday it will. Your contemporaries mostly just want to complain about their own aging problems. However, the positive thing about comparing your changes with your friends is they're usually going through age-related problems as well. You don't feel so alone, and you may be grateful you don't have it as bad as some of your friends.

## Coping with Aging

For some people, growing old can be a time of great creativity or a chance to accomplish things or connect with people in a way they didn't before when they were too busy raising families and/or working. When you're older, you can choose to focus on what is important, instead of what you no longer have. Staying healthy, spending time with family and friends, traveling, and volunteering are cited by older people as things they value.

survival strategies

Don't compare how you look and feel to others. There are always people who are more healthy and attractive and those who have worse physical challenges.

It's important to make mental adjustments to accommodate the changes in your body. Most middle-aged and older people have experienced doing (or attempting to do) something and realizing, "I'm too old for this." From time to time, stop, think about what you need to change because of aging, and let go of it. Allow yourself to grieve the loss, and then keep going. If you don't make the mental adjustment, you can have accidents—for example, climbing on ladders when you no longer have the balance and reflexes you did when you were younger. Your lack of adjustment (and perhaps stubbornness) can lead to an accident, which may be more debilitating (like breaking a hip from a fall).

Dwayne flew his own plane for years. But in his early 60s, he noticed he was losing his quick reflexes. To continue to fly would only put him and others in jeopardy. He took a few weeks to think about it, and (although he wouldn't admit it to anyone, including his wife) grieve. Then he sold his plane.

The best way to cope with aging is to practice good self-care. You will look and feel far better if you eat well, take vitamin and mineral supplements, and exercise—both cardiovascular workouts and weight-training. Part of aging well is having a well-rounded life, which includes different kinds of activities and pastimes. If you have to give up something you enjoy, you still have other areas of your life that bring you pleasure and fulfillment.

Don't focus on the past. Be someone whose life continues to evolve as much as possible. That means ignoring others who may try to define who you "should" be and what you "should" do at your age. Stay true to your own vision about what's possible. But it's not just others you need to be on guard against. Watch yourself. You could be the one holding yourself back.

## Chronic Conditions

A chronic condition can last from six months to permanently impacting your body. Whether you were born with a disability, developed an illness, or lost body parts due to an accident or other circumstance, you have experienced a loss—one that few people really understand unless they've been through something similar. The changes in your body force you to make alterations in your lifestyle and can be mentally, emotionally, and

financially draining. Chronic conditions aren't always disabling, but you
don't have to be disabled to grieve for the loss of your health in some way.

"The lack of control is a big thing. I can eat right. I can exercise. I can take
my vitamins. But nothing, and I mean nothing, is going to stop the disease
from progressing. It's not like getting bronchitis over and over because
you smoke, or being overweight because you eat too much. There's control there."

—Sheryl, who has multiple sclerosis

You can grieve what has happened or is happening to your body. A normal
part of grieving is dwelling on what you lost. And when you live with a
debilitating illness, chronic pain, or other physical loss, every day you
are faced with your loss. For some, moving beyond grief may be difficult.
People with chronic conditions may experience individual effects such as
the following:

- Varying levels of pain or fatigue

- Differing levels of disability

- Symptoms that interact with one another, which can compound the
  effects

- Varying activities they may have to give up

- Varying levels of a support network

- Different responses to treatment

- Social or environmental circumstances that exacerbate the condition

- Varying access to quality medical care

- Pain, medication, or stress causing memory or other impairments

- Varying side effects of medication

Ten years ago, Jenna didn't worry about where she was going or what she'd
have to do to get ready. She didn't think about how she would do all the mom
and wife things that needed to be done. Like everyone else, she just did
them. She went to the mall with her three kids. She shopped for groceries.
She cleaned the house and made meals.

Then her progressive disease worsened. Now she plans her days around important activities so she doesn't overdo it. She's still on her feet around the house, but she uses wheelchairs or electric chairs at the mall or stores. "There is nothing spontaneous about my life," Jenna says. "Mourning your health is like losing a person."

Some researchers and mental-health practitioners have conceptualized grief about a chronic condition or illness as chronic sorrow, and for some people, they may always feel grief about their physical or mental condition. However, for most people, a better description might be cyclical or periodic grief. You may grieve at any point, and then reach a place of balance. There may be times, even long times, when you don't feel grief. But then something happens, whether it's a series of painful or fatiguing days, not being able to do something you want to, seeing someone else who is healthy, not being able to interact with your family in the way you'd like, having a stranger give you a rude response that you know is about your condition, or any number of other things, and it sweeps you right into grief. You never know when you'll experience a cycle of grieving.

For Jim, his chronic condition is always in the back of his thoughts. But it comes to the forefront at times when he sees people doing things he used to be able to do, like when his extended family makes plans to go hiking or water-skiing. He knows they have to go on with their lives, even if he can't join them. He accepts it, but certainly misses the days when he could have gone, too. "I'm sad I can't be part of it," he says.

## Common Emotional Reactions

Some people experience many intense emotions about the changes in their body. Most people, at times, experience several of these feelings simultaneously, or they have one at a time. The type of chronic condition you have, the way it was acquired, your personality, how much support you have, and what you have to give up, all can make a difference in how you feel.

Often the initial response to a diagnosis is shock, fear, anger, or resentment. However, it's not uncommon to feel numb or disbelieving. Your emotions are frozen, and you might need to jump into a course of treatment, instead of allowing yourself to feel. However, if you've struggled for a while with symptoms that were difficult to diagnose, you also might initially feel some relief as in, "Okay, now at least I know what's wrong with me." Or, "I knew I wasn't crazy."

Once reality sets in, you can have a wash of feelings. You can feel betrayed by your body, or angry at yourself, God, doctors, or others who may have contributed to your condition. You may have various levels of fear and anxiety; for example, you can feel terrified about what's happening to you, or what may happen in the future (like the pain worsening). You can feel shame or embarrassment if your appearance changes. You may also feel or think that others are judging you, which feels shameful. You can feel ashamed about having to depend on others.

Mara's cancer treatments made her thick black hair fall out, and she had to grieve for her altered appearance. She hated the blatant stares from other people as she went about her business. There were plenty of times of pain and fear, like when she contracted a severe infection and thought she might die. She prayed and bargained with God, promising if she lived, she would do good for others.

Most people with chronic conditions go through mental and emotional readjustment. Then they reach an attitude of acceptance. It's almost a shrug of the shoulders and a "there's nothing I can do about it, so I just deal with it" attitude. If the illness is degenerative in some way, the individual may have to readjust to and accept it many times over the course of a lifetime.

> **Expressions of Grief**
>
> "I don't usually wallow in grief about my condition. It is what it is. People think I'm strong, but mostly I think why bother to live my life wishing it were something different. It's not. Buck up and deal. Everyone has *some* cross they bear and some people's are worse than mine. I could cry about everything I've lost, but that only gives me wet cheeks and puffy eyes ... it doesn't change anything. I choose to get up in the morning and be grateful I'm still on my feet, albeit unsteadily."
>
> —53-year-old Liz

## Secondary Losses from Chronic Conditions

When you suffer from a chronic condition, you may be hit with a long list of secondary losses you need to grieve. The chronic condition caused limitations, which can be minor or major. These changes can impact many, if not all, areas of your life. One common area is financial difficulties. You have medical bills and may also need things not covered by insurance, such as a specialized wheelchair, that you have to pay out of your own pocket. You may have to cut back on your work, or give it up altogether. Some other things you might need to grieve are the loss of the following:

- A pain-free body
- Mobility or ability
- Physical strength and stamina
- A former support system
- Independence
- Self-esteem
- A spouse through divorce
- Your role within your family
- Loss of hopes and dreams of the future
- Loss of certain activities you enjoyed

## Affected Relationships

The person with the chronic condition isn't the only one who may grieve because of his or her physical changes. Friends and family are also affected; their lives change, too. Marriages are especially impacted because the spouse needs to step in as the caregiver. Sometimes this happens abruptly, such as with a stroke or accident. Other times there's a slow deterioration. The relationship changes, and the spouse realizes what the wedding vow "in sickness and in health" really means.

Spouses, too, have to grieve the loss of the partner-that-was. They can grieve the loss of their former lifestyle. They can grieve for the hopes and dreams they had for the future that they now must let go of. The future looks different now. Perhaps bleaker. Perhaps more frightening. They may not allow themselves to feel grief or, if they do, to talk about it with their partner. They think, "My spouse is the one who's really suffering; how can I possibly grieve?" Some marriages may break under the pressure, and the spouses divorce—another loss. Others grow closer, and the two appreciate each other and value what they do have together. "One of the most important things I've learned from loss and grieving is that we don't really know love until we need it to live," said Rachael about her husband's illness. "That love is so much deeper and empowering when it's real—when it's tested."

## Caregiving

Caregiving can be a huge burden on a spouse or other family members. Sometimes they have to totally change their lives to accommodate their partner's condition. Caregiving can be physically, emotionally, and mentally draining. The caregiver may not sleep well from worry or because of the need to help their spouse throughout the night. They can give up some of the very things that reduce stress, such as exercise, personal time, enjoyable activity, and time with friends, so they may not replenish their energy.

> **cautions and concerns** Depression in the elderly and in people with chronic conditions can go undiagnosed. Many physical symptoms may be due to unresolved grief and depression.

The stress can take a toll on the caregiver's health. They may grapple with their own illnesses or conditions, yet still try to take care of their husband or wife. They can worry that enough of their spouse's needs aren't being met. If the time comes to move the mate into a facility for greater care, they can feel both relieved and guilty. They might have to grieve another loss—that of living together.

The needs of caregiving often isolate spouses. It's important for the caregiver to seek support from friends, family, and organizations. Support groups (whether in person or online) can be a lifeline for caregivers, helping them share and process overwhelming emotions. They can also receive coping tips for the condition. Look up caregiving resources online, or go to websites for the specific condition of the person you're taking care of.

## Parental Grief

When a child is born with a disability, the parents have a major adjustment to make. They expected a healthy baby. They had imagined life with their child and had so many dreams for his or her future. A child born with a disability can shatter those dreams. They may have to grieve the loss of the "perfect" fantasy baby they had imagined, before they accept and love their baby as he or she is.

For other parents, the baby is their longed-for child, no matter what, and they may not grieve initially. Regardless of their emotions, parents don't usually have much time to grieve. They're thrust into education about the baby's condition and treatment. They may have a lot more to learn and do in regard to taking care of their little one. The extra care and attention needed for the baby may last throughout childhood, adolescence, and beyond.

Other people's reactions can compound the parents' emotional reaction to their baby's birth. The parents may be seen as objects of pity. The baby's disability could be considered a tragedy, a burden, or a failure. The comments of family, friends, and co-workers can make the parents feel pain, shame, and resentment.

Parents (and other family members) of disabled children need to change their expectations of their baby. What might be a normal development in another child, such as walking, talking, or being potty-trained, can be a major achievement for their baby. Their emotions can range between grief for the child's suffering and all she can't do, to joy for the smallest achievement.

Parents can also grieve when a child experiences an accident or illness that gives him a chronic condition, perhaps causing mental and/or physical changes. If the situation was life-threatening, the parents can feel immensely relieved their child survived. They might also have been traumatized by the experience. They can be too caught up in the care of the child to realize they are grieving. They might not feel grief for a while. Or they might try to stop themselves, saying, "I should be grateful he's alive, not grieving what's changed."

Many parents report loving their child fiercely, perhaps even more than they would otherwise, because they have to fight so hard for every milestone. Depending on the illness or condition, they may also have the painful awareness that their child will probably die before them. Therefore, they cherish the time they do have. They feel their child teaches them so much, and they're better people because of their child's condition.

| Expressions of Grief | "Life is going to throw stuff at you. It's like paintball. If you get hit by a ball and start crying, you're just going to be a target. Keep on going, keep on going, then you're good." |
|---|---|

—16-year-old Hayley, who has celiac disease, vision problems, and speech disorders

## Finding Acceptance

Not all people will grieve physical losses. Some people are pragmatic. They accept what's happened and move on without needing to mourn their loss. Most others, though, will grieve. Grieving plays an important part in acceptance. Once you mourn the loss of who you were, you can accept the person you've become. But if you block your grief, then you might also block your path to acceptance. Acceptance involves making peace with who you are at this time. It's coming to the conclusion, "I'm not my body; it's part of me, but not who I am."

When you have a chronic condition, it's important to manage your physical and mental health. A good way to keep yourself on track is to keep an action journal. The journal is for yourself, and also helps your doctors and other health-care providers understand better what's happening with you. In addition to writing about your feelings, you can list the following:

- Symptoms, including the intensity and duration
- Medications, including the dosage and time taken
- Reactions
- What and when you eat
- Exercise, including when, duration, intensity, type, and how you feel afterward

- Other treatments you try

- Other medical information you receive from your doctors, and find through research

- Activities

- Amount and type of work you do

- Social engagement

It's good to participate in a support group, either in person or online. There you'll find other people who are going through what you are. They'll understand in a way those who are healthy cannot. In addition to support, you'll receive education, coping tips, and referrals to other resources.

"I really try to live by there is no 'I used to.' There's only 'I can now.' It really is a much more positive way of going through life."

—Larry, about his medical condition

Those who cope the best with their conditions (or those of family members) focus on what they can still do, instead of what they can't. They learn to accept their limitations and appreciate what's good about their life. They try not to live in the past, and enjoy their memories, instead of becoming bitter about how their lives are in comparison. They focus on being grateful they're alive and cherish the time with their loved ones.

## Essential Takeaways

- Aging causes changes in your body that you may need to grieve.
- When you have a chronic condition, you struggle with a loss of control.
- You can grieve for beloved family members who are coping with a chronic condition, as well as for the changes that take place in your life because of it.
- Finding acceptance means focusing on what you can still do, rather than what you no longer can do.

# Part 4

# Recovery

"Will I ever recover from my loss?" is a common question when people are grieving. You may wonder if (or worry that) your grief will never end. The answer is "Yes, it will." The journey may take some time (often far longer than you want). What you do (and don't do) along the way will make all the difference while you're grieving and aid you in your recovery.

This part helps you explore bereavement resources, such as groups. Others who are grieving, or who have been through the same loss as you, are often your best source of comfort. But books and grief materials can also help. You find plenty of tips for self-care, and also learn how you can help others to best help you. In addition, this part discusses how you can heal, and what will help you move on, so you can travel from grief into recovery.

# chapter 18

# Help from Others

How bereavement support can help

Getting professional help

Choosing your counselor wisely

Social support

Grief from bereavement can be bewildering because it's such a change from your normal experience and way of being. Suffering in silence and ignorance won't aid your grief journey; it will only inhibit it. Reaching out to others, and allowing them to support you, is a vital way to sustain you as you journey through your time of mourning. The reality is that, like most people, you'll depend on friends and relatives and may not feel the need for more support. However, if you do, there's a range of help available, depending on your needs.

Because much of our society has a death-denying mentality, the decision to seek counseling is often a very big step. It's not uncommon for grievers to live behind an "I'm fine" façade. To the external world they try to appear as if they've recovered. They may grieve in secret. Therefore, it's good for them to find other means of support to aid them in healing their grief.

## Grief Counseling

A grief counselor may be a psychotherapist or psychologist who has special training in grief. Or the counselor may be a minister/priest/rabbi or lay person who has taken classes and received training in grief. A hospice medical social worker or chaplain can also provide counseling support (whether or not your loved one died in hospice care). Often these types of counselors have also experienced their own losses, which propelled them into the grief recovery field. However, personal experience with loss isn't necessary in a good counselor.

People often have the (misguided) belief that they shouldn't burden others with their problems or emotions. Or they may feel guilty if they rely too much on someone. Perhaps they have family members or friends who are uncomfortable with their grief and unknowingly convey to the griever that they don't want to talk about the death, or they are selfish and don't care about the griever's feelings. With counseling, you can feel relieved of the guilt because you are paying a counselor to listen to you, seeing someone who already draws a salary from an organization, or is a volunteer who chooses to listen to other's grief stories. Thus, you don't have to feel like a burden to your counselor.

> **Expressions of Grief**
>
> "We all need someone—whether a friend, relative, or therapist, whom we can share everything with—our grief, despair, hurt, the 'why me?' questions. And he or she accepts and loves us through it all."
>
> —44-year-old Mark

## Bereavement Groups

A bereavement group provides an empathetic, supportive environment with people who understand what you're going through because they are, too. In the group, members discover what they're feeling is normal, and they provide comfort for each other. They can learn about grief reactions and acquire coping skills that can help them get through their time of mourning. They also see other people surviving their loss, which can give them hope. Sometimes members become friends outside of the group. Here are some of the first reassuring themes you find in a bereavement group:

- You're not crazy.

- You're not alone.

- You're not as different as you think.

- Nothing is "wrong" with you.

- You're not losing your mind.

There are several types of bereavement groups. One has members who have all suffered a similar type of loss—for example, the death of a spouse. The other kind of group has people in it who've lost all different types of loved ones, across a range of circumstances. These groups can be composed of people in various stages of the grief journey, or they may be for the newly bereaved. Both types of groups can be helpful.

Some groups are short term. They meet for a set number of sessions, and the same people stay together throughout, without new members joining. Other groups are open and continuous, and people rotate in, remain for as long as they need (which may be as short as a few weeks or as long as several years), and then leave. So the group can have a shifting population.

However, for more severe and unique losses, such as suicide or murder, it's more beneficial to be with people who've experienced the same loss and who share issues specific to that type of death. For example, with suicide, the grief response includes relief (because the deceased had severe drug abuse or mental illness), self-blame or guilt, the endless "why" questions, and the recurring, intrusive memory of the way the person died. (Chapter 5 discusses suicide in greater detail.)

Sometimes bereavement groups are more like meetings. They are free (or low cost) and open to the public. You can drop in when you want. Some of the people attend regularly, and others just come when they feel the need to.

After Honey's husband of 41 years died, she attended a bereavement group for two years. The group had about 50 members, and they met twice a month. During the meeting, they were divided into small groups, where they shared their stories and feelings. Honey met many people who had the same problems as she did. Some of the subjects the group members discussed were coping, positive thinking, taking care of themselves, stress reduction, and the various emotions comprising grief. When Honey finally left the bereavement group, she felt ready to go on with her life.

What really matters with bereavement groups is that the facilitator is caring and knowledgeable, and that everyone respects each other's loss and grieving process. It's important that the environment is emotionally safe, confidential, and supportive.

Usually bereavement groups are found in hospitals, churches, and mortuaries. However, individual counselors or a psychotherapy/grief recovery center may also have one or more groups available.

After the work of grieving is finished, the friendships made in the grief group can continue on. Sometimes the members realize they don't want to end the relationships, even though they've moved through their grief. So they find ways to step into the next stage of their lives together. They can travel together, or take up an activity, such as golf or bridge. One example I know of is several women from a bereavement class who decided to start a Red Hat Society group, and they continue to meet monthly.

## Internet Support Groups

The Internet has spawned a wave of groups and sites dedicated to educating and helping people with all kinds of losses, especially bereavement. The nice thing about Internet support groups is they are instantly accessible. If you want to connect with someone, all you have to do is get on the Internet through your computer or phone connection. This is important for those days and nights when you can barely function and can't bring yourself to get dressed and go out. The Internet is also helpful if you have what you believe are particularly shameful or embarrassing feelings, for example, feeling like you contributed to the demise of the person or are glad he or she is gone.

Even if it's the middle of the night when you can't call family or friends, others are on the Internet. Maybe they are from different countries, but are coping with similar feelings. You don't have to interact with someone online; instead, you can post about your feelings on a bereavement site, a place you know others will understand. Just the act of writing about your feelings and connecting with others can feel comforting. Also, the other people online are in various stages of their own grief journeys, and can give you support with yours because they've been there and survived.

Not every grief website is beneficial. Trust your instincts. If the messages seem critical or unproductive, don't go back to that site.

## Pastoral Grief Counseling

Pastoral counseling (from a priest, rabbi, or minister) in the grief process can play a significant role toward healing and restoring life to a person with religious faith. Pastors, rabbis, and priests often have resources that other grief counselors don't. If the person coming for counseling has been a part of the pastor's congregation, there's likely some level of a pre-existing relationship between them. Many times the parishioner feels a closeness and trust of the pastor because he has heard the pastor speak in sermons and classes for some period of time and interacted with him or her in the organization's social and community service events. The pastor also knows and cares about the griever and may also miss the deceased if she was a member of the congregation. Even if the pastor does not know the grieving parishioner well, the trust level may still be high.

The pastor and griever also have shared beliefs, which gives them a base of support and understanding. Because of the established relationship and trust, the griever may be more able to absorb the pastor's comfort and solace. Many pastors see their role as an attempt to be a tangible symbol of the love and presence of God. Pastoral counseling puts grief and loss into the context of faith and addresses the question, "Where is God in my suffering?" This type of counseling may also include prayer—either by both praying together, or by the pastor praying for the griever.

# Psychotherapy

Psychotherapy or counseling is a helpful way to understand and process your grief reactions with someone else who is trained to help you heal. You may choose to go to counseling just to receive the extra support. Whether or not you're aware of it, seeking help is a statement to yourself that you take your needs seriously. Here are other reasons:

- You're feeling stuck in your grief.
- You're having a hard time coping with your loss.

- You're having difficulty functioning in life.

- Your loss is causing relationship or family problems.

- You (or a family member) are abusing drugs or alcohol.

- You (or a family member) are having suicidal thoughts.

- You (or a family member) are having recurring, painful thoughts, or intrusive memories or images.

- You're having a hard time practicing self-care and you (or others) are afraid you're putting your well-being or even your life in danger.

Many people feel shame for being emotional following a loss, or because they can't "get over it" as soon as others think they should. People who are feeling shame about the intensity and duration of their grief often judge themselves as weak. Yet the capacity to seek out therapy is actually a sign of strength because it takes courage to acknowledge your feelings, especially when these emotions are filled with so much pain.

## Picking a Good Counselor

When you're seeking counseling, it's vital that you have a good clinician. You don't want to waste your time and money with someone who won't help you, and who may in fact be harmful. In your initial session, you want to feel three things:

- The counselor is knowledgeable about your issues, in this case dealing with grief.

- You feel the counselor understands you and what you're going through.

- The counselor gives helpful feedback. (You might not always *like* what's said or suggested, but deep down, you know it's right.)

If you don't feel these three things, then don't go back to the counselor. Go to someone else. Keep looking until you find the counselor who feels right for you. One of the best ways to find a counselor is a referral from someone else who has worked with a good one. Also check the Resources appendix for some websites.

## Healing Experience

People sometimes avoid psychotherapy because they think that seeing a "shrink" means something is "wrong" with them. Therefore, therapy is seen as a shameful experience. It's not until the grief becomes too much to bear, or there are too many negative consequences to their feelings and actions, that they are motivated to seek help. (Or someone else strong-arms them into it.) It's a case of the frying pan of pain becoming so hot that they jump into what seems like the fire of shame.

Yet, when they land in the fire, they find that the flames are just an illusion. With the right therapist, counseling is a healing experience. People who start out reluctant often become strong supporters. Counseling can provide you with the structure and context to help you on your grief journey. Counseling offers the following:

- Nonjudgmental support

- Validation of your feelings

- Release for blocked emotions

- Guidance

- New perspectives

- Help to process and heal old wounds that may tie in with the loss and your grief

- Help for relationship issues exacerbated or caused by the loss and reactions to the loss

- A chance to plan actions and evaluate how they work for you

# The Support of Friends

As I've said throughout this book, the support of others is one of the most important aspects of your grief journey. People can receive encouragement and emotional sustenance from relatives, friends, neighbors, co-workers, and people from church or temple and other organizations they belong to. People can aid you with various parts of your journey. Many will be there initially, only to fade away. Some may stay for the whole part, and some may enter later, or come out of nowhere at a certain point when you need them.

When Barbara's 2-year-old son Max died, she survived by having two women who'd also lost children scoop her up and take her to meetings held by Compassionate Friends (an organization that supports parents who've lost children; see the Resources appendix). The two stayed by her side throughout her long grief journey. Even though the three women hadn't initially been close, they became dear and lifelong friends.

Everyone grieves in his or her own way. It often takes individuals a long time to come to terms with a loved one's death. Yet many people expect the bereaved to "snap out of it" within a relatively brief period of time. Sometimes, people feel powerless and useless if they don't feel they can provide enough "help."

survival strategies

The worst thing an outsider or well-meaning friend can do is tell a person when or how to grieve or what he should do with his emotions. Understand that help doesn't have to come in the form of advice or solutions; it may simply be listening and empathizing. Don't try to take away someone's pain. Just be with her, acknowledge the person's pain, and offer support.

Develop a support network you can rely on. Sometimes reaching out is difficult when you're in so much pain, especially if you don't know how another individual and your social groups will react to your grief. You're vulnerable and more easily hurt when you're grieving. Unfortunately, many times the only way to know if someone can support you in the way you need is to interact with him. It's often trial and error with each person. Even a best friend, who knows you well and loves you dearly, might not be good for you at this time, especially if she is trying to control your grief journey in some way. However, your friend may be open to your feedback about what you need and adaptable in changing how she is with you.

Concentrate on the kindnesses of others, and do your best to let go of what you perceive as slights or criticism. People can be thoughtless or ignorant, but they usually don't mean to hurt you. They might feel bad if they knew they did.

Sometimes our good friends want us to hurry through our grief, not only so we won't be in pain, but so we'll return to our old selves—the one they're familiar with. They may not understand that, in some ways, you'll never be the same, although you might return to the person they enjoy spending time with. Sometimes, it's good to make friends or talk to someone new. They don't have expectations of you from before and may be more apt to allow you to just be who you are now.

As important as support is, people who are grieving need to balance interacting with others and taking time for solitude. Some individuals are introverts, who replenish by taking alone time and doing solitary activities. (You can be an outgoing introvert who's good with people. You just recharge your batteries by solitude.) Others are extroverts who feel revitalized by interacting with people. Therefore, individuals will often revert to their natural introvert or extrovert state when it comes to coping with grief.

Some people don't want to be alone at all for a while, and others just want to be alone. There are ways to support both introverts and extroverts when they're grieving. If you're friends with someone who wants solitude, you can quietly join them for walks or sitting and gazing out the window. Your silent presence can mean a lot. You're there if they want to talk or just think. However, if they truly need solitude, respect that. Don't pressure them to change. But do continue to let them know you're there if they want company. Send regular e-mails, texts, cards, and leave phone messages. Occasionally give them an invitation to do something, but allow them to start participating at their own pace.

Extroverts often can't have too much company and attention from others. They need friends and family to spend time with them, and they feel more upset when they're alone. Extroverts need to be careful not to get caught up in socializing as a way to fix their feelings or keep their pain at bay. While an occasional party is good, they need to balance people time with grief time. When you interact with a grieving extrovert, the best thing you can do is to enable him to talk to you about the deceased and his feelings of grief. This way, his needs for both companionship and processing his emotions are met.

## Essential Takeaways

- Sometimes seeking grief counseling is the best thing you can do to aid your grief journey.

- Psychotherapy offers professional assistance in helping you recover from your loss.

- Consider psychotherapy or counseling if you need extra support.

- Friends and family are often the best forms of support.

# chapter 19

# Children and Grief

| |
|---|
| Developmental differences |
| Helping children understand bereavement |
| Helping kids cope with the funeral |
| Confiding in trusted adults |
| Grief from divorce |

Children grieve, and children are affected by the grief of their family members. Children grieve the death of relatives and other people who are important to them. They grieve when they have to move. They grieve when their parents divorce. They grieve the loss of a pet. All of these situations can be emotionally damaging to the child. How the parent(s) prepares them for the loss and helps them cope afterward makes a big difference in their resiliency. The grief of children isn't necessarily going to look like the grief of adults. It's important to know how children grieve as well as find ways to help them deal with their changed circumstances and their emotions.

## Grief at Different Developmental Stages

In order to help a bereaved child, you need to keep in mind where he or she is developmentally. Each stage can have its own problems, conflicts, and adjustment issues. A toddler, for example, is going to react differently to a loss than a teen will. Children vary and so does their understanding of loss and reactions of grief. In addition to age, you need to consider the child's …

- Cognitive ability.

- Level of maturity.

- Self-esteem.

- Life experiences.

- Relationship to the person, place, object, or pet.

- Level of preparation beforehand.

- Support network.

## Telling the Truth

Truthful statements can diminish some of the child's anxiety about the loss because he or she understands (as much as possible) what has happened and what will come next. When it's time to break the news of the loss (or impending loss), have the person with whom the children are closest tell them what's happening. If the loss involves the departure of one of the parents—for example, in a divorce—it's best if both parents share the news as soon as the loss seems definite.

Children are sensitive to the stress and possible preoccupation or other changes in mood or behavior of the parents and other relatives. They may wonder what's wrong or think they are the problem. With advance notice, the child has a chance to get used to the idea, to ask questions, to grieve, and to say goodbye.

It's important to explain the loss in a straightforward manner. Use simple, age-appropriate terms. Be honest, but don't give children so many details that they are overwhelmed. Then invite questions by saying, "Do you have any questions for me?"

cautions and concerns

Don't tell children how (or how not) to feel. Saying "Be happy" or "Don't be angry" only teaches them that their feelings are wrong.

Children can take things in a literal manner. When talking about bereavement, use the word "died" rather then fell asleep, passed away, was lost, or is in heaven. You can say, "died and went to heaven." Don't say, "God took (name)." For younger children, also make sure you explain that the person can't come back home.

Sometimes the loss makes the child very emotional. She can cry or act out, or become dramatic, angry, or accusatory, all difficult reactions for parents to cope with during the best of times. But during a major loss, the parent is stressed, grieving, preoccupied, overwhelmed, and/or perhaps very busy. The parent may not have the patience, energy, and emotional fortitude to handle the child's grief.

Many losses involve partings, and children need permission and encouragement to say goodbye. Brainstorm how they are going to miss the person, place, object, or pet. You might help them formulate what they can say. Encourage them to make a goodbye card. Then give them the opportunity to say goodbye. For example, drive to the friend's home before the move, or the hospital to make a last visit to a dying relative. Afterward, talk to them about their feelings about the experience.

Like adults, children need to know that their feelings and reactions of grief are normal. Teach children the words for various emotions and what they mean. The larger vocabulary they have of "feeling words," the more they can communicate when they're upset and the less they have to act them out. Here are some examples:

- "Sounds like you're feeling (emotion)."

- "Are you feeling (emotion)?"

- "When I make a face like you just did, I feel angry. Are you angry?"

Sometimes children do have the words to express the feelings behind their actions, but no one asks them questions to elicit the answers. They may need help expressing their grief. Look for their anger, fear, or sadness in their play and help them talk about it.

When Andy was 2, his 4-month-old brother died of sudden infant death syndrome (SIDS). For the next months, Andy spent a lot of time shooting his cap gun at the sky. Finally, his mom asked him what he was doing, and he told her, "I hate God for taking Sammy, and I'm gonna kill him." By encouraging children to verbalize their feelings, you can see where they are struggling, and, like with Andy, if there's a misconception that needs to be addressed. Andy obviously required more conversations about God and death. He also needed other ways to express his anger, as well as his other feelings.

## Younger Children

Children 8 years old and younger almost universally react to a loss by regressing to a previous level. It's their way of coping. They rebuild by going back to an earlier time when they felt more secure. This stage can last from a few weeks to six months. Some regressive behaviors are the following:

- Clinginess
- Baby talk
- Thumb-sucking
- Wetting their pants, either during the day and night, or only at night
- Crawling into bed with a parent or siblings

As frustrating as the regressive behavior can be to the parents or caregivers, it's important for them to remain patient. Don't punish or shame the child for this behavior. Continue to comfort and reassure him or her. Gradually the child will progress to more advanced behavior.

People may think younger children don't need to be told the truth because they wouldn't understand it anyway, or they might become upset. However, children are very sensitive to the feelings of those around them. They can have limited and inaccurate understanding, and don't always get cause-and-effect relationships. When something feels bad to them, they might think their thoughts or actions caused the problem or situation. They need the reassurance that they are not bad and what's happened is not their fault.

Children in the 3- to 6-year age range have concrete thinking, which is very literal thinking. Children at this stage don't have the cognitive development to understand more abstract concepts. If you say, "We lost grandma last night," they might wonder why you're not going to find her. Young children also don't understand that death is a final event. They can wonder when the deceased is coming back. They repeatedly ask questions such as, "When is Mommy/Daddy coming home?"

## Tweens

When a loss occurs, tweens (9 to 12 years old) tend to shut down and not want to talk. They may not understand what they're feeling and need some help to talk about what's going on with them. You can leave them alone, but keep inviting them to talk to you. The invitation is what's important.

When a tween has a major loss, many of their friends don't understand what they're going through, which makes them intensely lonely. Finding other children who've endured similar losses is also a way to help them not feel so isolated. Put them in activities where you know other kids have endured the loss, or get to know some of the other parents and schedule play dates.

## Teens

Adolescence can be a difficult and complex time. Teens are trying to break away from their parents and assert their own individuality. Their bodies are developing and flooding with hormones. Because many teens appear physically mature, adults may think they can handle the loss like adults. Maybe adults don't realize the human brain continues to develop until the early 20s. Adolescents can be especially vulnerable to losses and grieving because so much in their bodies and lives is changing.

Teens often hide their pain from others. They may look like everything's okay on the surface, while on the inside they are in deep pain. Although they may confide in their friends (but sometimes with grief they don't) their family may not realize the teen is struggling.

| cautions and concerns | Sometimes children won't come to their parent for help or to ask questions because they're concerned about the parent's pain. They fear the parent will cry, and the children try to protect them. |
| --- | --- |

In the first weeks after the loss, adolescents can feel vulnerable from their grief. They may seek distractions to keep them from feeling, which can make them become stuck in their grief. Although some distractions may be healthy in themselves, such as sports or extracurricular activities, both, if done in excess, can suppress their pain. Even bigger problems come when the teen tries to push away pain—acting out in ways that can get them in trouble, such as drinking, doing drugs, and having promiscuous sex.

Kids may already have peer pressure to engage in these activities. A teen who feels empty inside, full of pain, and lonely is vulnerable to these temporary fixes and the lure of fitting in with a certain crowd. It's vital to help these grieving teens understand that these behaviors won't heal their pain. After the temporary "high" caused by drugs, alcohol, and sex, they'll return to their previous way of feeling, and perhaps even feel worse. They then may continue to indulge as a way to flee their grief and shame.

The behavior of a normal teen and a grieving teen can look the same— mood swings, becoming argumentative, isolating from the rest of the family and maybe even friends. It's difficult to know if she might be in trouble. Becoming too isolated—dropping out of activities or not keeping plans with friends—may be a sign that she needs more help. A prolonged (as opposed to a few weeks) drop in grades is another danger sign.

Not caring about anything is often a part of grief, and the teen should eventually move through these feelings. But the choices teens make while in this state may cause problems. Dropping grades and skipping classes can lead to further consequences. While they might not care about graduating and college now, when their grief passes they may be upset by the damage they've caused themselves.

**cautions and concerns**

Boys may have a harder time than girls because they may try to conform to the "manly" stereotype—macho guys don't show negative emotion (unless it's anger), and they certainly don't cry. Plus their male friends may feel uncomfortable with the griever's emotions and retreat or try to make him laugh, or pick on him, reinforcing the idea that it's not normal or safe for a male to cry.

Many schools offer peer-counseling groups, which can be a good experience for grieving teens to help process their feelings. Peer counselors are specially trained students who lead the groups. Because the group only consists of students, teens have an easier time opening up.

# Children and Bereavement

Children lose grandparents, parents, siblings, other relatives, teachers, friends, and pets. The way the person died, and the child's relationship with him or her, makes a difference in how the child initially reacts. If the death was expected, and the child was prepared beforehand, the passing impacts the child differently than if the loss was sudden.

When a person (or a pet) leaves or dies, very young children may begin searching for him or her. They look for the presence of the person in various places in the house. Or they may wait at the door, or crawl into a favorite chair and sit. Around ages 6 to 9, children start to understand that death is irreversible. They comprehend that all living things die. But they think they won't die. Middle school–age children understand death is inevitable, affects everyone, and is final.

Children have a primary need for security. They need to know they'll be taken care of and loved. They need both physical and emotional comfort. Physical comfort consists of hugs, snuggles, an arm across the shoulders, a shoulder squeeze, hand-holding, or a touch on the arm. Emotional comfort is about positive attention, reassurance, and receiving answers to their questions.

When children try to share their feelings, as much as possible, give them your full attention. You want to send them the message that they *and* their emotions are important to you. Validate their feelings by telling them what you understand. Sometimes it's not about the words. A hug, or the touch of your hand on their knee, arm, or shoulder, may be more important than what you say.

Children have a continuing relationship with the deceased, especially a parent. This relationship manifests in dreams, talking about her with toys or in play, talking directly to the deceased, thinking about her, and wondering what the loved one would say or do if she were present now. This relationship with the deceased isn't set in stone; it changes as the child matures and grows in understanding. As the child reaches different life stages or has certain life events, he or she can miss the loved one in a whole different way.

Children may feel anger about their loss and tend to act it out, which is unproductive. They need a healthy outlet for their anger. Sports are good. However, not all children are interested in athletics, so you might need to be more creative in order to help them.

When 12-year-old Jason's dad died, his mom could tell he was angry, but she couldn't get him to talk about it. So she went to a thrift store and bought a cheap set of ugly dishes. She brought them home and had Jason put on safety glasses and a long-sleeved shirt and pants. Then she had him go to the outside of the garage where there was a corner that had cement walls and floor. She had him stand about 10 feet from the wall. She told him to think of his dad's death, feel angry, and throw the dishes at the wall as hard as he could. (He had to sweep up the pieces afterward.) Then she left him alone. When Jason came back in the house, his face was red, although all he said was, "That was cool!" But for the next few days, his mom noticed that he seemed more like his old self and less angry. She told him to let her know if he ever wanted another box of old dishes. A few times over the following years, when Jason felt the anger build up again, he took his mom up on the offer.

| survival strategies | It's good for children of all ages to write about or draw pictures expressing their feelings. Parents and caregivers can use the writings and artwork as a way to facilitate discussion. Teens, however, may not want to share their journals or artwork with anyone. Encourage them to write a poem, eulogy, or song, which they can show to, or perform for, others. |
| --- | --- |

## Younger Children

When a death occurs in the family, it's an intense and perhaps chaotic time of upheaval. Younger children pick up on the cues around them. They can feel frightened by the strength of the grief around them. They may not receive the comforting they need.

People are often afraid to bring up the loss to children. Some may even think it's good they forget the person so they won't miss him. However, the opposite is true. Children need to feel a connection with the dead parent.

They need to express their thoughts and feelings about the parent and the death. Stories and memories are important to the child. The child needs the connection that stories provide to their deceased parent, both when they are young and as they grow.

Five-year-old Timmy's beloved grandfather, Joe, passed away early Christmas morning. When Timmy went to his grandparents' home, he hugged his grandma and told her, "Grandpa went to stay with God." A few months passed, and Timmy began getting stomachaches. His parents took him to several doctors, trying to find out the cause, and there was nothing. Finally, at the recommendation of the last doctor, they took him to a counselor. Everyone thought that perhaps his stomachaches had to do with starting kindergarten. Instead, Timmy told the counselor that his grandpa had died, and he missed him. He also asked the counselor, "When you die, why don't people talk about you anymore?" It made Timmy sad that everyone had forgotten about Grandpa.

Although the family still grieved for and talked about Joe, they rarely did so in front of the kids. It wasn't intentional, but when the kids were around, they kept on happy subjects. From that day forward, the family talked about Grandpa in front of and with Timmy. The next year on Christmas morning, the family and close friends went to Joe's favorite restaurant. They talked about Joe and laughed and cried. The experience felt so good, the family has since continued the tradition, and the attendees fluctuate every year, but the core group of relatives remains.

When Timmy was 12, he told everyone that his favorite part of Christmas was when he got to go with everyone for breakfast, walk on the beach and the pier, and remember Grandpa. He said it made him happy to know that Grandpa still spent Christmas with the family.

Young children can act out their grief through play. Sometimes they just do this a few times. Other times it lasts for a long time. The longer it lasts, the more they may need help in processing their loss.

After Lynn's baby brother died, she, her sister, and the other girls in the neighborhood spent most of their time playing "dead baby." They'd play with their dolls and give them diseases, kill them, and then have elaborate funerals. This went on for a couple of years. Once the girls were told to quit playing with their dolls and go do something else. So they moved the funeral and burial to the back alley where no adults ever came.

If the play continues for a while, talk to the children and try to help them process in other ways. Both Lynn and Timmy's story illustrate what can happen if the death isn't discussed in the family. In Lynn's case, her parents didn't talk about the baby's death, nor did she ever see them cry (although they did privately). The lack of discussion increased her need to dramatize the family pain through her play. The duration of the play mirrored the length of her parents' grief.

Create a way for the child to say goodbye, especially if he is younger. A good ritual is to have the child write a letter or draw a picture for the deceased. Then tie the message on a balloon that the child releases into the sky. The balloon is used as a symbol of letting go. It helps the child realize the person who died is apart from him. The balloon gives meaning to the death because it's a ceremony at the child's level.

## Older Children

When someone they love dies, adolescents are often surprised at the level of pain they feel. They may have no reference for it. Nor do they have the experience of adults—which tells them that they will get through this. Adolescents need to be educated about grief, especially how everyone grieves differently. They need to know the grief journey may take a long time. Reassure teens of the following:

- Numbness is a normal reaction. (Adolescents are often confused when they see others being emotional, and they aren't.)

- It's okay to go on with their lives.

- Their circle of friends may change if others are uncomfortable with their grief.

- Going to a grief counselor or therapist is like going to any other doctor (except they don't get stuck with needles).

When 15-year-old Tessa's mother became ill and died after an emergency surgery, she didn't know how to feel. In her family, she and her mom were close, and her younger sister was more connected with her father. She'd not only lost her mom, but the person in the family she felt was on her side. The balance between the four of them was gone, and the family was off-center. Part of Tessa's grief journey involved working issues out with her father, and the two of them becoming closer. Although Tessa's friends were caring, she knew they didn't understand what it was like for her. She alternated between periods of acting like everything was okay, even though she felt empty and hurting inside. Other times, she could forget her pain, and just be a teenager with them. She welcomed the chance to forget her sadness for a while.

Older children have friendships that can be deep and intense. Often they feel more connected to their friends than their family. Therefore, they can feel deeply affected by the death of a friend. Even though they're grieving, everyone's attention goes to the bereaved family; the teens' loss may be overlooked. Just acknowledging her grief is important. Say, "I know you've lost a good friend, and you're grieving for him."

Teens may suffer more from the isolation—no one's talking about the death. Put yourself in your teen's shoes. Ask yourself what it would have felt like if you'd lost your parent or other loved one at that age. Try to think about how your teen might feel. Then create opportunities to talk. Sometimes kids open up if you're doing something together such as folding laundry, driving home from school, or taking a walk. You might try saying to them, "If you want to talk or if you're struggling or having problems, I want you to tell me. The talk might make us both sad, but it's still important." Then you need to demonstrate that it's safe to do so. It doesn't help if they share something you don't like, and you blow up. You've broken the trust. It's doubtful if they'll share with you again.

Besides talking, there are other things you can do to help your older children process their grief. Provide activities for them (and their younger siblings) to remember the deceased and perhaps share about him or her. Some ideas are to …

- Make a scrapbook.

- View pictures and movies of the deceased.

- Tell a story about him or her.

- Visit the grave.

- Light a candle for the deceased at church and/or at home.

- Plant and care for a memory garden.

## Attending the Funeral

A funeral can be frightening, confusing, and overwhelming to a young child. They are not used to seeing adults cry. They may not understand what's going on. They don't grasp why adults are crying. They may be afraid of the body in the casket.

**cautions and concerns** Don't criticize children for playing after the death or on the day of the funeral. That will only make them ashamed and confused.

Invite children to attend the funeral if they have the capacity to understand what's happening, but leave young children at home. A funeral gives children a chance to formally grieve and say goodbye. However, if children don't want to attend, don't force them. Make sure you prepare them beforehand. Explain what will occur during the funeral. Tell them they will see adults cry and become very emotional because they are sad and miss the deceased. Explain about the casket (if there is one) or the urn with the ashes. Don't take children up to the casket during the viewing or the funeral. Seeing the body can give them fear fantasies and nightmares. Allow adolescents to make their own choice about viewing the body.

The child may not cry because she doesn't have an understanding about the finality of death. It takes time and maturing before she understands and grieves. Younger child won't grasp the finality until they're older. Don't feel bad about or reprimand the child for not grieving.

**survival strategies** Have an adult whom the child knows and likes, such as a favorite babysitter, attend the funeral to be with and take care of the child in case his or her parents are overcome with emotion.

# What Others Can Do

Children need trusted adults they can confide in about their feelings and concerns to help them emotionally, especially if they've lost a parent or if both parents are grief-stricken. They need someone who'll encourage them to talk, won't become upset by what they share, and will answer questions, such as a teacher, clergy member, babysitter, relative, or a parent of a friend. This person can also provide coping suggestions.

Other families, especially if they have kids of a similar age, can include the bereaved child in outings. It's good for them to be around families who aren't grieving and just have fun. And if they've lost a parent, they can receive some needed "mothering" or "fathering" that they no longer get at home.

Teens rely heavily on their friends for support. Yet many friends may not have experienced loss and may not know how to help. That's why counseling groups for bereavement with their peers can be helpful (see Chapter 18). They have a safe place to share with other kids their own age. They can see others who are going through what they are, so they don't feel so alone.

# Helping Kids Cope with Divorce

Children need to grieve the loss of the intact family. Even if they knew things were bad between their parents, they might still have wished for one or both of them to change and get along. They grieve not having a mom and dad in the same home. They can grieve not seeing one parent as much.

Often there are secondary losses the child has to grieve, such as the loss of their home, and thus a familiar neighborhood and their friends. It's also common after a divorce for a parent to have a lower financial status. If money is tight, they might not live the lifestyle they had before and consequently may have to give up activities they enjoyed (and the friends they made through them). There might also be a loss of a planned-for future—for example, going to college—that now might not be affordable.

**cautions and concerns**

Sometimes parents don't know what to say to their kids about the divorce, so they don't say anything. This is the wrong reaction, and may cause some emotional damage as the kids are left to wonder what's going on and struggle to cope on their own.

Parents may have a hard time with a child's grief, especially if they're angry with the ex or feel good about moving on without their former spouse. They can take the feelings personally and become hurt or angry. They can direct their reactions at the child. When they behave in this way, they don't provide their child with the safe haven he or she needs to process the grief.

Taking care of yourself emotionally helps you help your children. The more you practice emotional self-regulation, the more your children will feel secure about you and about talking to you about the other parent. Make sure you have people you can talk to so you don't have to make your child your confidante. Seek counseling to process your emotions and learn healthy coping skills. That doesn't mean you can't tell them, "I'm feeling sad about the divorce today." You can. It's good for you to explain why you might be in a certain mood around them. Just don't dump your thoughts and feelings about your ex on them.

The best way to help your child cope is to have an amicable relationship with your co-parent. You might hate your ex's guts, but you don't show it—not to your ex and not to your kids. Avoid putting your child in the middle of parental arguments, or forcing your child to take sides with one parent. As much as possible, explain any hurtful behaviors on the other parent's part in a matter-of-fact, but not disparaging, way.

Parents need to reassure the child that the divorce is not their fault. They didn't cause it, nor can they fix the parents' relationship. They need to discuss the changes that will be taking place. They must reassure the child that, no matter what, he or she is loved.

When the parents of my 4-year-old goddaughter, Lauren, first separated, I took her for a walk to find out what she understood about the impending divorce. She told me her mommy and daddy weren't going to be married and live together anymore. We discussed how she felt. I talked about how mommies and daddies can sometimes stop loving each other. I made sure she knew the divorce wasn't her fault. Then I reassured her that while mommy and daddy had stopped loving each other, they would never stop loving her. I also let her know she could always talk to me if she had questions or something she wanted to talk about.

**cautions and concerns** If the child's response is extreme, goes on for a long time, and/or the parent or caregiver is concerned, seek professional help.

If the children's other parent is no longer very involved (or at all involved), the kids can take that personally. Children can easily feel unlovable and believe that's why daddy or mommy left. They need assurance that the problem isn't them, but the other parent's. Also reassure them as they grow older. They have the right to grieve the fantasy mom or dad—the one they didn't have, but still want.

Children are resilient. With the love and support of their family, caregivers and teachers, and others, they can get through their loss. It will always be a part of them and shape who they become. They may re-experience their grief at other stages in their life. Yet they'll know they can recover because they have before.

## Essential Takeaways

- Children respond to a loss in varying ways, depending on what developmental stage they are in.
- If your children are going to attend the funeral of a family member, it's important to help them understand what they will experience.
- After a divorce, children need comforting reassurance that they're loved—by both parents.
- Encourage children to express their feelings through talking, drawing, writing, or playing.

# chapter 20

# Self-Care

Taking good care of yourself

Enlisting in causes

Finding comfort

Spirituality for solace

We all have some experience with stress and have familiar coping mechanisms we use when times are tough. When an important loss occurs, it's often such an extraordinary stress, it overwhelms our normal ways of coping, plus it piles additional tasks, emotions, and symptoms on us. We're left flailing for something that might work to make us feel better. Yet even when we're in crisis, we can take positive actions that support us in our grief and speed our recovery process.

## Caring for Your Body and Soul

Much of our ability to deal with extreme stress is based on our pre-crisis/pre-loss lifestyle. If we've followed a healthy routine, which includes a healthy diet, exercising, a strong support system of trusted people, the ability to communicate thoughts and feelings to others, and a healthy dose of self-esteem, we'll probably fare better. These pre-loss habits give us a strong base on which to function when we're hit with a loss or crisis.

However, the impact of a loss and the grief you experience can knock even the most self-disciplined person off his or her center. When you have a "knot" in your stomach, you might not want to eat. Or you can feel emotionally empty, and find yourself diving into all the food your friends and neighbors dropped off for you. You may feel so exhausted, you don't have the energy to shop and cook, much less exercise. You might grab fast food or skip meals.

In the 12-step program of Alcoholics Anonymous, there are two sayings that apply to the grief journey. One is "Just for today." The other is "One day at a time." Both these statements have to do with focusing on the here and now. For someone newly sober, the idea of giving up alcohol for the rest of his or her life is impossible. But thinking about committing to that goal just for today seems doable. Grief is the same way. When you think of spending the rest of your life without your loved one, having to carry the unbearable burden of pain forever, it can feel impossible to go on. But if you focus on surviving this day only, you can do it. Sometimes the idea of a whole day seems too much, and you might have to narrow your focus to the next hour, or even the next 10 minutes.

> **survival strategies**
>
> Big goals or tasks may seem too overwhelming, especially if you can barely function. Set daily goals, no matter how small. They might be as basic as getting out of bed, showering, and getting dressed. Then cross them off your list and congratulate yourself for obtaining each goal. Studies show that when you achieve your goal, the brain releases chemicals that give you pleasure.

You need to be aware that you're "in mourning" for your loss. Be tolerant of your physical, mental, and emotional limits. You might easily become exhausted and have difficulty making decisions. Stop to rest. Take naps. Watch a movie or read a book. Once you've recharged a bit, you can go back to doing what you need to do.

As much as possible try to return to your regular routine (especially if you have children at home) or develop a new one. However, don't force yourself to keep to the old schedule if you're not up to it. Pay attention to those parts of your routine that you previously enjoyed, and do them.

For many people, going back to work is a way to find some normalcy in their life and get back to a familiar routine. Other people need to be careful about rushing back to work before they're ready. Returning to work for the first time is hard. Your co-workers may not know what to do or say, or they're afraid mentioning your loss may upset you, so they either steer clear of you, or avoid saying anything to you. You may struggle with unexpected emotional surges, or have periods when you can't concentrate or think clearly. You may make mistakes. All this is normal. Be kind and patient with yourself.

## Eat Well and Exercise

During your grief journey, it's important to eat nourishing food to sustain your body and health. When you're grieving, you may not have the inclination or energy to cook. You may subsist on fast food or junk food because it's easier and the high salt and sugar content satisfies cravings. It's also very addicting and a good way to pile on the weight. Letting yourself go physically can contribute to low self-esteem and make you feel bad about yourself at a time when you need all your mental and emotional resources to cope with your grief journey.

> **cautions and concerns**
> Stress and anxiety, as well as emotions such as grief, fear, and anger, can produce temporary changes in the brain, which cause cravings for food, even if you're not hungry.

If you don't want to cook, stock up on frozen meals that you put in the oven or microwave. Keep on hand what I call "grabables," healthy food you don't have to cook. Apples and bananas, nuts, yogurt (especially plain Greek yogurt, which has twice the amount of protein), baby carrots, hard-boiled eggs, string cheese, cottage cheese, protein shakes, and protein bars are all good choices. Then when you're hungry, you can reach for something healthy instead of snacking on junk food.

Exercise is often one of the first healthy habits to fall by the wayside when you're on your grief journey. At first you may be too busy attending to all the tasks regarding your loss. But you may also feel you can't muster up the energy to make yourself work out. However, exercise is an important part of self-care, and after your workout, you can feel more energized. Among other benefits, exercise …

- Reduces the release of stress hormones.
- Increases mood-boosting endorphins in the brain, which reduces the sensation of pain and increases your sense of well-being.

- Can help you forget about your pain for a while.

- Helps keep your weight down.

- Helps keep you mobile and flexible, and increases your strength and stamina.

- Gives you an adrenaline rush, which can make you feel happier and more energized, and fights stress, anxiety, and depression.

- Boosts brain power, improving cognitive function and helping you stay more positive, focused, and alert.

- Improves your immunity against common colds, the flu, and other illnesses. (After bereavement, people often are more susceptible to illness and increase their visits to the doctor.)

- Encourages a better night's sleep, often helping you fall asleep faster and sleep more deeply. (Sleep is often a problem when you're grieving.)

If you haven't exercised before or can't bring yourself to do much, it's good to take walks, especially when you're bereaved. Aside from receiving the benefits of exercising, walking gives you time to yourself. Many people use the walk to think of their loved one, almost as if he or she were present. Some people might also stop at a park bench or another quiet spot, just to have an opportunity for quiet grieving.

## Limit Stress

When you're grieving, you don't have much, if any, tolerance for pressure and other things going wrong. What under normal life circumstances might not be a big deal, can adversely affect you when you're grieving. Perhaps the stress can cause you to burst into tears or fly off the handle. You don't have your usual perspective, stores of energy, and coping ability, and you may not be getting enough sleep. Therefore, you are far more vulnerable to stressful situations.

After a loss, as much as possible, avoid making major changes, which tend to increase stress. You're already under so much stress from the loss, you don't need more, no matter what well-meaning friends and family members may say. Wait to make big changes until you feel more clear-headed and ready to tackle them.

**survival strategies**   Studies show we enjoy almost every activity more (even those we dislike) when we're with people we like. Include a friend or relative when it comes to things like exercising or tasks you haven't done on your own before, like preparing your tax return.

There's nothing wrong with using some of your favorite short-term indulgences if you need a break from stress. When I need some comforting, I allow myself one temporary fix: Mexican food and my favorite chocolate for dessert, which I eat while reading a novel. Then I take a nap. Giving myself a little emotional distance frees me to process my feelings when I'm more centered. However, I'm careful to do this knowingly, instead of unconsciously acting out. And I limit my indulgence to once.

Meditation and yoga are good ways to relax and help you manage stress. Both practices involve centering yourself in your body and taking calming breaths. Studies show yoga and meditation can ease anxiety, help you sleep better, and enhance emotional stability. Even if you don't do either, it's good to remind yourself to take deep breaths, which can help your body relax.

## Laugh

How can laughter be part of grieving? The grief journey seems like a joyless, endlessly sad path. And for many, it is. People who are mourning may go for a long time without laughing. They often feel surprised when they laugh for the first time since the loss occurred. They tend to remember that moment for a long time.

However, laughter can also be part of the grief journey from the very beginning. I often facilitate grief groups for companies that have just lost an employee. In the group, people tend to tell stories about the deceased. Some stories are well known to everyone, while others are individual to the narrator. Sometimes the whole room erupts in laughter. It's not uncommon for people to laugh through their tears at a certain anecdote. Yet the very fact of laughing and grieving together bonds the employees and helps them feel better—still sad, but better.

Research shows the importance of laughter for our health. Seek out situations that might tickle your funny bone. Read comics, watch a funny movie or television show, and look for humor in life. Maintaining a sense of humor isn't going to fix your grief, but it can give you a little time, maybe only a few seconds to chuckle and to feel a little lighter. Those moments of laughter can provide a break from your pain, give you hope that you'll not always feel this way, and sustain you along your grief journey.

The night my father died, I read a historical romance novel written by a friend. The book had some humor in it and had me laughing in several places. I *so* appreciated journeying to another time and place far away from my grief. The laughter was a nice end to a painful day.

## Being of Service to Others

Most grievers don't set out to become philanthropists. Yet when they lose a loved one, they often use their sadness, or anger, or a sense of injustice about the circumstances of the deceased's death to try to make an impact on the world, as well as keep the memory of their loved one alive. Sometimes family and friends join an already established organization, sometimes they form their own, and other times they just try to help individuals. Volunteering offers physical, mental, emotional, and spiritual benefits. Helping others …

- Improves the functioning of the immune system.
- Stimulates the production of serotonin (the feel-good brain chemical) in both the recipient and the person volunteering.
- Lowers stress, depression, and anxiety.
- Contributes to longevity.
- Puts your problems into perspective.
- Gives your life meaning and satisfaction.
- Can foster joy and gratitude.
- Helps get you out of your pain for a little while.
- Keeps you involved instead of isolated.

**Mothers Against Drunk Driving**

MISC.

One of the most well-known charitable organizations is Mothers Against Drunk Driving (MADD) founded in 1980 by Candy Lightner, whose 13-year-old daughter, Cari, was killed by a repeat-offender drunk driver. Candy was soon joined by Cindy Lamb, whose baby daughter, Lauren, became the youngest quadriplegic in the nation after a car accident that involved a drunk driver. Lauren died from complications of her injuries at age 7. Other grieving parents (and family members) flocked to the organization. Largely because of MADD's efforts, annual alcohol-related traffic fatalities have dropped from an estimated 30,000 in 1980 to 17,000 today.

While taking up a cause can be a helpful part of your grief journey, don't immediately jump into one. If you focus all your emotions and energy on volunteering, you may avoid the grieving process and detour from some necessary grieving. Give yourself some time to mourn first, and then ease in slowly.

# Healing Tools

Along your grief journey, you're going to receive a truckload of advice for what to do with yourself. Some of the suggestions may be helpful, but many, if not most of them, won't. However, there are some common "tools" people have used to comfort themselves. Remember, everyone is going to be different in what works for them. You may have to experiment to see what's most effective for you.

## Find Comforting Rituals

The word "ritual" has a spiritual connotation and is often used as a way to connect you with God. However, a ritual can also connect you with yourself, and may or may not be spiritual. The familiarity of doing the ritual on a frequent basis, perhaps every day, can calm you, especially when so much of your life may be filled with chaos. Although performing the ritual won't "fix" your pain, it may soothe your mind and emotions enough for you to get through your day.

Anything that's repetitive or calming can help. I've already discussed walking, yoga, and meditating. However, other activities can soothe you. Some possibilities are these:

- Quilting, knitting, sewing, or crocheting

- Fishing

- Working on a puzzle or playing Solitaire

- Baking or cooking

- Woodworking

- Gardening

- Singing

After Lee's baby daughter died, she started having panic attacks. She went to a psychiatrist, who gave her a biofeedback tape of relaxing statements and sounds to listen to. She played it every day for several months. Soon she could calm herself and bring her heart rate under control within one minute.

When you're upset, especially with the death of a loved one, another ritual that may help is to talk to him. Favorite places to have conversations are the gravesite, a tree or bush you planted in his memory, or a favorite picture or a place. You can also talk to pets when you're grieving. They also offer silent support.

> **Expressions of Grief**
>
> "I talked to my dog whenever I was upset about my job loss. He's my counselor! He'd lean against me, listen to everything I had to say, and try to lick my nose. Sometimes he even made me laugh."
>
> —31-year-old Ted

## Journaling

Writing in a journal is one of the best ways to process your feelings. Research shows that journaling may also keep you physically healthier. Writing about your emotions can give you insight by helping you understand and assimilate your grief. Journaling is good because it does the following:

- Helps you sort out your thoughts
- Gives you insight and perspective
- Defuses intense emotions
- Gets your feelings out in the open
- Changes how you see things
- Gives you a reference point to come back to later and see changes or patterns
- Helps you understand and assimilate your grief
- Helps you work things out with someone (living or dead)

When writing, you have the freedom to express whatever you think or feel. No one needs to see it unless you choose to share, for example, posting your feelings on a blog. Therefore, you can write anything you want, maybe some things you'd never say out loud. So you can say something mean, use profanity, or endlessly repeat yourself, all of which can feel emotionally freeing.

In the journal, you can also enter inspirational sayings, poems, Bible verses, lyrics to hymns or songs—anything that comforts you. You can write about certain memories that have meaning to you. You can reread those pages when you're in need of solace.

**cautions and concerns**    In the short run, writing about your feelings may make you feel worse because it brings everything up for you. But over time, it helps you work through your loss.

Writing letters is another way to channel your feelings onto paper (or whatever technological gadget you use). You can write letters to the deceased, to anyone you're upset with, or to God. As in journaling, you can say anything you want because no one will read it. (If it's about a living person who has access to your home, tear it into tiny pieces afterward so he or she can't accidentally find it.)

When someone dies, or a relationship breaks up, or a friend disappears, often you're left with things that are unsaid, which means that you might lack closure or completion with that person. Writing a letter gives you a chance to find that completion. (You can also write a letter to a pet, or a home, a job, or anything else you've lost.)

You can write a free-flowing letter, or, if you want one that can help you process your feelings and may bring some relief, you can write a structured letter. I have people use the following outline (adapted from the work of American author and counselor Dr. John Gray). Write your emotions in the following order:

- Anger
- Fear
- Shame
- Sadness
- Any other feelings such as betrayal, remorse, yearning

Then ask for forgiveness (if necessary), and add anything else you want to the letter.

The next step is to write a response as if you were the other person responding to you. On the bottom, or back of the paper, or in a new letter, write to yourself, as if you were the person, pet, object, or situation. Say what you understand. Express forgiveness, love, and encouragement. Also apologize if necessary.

## Reading

Reading is a favorite occupation for many people. Reading good books is a great way to escape into another world for a while. Whether or not a griever likes to read, after a death they often find themselves searching for literature that can help them. Or helpful friends and relatives may give them books on grief. (See the Resources appendix for some suggested books and websites.) Reading a book on grief provides a way to …

- Temporarily escape your pain.

- Gain knowledge and understanding.

- Receive comfort.

- Relate to others' stories.

- Realize others have survived what you're going through.

- Find suggestions for coping.

# Embrace Spirituality

Since the time of primitive humans, religion has given inspiration and solace to untold millions of people. Most religions provide a belief system for dying and death that includes a conviction of some form of afterlife. For many people, faith is an integral part of their grief journey. Just like you have physical and emotional needs, you also have spiritual ones. Understanding those needs and making sure they are met is an important part of the grief journey.

After a loss, isolation can be a painful experience. If your personal belief includes the idea that God is always with you, you have "someone" to talk to when you're lonely and in pain. You can feel guided by God. You can also believe there's a purpose to your loss, even though you don't know what that is.

The day before her 19-year-old son, John, died of cancer, Chris spoke to her pastor, reflecting on how unfair life is and about the burdens that many people carry. She talked about how there were times during John's long illness when she felt so alone. Then she said, "As I look back, I wouldn't have wished this cancer on John, but in looking back, I see this burden has been lined with blessings from God every step of the way."

Studies have shown that prayer can heal and help us to cope with crisis and loss. Spirituality that promotes love and forgiveness can increase mental and emotional well-being and also reduce anxiety, depression, and substance abuse.

**The Serenity Prayer**

One of the most popular and well-known prayers is the Serenity Prayer, adapted from a sermon by Reinhold Niebubr, an American theologian. The modified (and most popular) form of the prayer is this: "God, grant me the serenity to accept the things I cannot change, the courage to change the things I can, and the wisdom to know the difference." The Serenity Prayer can be a helpful reminder of what to focus on. It reminds you to evaluate your life in terms of what's doable and what you can let go of. If you're not spiritual, you can take out the reference to God and say it as a wish or affirmation.

## Organized Religion

If spirituality is a part of your life, continuing your involvement with your religious community is important. The organization usually has people who …

- Care about your well-being.

- Pray for you, which can feel comforting.

- Support your spiritual beliefs.

- Provide companionship.

- Give concrete assistance (depending on the type of loss) such as food and lodging.

When several families in Jackie's church lost their homes in a fire that ravaged the community, the congregation stepped forward with donations of money, household items, and clothes. Six months later, at Christmas time, the minister requested every member bring an ornament to the church. These were donated to the families, so they could each have a Christmas tree decorated with ornaments given in love.

In some religions, specific ceremonies to honor the dead or mark periods in the grieving process may be helpful. For example, in the Jewish tradition, after the death, the family "sits" Shiva (meaning "in mourning"). Traditionally Shiva lasted seven days, although now it may be from one to seven. Relatives and friends of the deceased pay a Shiva call to the family, sitting with them and sharing memories of the deceased. This can help mourners cope with the immediate loss.

A religious organization also offers tangible ways to remember and honor a loved one. In Catholic churches, you can light a candle for the deceased or have a mass said for him or her. In many churches and temples, you can dedicate flowers on the altar, or make a donation in the loved one's name to a charity the organization supports.

## Other Perspectives

People may be spiritual without belonging to a religious institution. They may not even believe in "God" but in a force of nature or universal power. Other ways to express spirituality are the following:

- Spend solitary time in prayer, meditation, or thought.
- Quietly listen to your inner voice.
- Spend time in nature.
- Attend spiritual, motivational, or inspirational lectures and classes or listen to them on CDs.
- Read inspirational books, articles, and poetry.
- Listen to inspirational or soothing music.
- Seek out individuals who serve as symbols of hope and inspiration.
- Plant a tree or bush that you can visit to think about or talk to your loved one.

## Forgiveness

Forgiveness (whether or not you're a spiritual person) is an important part of the healing process for grief. Yet it's also extremely personal. You can't just forgive because someone tells you to, or because you think you should. You come to a place of forgiveness when you're ready.

Self-forgiveness is also a part of healing. You need to remember this as you look back at your pre-loss life with all the wisdom that comes from hindsight. You have to make peace with the fact that you did what you did at the time with the knowledge that you had *then*. You need to forgive yourself for who you were at the time and for what you did or didn't do. Otherwise you may become stuck in your grief.

You may need to forgive the deceased for leaving you or doing something that contributed to the death. Sometimes you have to forgive others for actions that caused or contributed to your loss. Forgiveness doesn't mean you condone the action. For example, you can forgive a person who killed your loved one, but you don't have to forgive the action of murder.

Although sometimes forgiveness is an act, when it comes to loss, forgiveness often is a process that may take a while, sometimes many years. Forgiveness occurs in both your mind and heart. Often people jump to mentally forgiving someone, but emotionally, they're still angry or bitter. It you're spiritual, pray for the *willingness* to forgive.

## Signs of Hope

Whether or not people are very spiritual, after bereavement, it's common for them to see or hear signs that they choose to interpret as communications from the deceased. They may believe that these are the deceased's way of letting them know he or she is okay and is still present in their lives.

Sometimes people keep these encounters secret because they're afraid others will scoff at them. The connection, whether real or imaginary, feels too important and fragile to submit to the scorn of disbelief. Other individuals love sharing stories about signs of hope with their family and friends. Sometimes friends and relatives bring signs they see, feel, or hear to the family as a way to give them hope. Here are some common signs of hope:

- A meaningful song comes on the radio as you think of the deceased.
- You see a rainbow, or a cloud in the shape of a heart.
- The lights in your home flicker or other electronics turn on and off.
- You catch a whiff of his or her scent.

- You hear a noise in his or her room, or the sound of a door opening and closing.

- Your dog or cat seems to hear or see someone who's not there.

- You have a loving dream of the deceased.

These little reminders of the deceased are often enough to keep loved ones going when the pain of the loss becomes too much to bear. The hope that the deceased lives on and continues to connect with them gives them hope when they are in the midst of despair. For that reason, if a bereaved individual mentions a sign of hope to you, and you have a negative reaction, don't say so. Instead, say something like, "It sounds like that experience was comforting for you."

## Essential Takeaways

- Self-care of your mind and body helps you better manage your grief reactions.
- Philanthropy is often a way for grievers to give their life meaning.
- It's important to seek out rituals that help you cope with your loss.
- Using some form of spirituality can bring you comfort.

# chapter 21

# Healing and Moving On

| |
|---|
| Benefits of gratitude |
| Healing in all areas |
| The path toward recovery |
| Finding a sense of meaning and purpose |
| Finding peace and acceptance |

Grief creates change. It may be difficult, if not impossible, for us when we're in the throes of intense grief, especially that of bereavement, to believe that someday we will recover. In the process, we may become stronger, more empathetic, and more grateful. We will find a place of balance and a way to redefine ourselves and learn to live with our new circumstances. We may end up with a life that's satisfying, although perhaps very different, from our former one. Holding onto hope for renewal can help guide us on the path toward recovery.

## The Power of Gratitude

Several days after the earthquake and tsunami that devastated the coast of Japan in 2011, one survivor of the hard-hit port city of Sendai was quoted in the newspaper as saying, "My family, my children. We are lucky to be alive. I have come to realize what is important in life." Such comments are common after a disastrous loss has destroyed everything you own—a time when the last thing you'd think survivors would feel is gratitude. Yet our ability to feel gratitude during tough times is one of the attributes that helps get us through them.

Research has shown how gratitude—a positive appreciation for the blessings in our life—is an important attitude to have. It can keep us mentally and emotionally content. People who regularly practice gratitude …

- Are healthier.

- Have an easier time letting go of traumatic memories.

- Are more optimistic.

- Tend to have more energy and alertness.

- Create more joy in their lives.

- Are more helpful to others.

- Make more progress toward their goals.

- Are less vulnerable to clinical depression.

Gratitude may well up from a place of joy; other times it comes from surviving or overcoming an experience of great pain. Sometimes gratitude comes out of nowhere and strikes a cord in your mind. Your grief shifts a little, or maybe a lot. You feel a lift to your spirits. That surge of gratitude seems to help grievers turn a corner on their grief journey. They've come into the light, if only for a while. That doesn't mean they won't feel sad again. They will. But they now know they'll eventually recover. The following two stories illustrate a gratitude turning point after bereavement:

- Paul lost his wife to cancer a year ago. Up to that point in his grief journey, Paul had been despondent and tended to ask, "Why me?" While driving with his 16-year-old daughter a few weeks before Christmas, they saw two homeless people. Paul was struck with the realization that there were other people struggling with far greater problems than he had. "I have a good job, great children, a nice house, and I had good years with my wife," he thought. Paul turned to his daughter, and said, "We think we have it so bad, but we don't. We're always going to miss your mother, but we're fine."

- When Melody's mother died after a long, slow dwindling away, she worked out her feelings of grief and loss by running on country roads. As she was out jogging one morning, a month or so after her mom passed away, she was suddenly bowled over by a strong sense of gratitude. She was grateful that she could still run at age 51, and that she could work out in such beautiful countryside. The more she ran and pondered, the more things she became grateful for.

## Brain Changes

Research on the brain using *SPECT* scans shows how gratitude can affect the brain in positive ways. Fear or negativity decreases activity in key areas of the brain involved in thought coordination, integration of new information, mood, memory, and temper control. Thoughts of gratitude change the brain. These changes show up on the SPECT scan, demonstrating there's more activity in these important brain areas.

Definition

**SPECT,** short for single photon emission computed tomography, scans the brain to see the blood flow and activity patterns and provides 3D images.

What this research means is that when you dwell on things you fear or have other pessimistic thoughts, you'll also feel "blue." You may have trouble processing your thoughts, and won't be able to make decisions easily. You also may be more irritable than usual and become clumsier.

When you have pessimistic thoughts, your brain releases negative chemicals, which cause physical reactions that respond to your thoughts. For example, fear makes your stomach muscles tighten, your breathing becomes shallow, and your heart beats faster. As your body responds to the chemicals, your feelings intensify, which can also increase your negative thoughts, strengthening a vicious cycle. On the other hand, when you think thoughts of gratitude, your brain releases dopamine, the "feel-good" chemical.

## Mood Changes

When you're grieving, your mood can be all over the place (which can feel disconcerting), but it's often down. While it's important to process your sad emotions, a low mood is often caused by a negative or pessimistic state of mind. There are ways to keep your mood up when you've suffered a loss. Practicing these techniques doesn't mean you won't have waves of grief; it just means you'll be able to return to a more centered place afterward. Try doing some (or all) of the following:

- Every day, write down five things you're grateful for. Even better, write them twice a day—once in the morning when you first get up and again before you go to sleep.

- Savor positive moments.

- Engage in meaningful activities.

- Tell people you love them every day.

- Acknowledge others.

- If you're spiritual, give thanks throughout the day when you feel blessed in some way, no matter how small.

## Integrated Healing

Many people have innate personal strengths. Other people develop them. While it's possible to enhance personal strengths by reading books, attending seminars, being mentored and coached, having good role models, and helping others, many people develop personal strength through adversity.

Grief pushes you to utilize your personal strengths and abilities as well as develop new ones. Like the caterpillar enduring the painful process within the cocoon—its body being broken, and then rebuilt to emerge as a butterfly—you, too, can become a better, stronger person as you pass through your time of mourning. After a major loss, a time of detachment (or "cocooning") can be normal as you reflect on the changes in your life, feel your grief, struggle to find meaning, and redefine yourself. From this process, you may experience creative urges. You may shift your priorities and head in new life directions.

In order to emerge into any kind of butterfly state, you have to support yourself while you're in your cocoon (and afterward). Throughout this book I have discussed ways to help yourself stay physically healthy, but it's also important to take care of yourself mentally and emotionally.

| Expressions of Grief | "Even though my son has been dead for eight years, I miss him more today than I did yesterday, and will miss him more tomorrow than I did today. I think that's how it always will be for me. I gather my life back in a new form, and I give to others. I'm probably a better person because of his death, and that gives me comfort." |
| --- | --- |

—Nan

## Mentally

As you've seen from the section on gratitude, your mental state plays a huge part in your recovery. Research shows that pessimism can override the effectiveness of even powerful healing treatments. Most negative thinking is automatic. You'll have pessimistic thoughts and won't even be aware of it. But your body will know and react.

Mental self-discipline is the precursor for changing attitudes or habits, pushing through fears and past your usual limits, and accomplishing goals. This means you have to pay attention to what you think, and catch yourself when you have a negative thought. Then ask yourself questions like these:

- Is this *really* true?
- Do I know this for a fact?
- Is this true 100 percent of the time?
- What if I were to switch my thoughts to something positive?
- What if I were to think the opposite?

Let's take a real example to demonstrate. A common thought after the death of a spouse or the breakup of a relationship is: "I will always be alone. I'll never have another romantic relationship." Ask yourself the following.

- Is this *really* true? "Well … I don't know. Maybe."

- Do I know this for a fact? "Well … no."

- Is this true 100 percent of the time? "No."

- What if I were to switch my thoughts to something positive? "I can find love again."

- What if I were to think the opposite? "I'll have a happy, loving relationship that lasts for the rest of my life."

You see how moving through these questions can make a difference? What starts out as a pessimistic, painful thought can transform within a few seconds. You just need the determination to confront your own negativity.

"There are things I have to do to live a productive life. I have to function. I take the negative thoughts that are so easy to go for and flip them."

—Gail, whose 14-year-old daughter died suddenly

When we're grieving, we tend to focus on what's difficult and painful. It will take mental self-discipline to change your thinking, and that's not easy to change because your negative thoughts have worn a groove in your mind. Sometimes you'll have to wrestle them in a new direction. When the discouraged thoughts come to you such as, "I'll never get over this loss," or "I'll grieve forever," say to yourself, "I *will* recover; it will just take time."

One of the ways you know you are getting better is when less of your thoughts are negative, despairing, or self-destructive. You'll find you're more able to let go of them when they do come. You may even think optimistic thoughts much of the time. The change in your thinking patterns will correspond to positive changes in your emotions.

## Emotionally

We are created to be emotional people, yet often we don't know what to do with our feelings. Many people have been taught to only feel the "good" ones. However, emotions are made to be felt. Denying your grief can make it more confusing and overwhelming.

When a wave of emotion hits, our body is designed to experience the feeling, and then have it fade away. However, that's not what most people allow to happen with the "difficult" emotions. They usually try to suppress or avoid them. Unresolved emotions can cause other damage. They can weaken your immune system, come out in other ways, such as arguing with a partner, or surface months or years down the line. What we need to do with our painful emotions is "sit" with instead of avoid them. As we think about, explore, and accept the emotion, that wave recedes.

As I've discussed in previous chapters, your grief journey will be up and down, sideways, and sometimes one step forward and two steps back. Give yourself the time you need to grieve, cry, talk about your feelings, and tell stories about your loved one. Don't judge your emotions. They are what they are. Feel them and let them pass through you. Don't compare your loss or your grief to another's. Everyone has his or her own pain, and to judge yours as less worthy does disservice to the love you felt for the person, pet, object, or job.

**survival strategies** | If you become too wrapped up in guilt and regret, there may be something you're avoiding. Ask yourself, "If I wasn't focused on regret, what emotion would I be feeling?"

## Socially

As I discussed in Chapter 20, most people are either introverts or extroverts. Just by knowing the way you replenish your energy will guide you in your social activities. As an introvert, when you feel the need for friends, love, fun, and connections, you spend time with others. But when you need to recharge, you head for solitude. Extroverts, on the other hand, need to make quiet time for introspection and grieving, and then find people to help them recharge. One of the ways you'll know you're healing is when you have the ability to tolerate and even enjoy both social and quiet times.

Your friends may fumble around, uncomfortable with your grief. Their efforts to connect and their actual words may be way off base. As much as possible, try to look at their intentions.

cautions and concerns Back away from contact with individuals you believe are insensitive or deliberately hurtful. These kinds of people aren't good to be around during the best of times, but certainly not when you're grieving.

This might be a time when you re-evaluate your friendships. If you have a difficult or critical person in your life, why have you allowed that individual to remain in your social circle? Do you still want him as a friend? What are you going to do about friends with shared interests that now seem unimportant? Do you really want to hang out with someone who just talks about himself? As you let go of certain friends, keep close in your heart those who have been there for you, and allow yourself to be open to new people coming into your life.

No one emerges from a grieving period without some change within herself, no matter how small. How you've handled your loss and adjustment period makes a difference. If you've acted in ways that were unhealthy, or caused harm to yourself or others, then you still might have some shame to process and repairs to make in your relationships. Take the time to work through your feelings, make amends to others, and forgive yourself.

## Moving On Doesn't Mean Forgetting

It's important to practice patience with yourself. It may take you months or even years to absorb a major loss and accept your changed circumstances. With bereavement, it may be difficult to face the fact that a loved one will never again be part of the family. As time goes on, you'll realize that, in some ways, the deceased remains with you and is still part of the family.

Recently, I was driving my younger cousin on an errand. We were talking about how her baby was due on our grandmother's birthday. I suggested that Wulf, our great-grandfather's name, might be a good middle name for the baby. Mindy said she didn't know anything about him. Because I'm the family historian, I started telling her about our great-grandfather, and then went on to share one of the funniest stories I know about our grandmother's childhood. As I related the story, Mindy laughed and laughed, and I joined her. In those wonderful moments, our grandmother's presence was so strong, it was almost as if she were present.

Somewhere along the way, you'll find yourself feeling better. You'll compare your "now" to how you were "before" and see the differences. The changes give you hope for further recovery, although you might have some sadness or guilt because you're moving on, and you think you're leaving someone or something behind. If you've grieved the loss of a person (or a pet), you may find that the time comes when you can remember him or her with love and gratitude, instead of with pain and sorrow.

# Finding Meaning in Loss

In challenging times, it can be a struggle to find the good in our loss. (Some people don't even try.) Yet they can miss out on the healing that comes from surviving loss. Facing a major loss can cause us to ask, "What are my priorities, dreams, and goals, and what should I do to accomplish them?"

We can learn lessons from all aspects of life. Some of the most profound lessons can come from agonizing losses. Although we're too close to the event initially, eventually we can come to see the lessons we learned from the experience and the good that has come out of it. We can use what we've gained to live a more meaningful life and be better people.

Trust that the lessons are there, and at some point you may be able to look back and say, "Ah, now I understand." That doesn't take the hurt of your "now" away. Instead, it places your loss in a different context, which can make it easier to bear and recover from. You'll find that a sense of meaning and purpose does return, especially if you seek ways to enhance these concepts.

> **survival strategies**
>
> Focus on activities that bring pleasure, peace, and joy into your life and the lives of others. Helping others can give you richness, purpose, meaning, and a sense of gratitude.

We may come to like the new person we are far better than who we were before. Our new circumstances may suit us more than the old ones. We can become …

- More philanthropic.
- More appreciative.

- Less materialistic.

- More generous.

- More focused on living in the now.

- More family oriented.

## Peace and Acceptance

Too much emphasis is placed on getting "over" a loss versus getting through your suffering and grief. With many losses, such as bereavement, you don't "get over" them, yet you do get through them. We reconcile ourselves to living with the grief, and most of the time we move beyond it.

Sometimes, our grief journey is a step-by-step process or maybe even an inch-by-inch crawl. The sorrow and suffering do pass; however, the missing feeling or the empty place may not. But eventually you come to terms with the changes in your life. You make peace with who you are now—a person who you wouldn't have become without the loss in your life. You come to some feeling of acceptance.

Because of your loss, you can feel a newfound sense of gratitude. You have come to realize life is precious, and you don't want to take it for granted. You focus on enjoying today. You now know the time you have with family and friends is truly irreplaceable. The memories you make together last your lifetime and, as my story of my grandmother shows, beyond.

Although you move on, your struggle with your loss (especially that of bereavement) may occasionally resurface. As your circumstances change and you travel through different life stages, you may have to grieve anew. Let your sadness bubble up, wash over you, and drift away on the tide of your memories.

Although in some form you carry the past with you, it doesn't have to hold you back. As you heal, your "old self" will return (to the delight of your friends and family). However, this self will be tempered by your experience, and you may see things differently and appreciate who and what you do have. Having faced adversity and survived, you've learned that you are wiser and better prepared to deal with potential challenges. You now know you have the strength and ability to persevere in the face of problems. You possess the power to move forward into the future—one of your own making.

## Essential Takeaways

- Thinking grateful thoughts is one of the best things you can do to lift your mood and keep you healthier.
- It's important to take care of yourself mentally, emotionally, and in social situations.
- After a loss, you may need to find new meaning in your life.
- Recovering from a loss can make you a stronger, better person.

# Resources

Following are some books and websites you can consult to help you through the grieving process.

## Books

Aleskire, Liz. *101 Ways You Can Help: How to Offer Comfort and Support to Those Who Are Grieving.* Illinois: Sourcebooks, Inc., 2009.

Gilbert, Allison. *Parentless Parents: How the Loss of Our Mothers and Fathers Impacts the Way We Raise Our Children.* New York: Hyperion, 2011.

James, John W., and Russell Friedman. *The Grief Recovery Handbook: Action Program for Moving Beyond Death.* New York: HarperCollins, 2009.

Kübler-Ross, Elisabeth, and David Kessler. *On Grief and Grieving: Finding the Meaning of Grief Through the Five Stages of Loss.* New York: Scribner, 2005.

Kurz, Gary. *Cold Noses at the Pearly Gates: A Book of Hope for Those Who Have Lost a Pet.* New York: Citadel Press Books, 2008.

Kushner, Harold S. *When Bad Things Happen to Good People.* New York: Random House, 1984.

Redfern, Suzanne, and Susan K. Gilbert. *The Grieving Garden: Living With the Death of a Child.* New York: Hampton Roads, 2008.

Rosof, Barbara D. *The Worst Loss: How Families Heal from the Death of a Child.* New York: Holt, 1994.

Telpner, Heidi, R.N. *One Foot in Heaven.* Iowa: Jupiter Gardens Press, 2010.

Van Praagh, James. *Healing Grief: Reclaiming Life After Any Loss.* New York: New American Library, 2001.

Winter, Aurora. *From Heartbreak to Happiness.* Free ebook and CD, www.aurora.com.

Wray, T. J. *Surviving the Death of a Sibling: Living Through Grief When an Adult Brother or Sister Dies.* New York: Three Rivers Press, 2003.

# Websites

www.aamft.org (American Association for Marriage and Family Therapy)   A national website for professionals and couples looking for marriage and family advice.

www.aarp.org/families/grief_loss (American Association of Retired Persons)   Grief and loss articles, and support for seniors.

www.apa.org (American Psychological Association Help Center)   Helpful resource on relationships and mental health.

www.aplb.org   A website for pet loss.

www.cancer.net   Cancer resources, including help for planning end-of-life care.

www.compassionatefriends.org   A nonprofit, self-help support organization offering friendship, understanding, and hope to families after a child dies.

www.counseling.org (American Counseling Association)   A comprehensive website for professionals and people in need of a therapist.

www2.ed.gov/programs/dvppserv/index.html   U.S. Department of Education's Project SERV (Schools Emergency Response to Violence) helps schools recover from a violent or traumatic event. You can also reach them at 202-260-1856.

www.goodtherapy.org   Assists people in finding a therapist.

www.grief.net   A website for helping people move beyond loss.

www.griefhealing.com/comfort-grieving-animal-lovers.htm    Assistance for people grieving the loss of a pet.

www.griefwork.org (The National Catholic Ministry to the Bereaved)    A faith-based bereavement ministry.

www.growingthroughgrief.com    Helping people move through loss.

www.iamfc.org (International Association of Marriage and Family Counselors, a division of the American Counseling Association)    A website for help with divorce and marital problems.

www.lightning-strike.com    Support with the loss of a pet.

www.livingwithloss.com    Website for ordering *Bereavement Magazine: Hope & Healing for the Body, Mind & Spirit.*

www.mayoclinic.com/health/marriage-counseling/MY00839    Marriage advice from the Mayo Clinic.

www.memory-of.com    A website for creating an online memorial.

www.myadultsiblinggrief.com    Online community for people grieving the loss of an adult sibling.

www.nahc.org/haa (Hospice Association of America)    For caring assistance with dying; comprehensive list of hospices provided.

www.nasponline.org (Association of School Psychologists)    Finding counseling and psychiatric help for children.

www.ncfr.org (National Council on Family Relations)    A website for professionals regarding family and marriage issues.

www.nfcacares.org/caregiving_resources/ (National Family Caregivers Association)    Offers information and educational articles; also provides opportunities to connect with other caregivers.

www.nhpco.org/templates/1/homepage.cfm (National Hospice and Palliative Care Organization)    For information and support of end-of-life care.

www.nimh.nih.gov (National Institutes of Mental Health)    Offers resources and links for mental illness, marital problems, and more.

www.opentohope.com   Resource for helping people find hope after loss.

www.petloss.com   Resource for those grieving the loss of their pet.

www.pomc.org (National Organization of Parents of Murdered Children)   Information and support for families whose child was murdered.

www.psychcentral.com   Information on various psychological conditions.

www.psychologytoday.com   Offers a listing of therapists.

www.ptsdinfo.org   Information on post-traumatic stress disorder.

www.recover-from-grief.com   Help with creatively working through stages of grief.

www.sharegrief.com   Volunteer grief counseling offered for those grieving the death of a loved one.

www.suicidology.org (American Association of Suicidology)   Help with all issues of suicide, including those grieving the loss of a loved one due to suicide.

www.try-nova.org (National Organization for Victim Assistance) Assistance for victims of crisis and crime. You can also call 1-800-TRY-NOVA.

# Index

# D

**G**

# H

# M

# N

## R